5

Building New Competition Law Regimes

Selected Essays

Edited by

David Lewis

Executive Director, Corruption Watch and Extraordinary Professor, Gordon Institute of Business Science, South Africa

Edward Elgar

Cheltenham, UK • Northampton, MA, USA

International Development Research Centre

Ottawa • Cairo • Montevideo • Nairobi • New Delhi

Published by
Edward Elgar Publishing Limited
The Lypiatts
15 Lansdown Road
Cheltenham
Glos GL50 2JA
UK

Edward Elgar Publishing, Inc.
William Pratt House
9 Dewey Court
Northampton
Massachusetts 01060
USA

International Development Research Centre
PO Box 8500
Ottawa, ON, K1G 3H9
Canada
www.idrc.ca / info@idrc.ca
ISBN 978-1-55250-552-6 (IDRC e-book)

A catalogue record for this book
is available from the British Library

Library of Congress Control Number: 2012953537

This book is available electronically in the ElgarOnline.com Law Subject Collection, E-ISBN 978 1 78195 373 0

MIX
Paper from
responsible sources
FSC® C018575

ISBN 978 1 78195 372 3 (cased)

Typeset by Columns Design XML Ltd, Reading
Printed by MPG PRINTGROUP, UK

Contents

Contributors

Janice Bleazard is an Advocate of the High Court of South Africa and a Member of the Johannesburg Bar, South Africa.

Heidi Claudia Sada Correa is Director of Planning and International Affairs at the Mexican Federal Competition Commission.

John Fingleton was the Chief Executive Officer of the UK Office of Fair Trading from 2005–2012 and chaired the International Competition Network's Steering Group from 2009–2012.

Eleanor Fox is Walter J. Derenberg Professor of Law at New York University School of Law, USA.

Alberto Heimler, on leave from the Italian competition Authority, is Professor of Economics at the Italian School of Public Administration in Rome and is Chairman of the OECD Working Party on Competition and Regulation.

Frédéric Jenny is Professor of Economics at ESSEC Business School in Paris, France, and Chairman, since 1994, of the OECD Competition Committee. He was Chairman of the WTO Working Group on the Interaction between Trade and Competition from 1997 to 2004.

Thula Kaira was at the Zambia Competition Commission from 1998–2011, during which time he rose to become the CEO. He is now CEO of the Competition Authority in Botswana.

Csaba Kovács has been a member of the Hungarian Competition Authority, in various positions, since 1992.

Sophie Mitchell is International Competition Network counsel and Assistant Director at the Office of Fair Trading, UK.

Eduardo Pérez Motta has been Chairman of the Mexican Federal Competition Commission since September 2004, and in April 2012 he was selected Chair of the International Competition Network.

Deunden Nikomborirak is Research Director at the Thailand Development Research Institute.

Andreas P. Reindl is Professor at Leuphana University, Lüneburg, Germany, and of counsel at Öberg & Associés, Brussels, Belgium.

Preface and acknowledgements

If development economics has taught us anything, then it is that institutions matter. And yet writing which examines the functioning of particular institutions and the factors that influence the trajectory of their development, including their success or failure, is relatively rare. In the world of competition law there is a huge treasure trove of scholarly literature dealing with case law and with substantive issues in competition law and economics, but, albeit with significant exceptions, little that focuses on the institutions responsible for applying the law. It is, perhaps predictably, an area where practitioners – and by that I mean largely agency officials – lead the rich community of antitrust scholars. Institutions like the Organisation for Economic Co-operation and Development (OECD) and the United Nations Conference on Trade and Development (UNCTAD) have, for some time now, produced a growing library of institutional peer reviews and the International Competition Network (ICN) is deeply concerned with questions of agency effectiveness. The essays in this book focus on institutions. The authors are, for the most part, either practitioners or scholars who have a particularly strong record of engagement with agencies.

The most significant development in international competition law in recent times is the extraordinary burgeoning of national competition authorities. While competition statutes and their accompanying institutions were, until the 1990s, the preserve of a small number of the most developed economies, they are now commonplace across the globe, from Australia to Zambia and most countries in between.

This volume is effectively the companion to a book authored by the editor. That book – *Enforcing Competition Rules in South Africa: Thieves at the Dinner Table*, also published by Edward Elgar – is concerned with the development of the South African competition agencies. A principal thesis of that book is that while global markets and essential similarities in the character of many national markets do permit a degree of homogeneity in national competition laws and the approaches of enforcers and adjudicators, particular national circumstances, both historical and contemporary, are enormously influential. They are, or should be, the factors that underpin governments' key policy objectives; they account for the public's very understanding of the notion of competition; they determine whether and to what extent non-competition objectives are incorporated into the legislation and the decisions of adjudicators; they determine the reach of competition law; they influence the extent to which the conduct of dominant firms is investigated and prosecuted; they lend legitimacy – or otherwise – to merger regulation.

To the extent that it is possible and helpful to generalise – and the essays in this book demonstrate the limits of useful generalisation – the spread of competition law enforcement is largely a product of the economic liberalisation that swept the globe in the last quarter of the twentieth century. The reduction of barriers to international trade and investment – or, expressed otherwise, the internationalisation of many key markets – coupled with the sweeping away of rules that stifled the development of markets in many national economies exposed the rank idealism that underpinned the celebration of 'free' markets. If markets were to function efficiently they required enforceable rules, and front and centre of the rules required were those governing competition.

However, those who seek the origins of national competition laws purely in the imperatives of economic efficiency will also find that many, if by no means all, national competition laws are rooted in considerations of fairness and equity. In some countries, particularly those in which markets had been comprehensively supressed, liberalisation simultaneously led to sharp price increases, the disappearance of social safety nets and the rise of a conspicuously wealthy elite; and so competition authorities were established, or at least expected, to re-introduce a semblance of protection and equity. In countries where protectionism and strong elements of state ownership had given rise to a business class strongly supportive of a previous repressive regime, competition laws were introduced, in part at least, to level the playing field between these established business interests and other social interest groups, such as new business entrants and, particularly, small and medium-sized enterprises.

Purists may disapprove. They may insist that protecting the poor and hungry or small farmers and retailers from competition or neutralising powerful dominant firms, even those whose dominance has been secured by past privileges and connections, will come at the expense of the very economic efficiency that competition law is intended to promote, and may ultimately be at the expense of the very interests that they ostensibly aim to support. They would certainly insist that even if government deemed it appropriate to support particular interest groups then this should not be done by burdening competition law with multiple and conflicting objectives.

However, these imperatives are powerful and the legitimacy and, hence, efficacy of the competition law and its enforcement may well be contingent upon it finding an accommodation with these conflicting values and objectives, if indeed they are in conflict. My point is simply that these historical and contemporary environmental factors will inevitably inform the drafting and the application of a statute as socially and economically significant as that governing market rules. This does not mean that the economic textbooks should be discarded any more than that the accumulated wisdom acquired through decades of enforcement, scholarship and jurisprudence be ignored by the newer competition regimes. It simply means that economic rules are applied in concrete and particular contexts, including equity considerations and objectives, which cannot be ignored either.

This collection comprises five country studies – of Hungary, Mexico, South Africa, Thailand (with a comparative perspective on South Korea) and Zambia – and two essays that explore multinational issues in antitrust. From every conceivable perspective the countries chosen represent a diverse range of national economies and societies. However, the choice of these five – or six if the South Korean component is factored in – is dictated by particular features of both their economic and political environments that bear significantly on the nature of the competition law project and the prospects of its success.

The essays will speak for themselves and no attempt will be made to summarise or synthesise them here. However, in each instance the form that the competition law project took and its successes and failures are deeply rooted in particular characteristics of each of the countries in question. These range from Hungary's place in the erstwhile Soviet bloc; periods of severe economic crisis and a historically powerful business elite in Mexico; Thailand's periodic swings between a government dominated by a thoroughly corrupt, anti-reform business elite and reformist, repressive military rule; Korea's adherence to powerful, state-driven industrial policy and subsequent and largely successful attempts, in which the application of competition law played an important role, to reverse this state-centred approach to economic development; and in Zambia the simultaneous presence of a resource-extractive formal sector dominated either by foreign-owned multinational corporations and state ownership, on the one hand, and a largely informal small business sector. While the particular South African features that influenced its competition law are extensively dealt with in *Enforcing Competition Rules in South Africa: Thieves at the Dinner Table*, the South African essay in this collection analyses recent court decisions whose lack of appreciation of some of the key features of competition law has challenged and undermined an otherwise largely successful introduction of a competition law regime that enjoys significant public support. It serves to underline that in promoting a competition culture, it is the courts and the legal system that may be least capable of departing from deeply engrained and inappropriate practices and approaches, characterised by an overbearing emphasis on procedure and a black letter approach to the interpretation of social and economic statutes.

The volume is rounded off by two studies of key multinational themes in competition law. Both are concerned with the institutional response in the arena of competition law to the internationalisation of markets, essentially with the question of how nationally fragmented competition rules deal with markets that traverse national boundaries. The first of these two essays is principally concerned with global institutions – in particular the International Competition Network (ICN) whose very composition ensures that while it is bound to recognise the powerful imperative that international markets give towards convergence in the application of national competition law, it must simultaneously recognise the salience of national circumstances and concerns. The final essay in this volume considers the possibility of utilising regional agreements between countries as a mechanism for strengthening the application of competition law, particularly in developing country regions.

I am grateful to the International Development Research Centre for funding this project and to the Gordon Institute of Business Science for providing me with a supportive and stimulating home. My editor, Catherine Garson, is owed an enormous debt of gratitude for undertaking a challenging task, as are Laura Seward and Nicolas Wilson, the Edward Elgar editors responsible for producing this volume. Above all, though, I would like to express my gratitude to the contributors to this volume, all friends and colleagues in the always stimulating and collegial international community of competition practitioners and scholars.

David Lewis
Johannesburg, South Africa

PART I

Country studies

1. Competition policy in Mexico

Eduardo Pérez Motta and Heidi Claudia Sada Correa

INTRODUCTION

There is no doubt that the enactment of a competition law and the creation of a specialised agency to enforce it are key conditions for the development of a favourable economic environment in any country. Mexico started this process in the early 1990s, with the approval of the Federal Law of Economic Competition (FLEC[1]), and the creation of the Federal Competition Commission (CFC[2] or Commission).

This chapter seeks to tell the story of the economic context that preceded the enactment of the FLEC and the creation of the CFC. It describes the environment in which the competition regime was adopted and explains how the Mexican competition authority became a strong and active agency, with a stable institutional structure that, combined with technical and operative autonomy, guarantees the independence and impartiality of its actions.

THE EVOLUTION OF COMPETITION POLICY IN MEXICO

Mexico's Industrial Policy Between 1940 and 1980: Inward-looking Industrialisation

For decades, the Mexican economy was characterised by strong protectionism and heavy government intervention. In the latter part of the 1940s, following World War II, the country subscribed to import substitution industrialisation as its main economic policy. The aim of this economic model was to use trade policy as an instrument to limit foreign competition by applying ad valorem tariffs, import tariffs, custom valuations, and import licences to protect the infant domestic industry.

During the 1960s and late 1970s, a stabilising development policy was adopted to modernise the manufacturing sector. The aim of this model was to protect existing domestic firms from competition by supplementing trade protection with additional protective measures and subsidisation programmes.

During this period, the state was very involved in regulatory activity in almost every economic sector. The state controlled the entry and exit of competitors, applied price controls, and imposed restrictive regulation on foreign investments that were destined for the production and distribution of products and the exploitation of natural resources. In addition, the government channelled subsidies to specific activities, particularly in industries where large-scale production was prevalent, such as telecommunications, transport, chemicals, petrochemicals, rubber, and machinery and industrial equipment.

However, the irony of the application of the stabilising development policy was that in most cases, the criteria for the allocation of subsidies were based on the political importance of the favoured industry, and not on efficiency or productivity. Meanwhile, during the same period, the government's dominant role in the economy intensified as it took over the control of a number of private firms. This nationalisation initiative was justified on the grounds that it was either preserving employment or averting bankruptcies.

As a result, these economic policies created conditions that favoured rent dissipation, discouraged efficient resource allocation and innovative production methods, and shielded domestic firms from foreign competition. The net effect was that entrepreneurial creativity was essentially discouraged and the country was led down a path of lagging competitiveness. By the mid-1980s, the Mexican economy was highly concentrated, with poorly-performing industry using its resources inefficiently.

Industrial Policy Since the Mid-1980s: Economic Liberalisation

In 1982, the last year in office of President José López Portillo, state-owned or state-linked economies had largely replaced many private sector enterprises in productive areas of the economy, with more than 1100 state-linked companies across the economy.[3] In addition, the country faced an intolerably high fiscal debt, and its international reserves were almost zero. These conditions motivated President López Portillo to nationalise the bank system just before the end of his term, which had the unfortunate result of worsening the macroeconomic conditions of the economy.

When President Miguel de la Madrid took office after President López Portillo, the Mexican government was facing serious economic and fiscal problems. The new administration had no choice but to devise a set of urgent economic reforms to replace the poorly-performing state-led development strategy. A poorly-performing manufacturing sector and the macroeconomic instability that arose from the growing reliance on petroleum revenues and increased indebtedness meant that even the groups that had benefited from the previous policies – such as state monopolies, unions, government contractors, and chambers of commerce – understood that the government needed to change its approach. Important reforms began to be implemented. These included the renegotiation of the terms of the foreign debt, the devaluation of the peso, the divestiture of non-strategic state-owned enterprises through sale, merger or liquidation, and other efforts aimed at restoring the confidence of international investors and markets. The new reforms were characterised by a move away from targeted policies for specific sectors to a horizontal approach to trade and financial liberalisation, foreign direct investment, deregulation, and privatisation.

This new approach was called the Restructuring Programme, whose main purpose was to improve the overall efficiency of the public sector. The process was supported by constitutional reforms that allowed the government to close around 300 state-owned companies and privatise 157 companies.[4]

The policies were based on the theory that, through market mechanisms, firms would attain productive efficiency by better deciding on their choice and mix of technology and factors of production, such as labour and capital, to maximise their profits. Through this process, the whole economy would attain allocative efficiency, minimizing costs and waste in production, and resulting in improvements to social welfare.

The idea was that the government's role would be simply to create conditions conducive to ensuring that the economic environment favours the efficient functioning of markets and encourage private investment to generate productive employment, while minimising distortions, including subsidies. Nevertheless, there were three necessary preconditions: macroeconomic stability, open trade, and deregulation.

For this reason, the new industrial policy saw trade openness as an instrument for encouraging economic efficiency and industrial competitiveness. Deregulation measures at this time included: the elimination of sectoral programmes based on fiscal incentives and subsidies; the elimination of price controls and obsolete regulations in sectors such as transport, roads, railroads, and customs; the elimination of government's discretionary powers to allow or veto majority foreign investments, and allowing complete foreign participation in most economic activities (banking and finance, as well as reserved activities for the State excepted); the elimination of legal provisions on technology transfers, making the laws and regulations more flexible in these matters; and the modernisation of the industrial property system.

In 1994, during President Carlos Salinas de Gortari's administration, the pace and depth of reforms increased, following international commitments such as the signature of the North American Trade Agreement (NAFTA), which had formalised Mexico's trade liberalisation process with its main trading partner, the United States, and Canada. NAFTA was followed by the accession of Mexico to the Organisation for Economic Co-operation and Development (OECD) and to the predecessor of the World Trade Organisation (WTO), the General Agreement on Tariffs and Trade (GATT), as well as the signature of free trade agreements with other parties such as the European Union and some Latin American countries.

Also during the 1990s the government continued privatising hundreds of state-owned commercial enterprises. The largest efforts were made in 1990, when the telephone monopoly was sold for US$6 billion, and in 1991 and 1992, when 18 commercial banks were privatised for a total of US$13 billion. Public firms in steel, sugar processing, airlines, TV broadcasting, satellites, airport and seaport facilities, and railroads were sold to the private sector. In addition, activities formerly performed by the state, such as seaport services, and the storage, transportation and distribution of natural and liquefied petroleum gas were auctioned for licences and concessions. All these measures contributed to improving the economic conditions of the country. A clear example of this is evident in the period between 1989 and 1993, when the government's fiscal budget passed from a high deficit to a slight surplus.[5]

At the same time that the Mexican government was pushing for trade liberalisation, it was introducing certain deregulation measures. Deregulation efforts were guided by the following priorities: standardising the rules affecting all sectors across the economy in relation to standards, quality requirements and operating rules; focusing on those activities in which deregulation would have an immediate effect, or where the cost of not deregulating is very high; and facilitating the systematic reduction of the role of monopolies in the economy.

Despite these efforts, deregulation did not eliminate all distortions in the economy, particularly those in the so-called strategic areas, such as telecommunications, airports, seaports, railroads and roads. Furthermore, deregulation alone did not prevent anticompetitive practices, and in many cases privatisation was done without regard to competition criteria, allowing public monopolies to be transferred to private monopolies. As mentioned above, the main reasoning underlying the privatisation processes that effectively allowed publicly-owned monopolies to be substituted by privately-owned monopolies was to maximise fiscal revenues and re-allocate these revenues to tasks related to the stabilisation of macroeconomic variables.[6]

As privatised sectors exhibited monopoly characteristics, regulatory regimes were instituted to deal with any defects in market operations. However, difficulties arose in most of these sectors because regulatory frameworks were neither sufficiently well designed nor implemented in a timely fashion. One example of the weaknesses is the telecommunications sector. Aiming to maximise revenues, the government sold the entire existing infrastructure to a single entity in 1991, but did not establish a regulatory agency until 1996, 5 years after the concession was awarded. During these 5 years there was little to no oversight, resulting in disputes over network access by competitors on long-distance and mobile telephony services.

By the end of the 1990s, supporters of deregulation began to emphasise the creation of regulatory agencies with some degree of independence from the executive branch of government. At the same time, the government was involved with revising the legal frameworks governing many sectors to eliminate unnecessary burdens and reduce barriers to investment, trade and credit, particularly for small and medium-sized enterprises (SMEs).

During this period, important steps were taken to remove rent-generating restrictions and to eliminate red tape at the level of the federal government. By 2000, the Federal Law of Administrative Procedure (FLAP) was enacted with the aim of making regulatory reform continuous and permanent. The FLAP created the Federal Commission for Regulatory Improvement[7] to guarantee transparency in making and enforcing regulations, and to ensure that regulatory costs were offset by greater benefits to society. It also made mandatory the use of regulatory impact assessment to almost all ministries and federal government agencies, and set out the federal registry of formalities and services. Another powerful instrument for promoting industrial activity was standardisation, established by the Federal Law on Metrology and Standardisation. This law set a transparent procedure for elaborating standards and conferred an important role on the private sector both in elaborating standards and in verifying and certifying these standards.

The Adoption of a Competition Regime

As the removal of trade barriers could not assure competition if private barriers sprang up instead, and import liberalisation could not ensure rivalry in non-traded sectors, a key element in the government's economic reform was the adoption of a general competition law, the FLEC in 1993.

Thus Mexico's competition policy was introduced as part of a decade-long reform initiative to end central government control and protection of domestic economic activity, and to develop a market-based economy. This initiative involved putting an end to most domestic price controls, reducing entry constraints, and opening up the economy to foreign trade and investment. As part of this initiative the CFC was established to enforce the new competition law, the FLEC, and to develop the FLEC's implementing regulations. These implementing regulations were published in March 1998, and reflected more specific substantive and procedural aspects of the law's provisions.

The CFC, which has sole responsibility for applying the FLEC, was established as an independent agency with technical and operational autonomy, although it was attached to the economics ministry for the administration of its budget. The FLEC stipulates that the Mexican president appoints a chairman (or a president commissioner) and four commissioners, who together constitute the plenum, and who are, in effect, the CFC's decision-making authority. They are appointed for staggered 10-year terms and can be removed only for grave causes. The plenum makes determinations by majority vote and is presided over by the chairman, who also directs the CFC's work, represents the CFC publicly, and can appoint and remove personnel.

General Description of the FLEC

The FLEC is designed to give operational force to the anti-monopoly provisions set out under Article 28 of the Mexican Constitution, which opens with a broad prohibition of 'monopolies, monopolistic practices, [and] State monopolies'. The parameters of prohibition are subsequently narrowed when the article clarifies that functions exercised exclusively by the State in specified 'strategic areas' will not constitute monopolies. Also excluded from the prohibition are exclusionary privileges accorded to copyright and patent holders as well as labour associations and export trade associations. The strategic areas currently include postal services, telegraph and radiotelegraphy, petroleum and other hydrocarbons, basic petrochemicals, radioactive minerals, nuclear energy, electric power, and the functions of the central bank.[8]

The FLEC reflects and further details the boundaries of the constitutional exemptions. Article 4 restates the strategic area exclusion, but clarifies that state-owned enterprises are subject to the law with respect to activities that are not explicitly exempted by the Constitution. Articles 5 and 6 repeat that legally-constituted labour associations and export trade associations, respectively, do not constitute monopolies. However, the law adds several requirements for the export trade associations, including that association membership must be completely voluntary and that the organisation of the association must be in compliance with the law of the association's domiciliary state.

Apart from these exceptions, the FLEC is applicable to 'all economic agents', expressly including government agencies (Article 3), and to 'all sectors of economic activity' (Article 1). Thus, the state, its agencies, and all state-owned commercial enterprises operating outside the strategic areas are subject to the law. Nevertheless, the CFC ordinarily has no law enforcement jurisdiction when a government agency is acting as a regulatory authority and not as an economic agent, even if the government entity is engaging in regulatory conduct that inappropriately restricts competition. In these cases, the Commission may issue an advisory opinion to the agency in question, but this order has no legally binding effect.

Although the statute does not make any distinction between foreign and domestic actors and the law 'applies to all agents whose actions impact markets in the Mexican territory', the CFC recognises that enforcement based on an 'effects' test faces a range of difficulties. The Commission has addressed transnational enforcement issues by voluntary submission of the parties, through cooperative agreements with foreign antitrust enforcement authorities, and by adopting regulations designed to exempt certain foreign transactions from its pre-merger notification requirements.

The main objective of the law is economic efficiency. In 2006, this objective was strengthened by amendments to the FLEC, which explicitly introduced the efficiency defence for unilateral conduct and mergers. That is, practices or mergers that would otherwise be anticompetitive may be allowed in view of the efficiency gains they bring about.

For the purpose of law enforcement, economic efficiency is interpreted as the maximisation of consumer welfare. This interpretation was clarified by the 2006 amendments, which specified that in determining whether a unilateral conduct is illegal, the CFC must evaluate the pro-competitive efficiency gains it produces, as well as its net effect on consumer welfare. A similar interpretation applies to mergers: Article 16 of the regulations deems a merger as efficiency-enhancing if it increases consumer welfare. Article 5 of the law exempts intellectual property rights (IPRs) from the monopoly provision, thus implicitly allowing monopolistic exploitation of IPRs for the sake of promoting long-term innovation. This exception, however, does not include leveraging IPRs to exclude competitors in related markets.

Enforcement of the FLEC

The FLEC implements the Constitution by prohibiting and sanctioning the practices by which monopoly power might be obtained or strengthened. Under the FLEC, monopolistic practices are classified as either 'absolute' (Article 9) or 'relative' (Article 10).

Absolute monopolistic practices are prohibited *per se* and agreements to undertake them are legally void. Such practices cannot be defended by claiming that they are efficient, as their inefficiency is established by the law. In contrast, relative monopolistic practices may not be found illegal unless the respondent is found to have 'substantial market power' in a defined relevant market and fails to prove efficiency gains derived from this practice.

The following sections discuss the CFC's experience in the three principal areas of competition law enforcement: abuse of dominance, cartels, and mergers.

Unilateral Conduct or Abuse of Dominance

Anticompetitive unilateral conduct is subject to a substantial market-power screen and demonstration of intended, actual, or potential harm to competition. The preamble of Article 10 of the FLEC provides a generic definition of relative monopolistic practices as those 'whose aim or effect is or could be to improperly displace other agents from the market, substantially hinder their access or that establish exclusive advantages in favour of one or several entities or individuals'. Article 10 then specifies 11 specific types of anticompetitive conduct: (1) vertical market division; (2) resale price maintenance; (3) tied sales and bundling; (4) exclusive dealing; (5) refusal to deal; (6) collusive boycott; (7) predatory pricing; (8) exclusive dealing in exchange for special discounts; (9) cross-subsidisation; (10) price discrimination; and (11) raising rivals' costs, hindering their production process, or reducing their demand.

In order to find a violation of the law the CFC must demonstrate that: (1) the alleged violator carried out one of the specific practices defined in Article 10; (2) the conduct concerns goods or services in the relevant market; (3) it can be determined that the alleged violator has substantial power (dominance) in the relevant market; and (4) the conduct has the intent or effect of displacing agents, hindering access, or establishing an exclusive advantage.

During its 17 years of existence, key actions have been conducted in three main areas in order to improve effectiveness in enforcement of competition law regarding abuse-of-dominance cases. First, a new criterion was adopted for choosing what cases will be initiated, investigated, and eventually sanctioned.[9] Second, an advocacy strategy aimed at strengthening communication between the judicial branch and the competition authority, and improving judges' understanding of competition issues, was developed. Third, and perhaps most importantly, the FLEC was amended in 2006 to clarify the conduct that could constitute an abuse of dominance.

Before the 2006 amendments, the FLEC defined specific conduct that could be sanctioned, including: (1) non-price unilateral restraints; (2) resale price maintenance; (3) tied sales; (4) exclusive dealings; (5) refusal to deal; and (6) exclusionary boycott. The FLEC then defined other types of anticompetitive conduct as conduct that unduly damaged or impaired the competition process and free access to production, processing, distribution and marketing of goods and services (Article 10, paragraph VII). This lack of precision became the subject of legal controversy that influenced one of the most important 2006 amendments.

By 2005, there were four judicial procedures in district courts where complainants challenged the open-ended nature of the provision on relative monopolistic practices as unconstitutional. In 2005, the Supreme Court analysed and resolved the constitutionality of Article 10, paragraph VII, concluding that this paragraph was unconstitutional, as it only included general criteria for the kind of conduct that can hinder free market access and economic competition, and failed to establish the parameters that the CFC must observe in order to sanction the relative monopolistic practices involved.

In order to overcome the Supreme Court decision on the unconstitutionality of Article 10, paragraph VII, the 2006 reforms to the FLEC included five additional relative monopolistic practices that were originally contained only in the FLEC's regulations. These were: (7) predatory pricing; (8) rebates and loyalty discounts; (9) cross-subsidisation; (10) price discrimination; and (11) raising rivals' costs.

The 2006 amendments also included specific economic concepts that firms can use to argue efficiency gains that offset the effects of anticompetitive practices.[10]

In nearly two decades of experience with abuse-of-dominance investigations, one important lesson from the CFC experience is that the criteria for selecting dominance cases are of vital importance for a competition authority. As the CFC has gained experience, the quality of the cases accepted has improved, as well as the CFC's analyses of the conduct under investigation. The rate of success before the courts has improved dramatically, in large part because the Commission has tried to understand the reasons for it losing cases in the early years. In addition to learning from its mistakes, the CFC has become very proactive with the judicial tribunals, and has been working actively to present its viewpoints throughout the appeal process, and generate a clearer understanding of competition issues among the members of the judiciary. These initiatives, which are part of the Commission's advocacy strategy, will be explained in more detail under the section on competition advocacy.

In 2009, 75 per cent of the CFC decisions that were appealed before the judiciary were upheld. Among the most important decisions that were upheld by the judiciary were those related to the sanctions imposed on several firms that are part of the Coca-Cola Group, in which the Commission decided that the Coca-Cola Group was abusing its market power by carrying out exclusivity contracts with retailers. The importance of these resolutions is that the concept of an economic interest group was confirmed by the judiciary. Another important resolution is that the judiciary confirmed the powers of the CFC to impose cautionary measures in order to force economic agents to provide information or appear before the CFC.

The Coca-Cola Export Corporation case began in 2000. The case involved Grupo Pepsi-Cola (PCM) and other companies filing a claim against several companies that form Grupo Coca-Cola (GCC), alleging a violation of the FLEC because of an exclusive dealing requirement that conditioned the sale of carbonated drinks on agreements not to acquire or sell the carbonated drinks produced or distributed by companies that are not part of Grupo Coca-Cola. From this claim, the Commission started an investigation as it deemed that the denounced conduct would fall within the practices contained in Article 10, paragraphs IV and VII, of the FLEC. Once this conduct had been proven to have taken place, and after determining that the defendants had substantial relevant power, it was established that the members of Grupo Coca-Cola may be responsible for these practices. Therefore, a warrant establishing the probable responsibility of the Grupo was prepared and the economic agents that form part of Grupo Coca-Cola were notified. The group then proceeded to submit its arguments and evidence to support its defence. In June 2005, after weighing the evidence before it, the Commission ruled that these firms engaged in a relative monopolistic practice established in Article 10, paragraph IV. The CFC sanctioned the group by imposing a fine of \$45 128 571 (forty-five million one hundred and twenty-eight thousand five hundred and seventy-one dollars). The sanctioned companies filed an appeal for review, challenging the definitions of the relevant market, the determination of substantial power, the existence of GCC as an economic interest group, and the legality of actions carried out by the Commission. In December 2005, the CFC decided on GCC's appeal, declaring it unfounded. The resolution was thus upheld. Contesting the resolution, the Coca-Cola Export Corporation promoted an 'amparo' suit,[11] which was granted because the judge considered that the Statement of Objections issued by the CFC lacked grounds and motives. The CFC filed an appeal before the Federal Circuit Tribunal on Administrative Matters, which was settled in April 2007 when the sentence issued by the judge was revoked, thus denying the 'amparo' to the plaintiff. In this sense, the court validated the resolution issued by the CFC and determined that the concept of 'economic interest group' has its basis in the FLEC.

Cartels and Mexico's Leniency Programme

The absolute monopolistic practices that are subject to *per se* prohibition under Article 9 are grouped into four categories of hard-core horizontal agreements among competitors:

- Price fixing: Prohibits information exchanges with the purpose or effect of fixing or manipulating price.
- Output restriction: Prohibits commitments relating to the volume or frequency with which goods and services are produced.
- Market division: Covers potential as well as existing markets.
- Bid rigging: Covers agreements respecting both participation in auctions and establishment of the prices to be bid.

These prohibitions have been a critical weapon in the elimination of publicly-sanctioned, but privately-arranged, price constraints. Until the mid-1980s, prices for most goods and services were fixed by law, and the ostensibly regulated price level was often the result of an agreement among industry members. Industries were organised into 'business chambers' subject to the supervision of the ministry of the economy.

Hence, in the early years of the Commission, much of its enforcement work with respect to these practices was focused on rooting out the endemic anticompetitive habits that these business chambers and price controls had encouraged.

Since 1998, the CFC has continued to bring price-fixing cases involving business chambers, but far fewer than in the previous 5 years. Recent cases have involved pursuing chambers of business operating in markets such as tourist transportation services, corn tortilla dough, customhouse brokerage services, services in the real estate market, and blue agave (the main ingredient used to produce tequila).

A good example of the CFC's current enforcement activity in the area of absolute monopolistic practices is in the provision of professional services in the real estate market. The case started in May 2007, when Bella Vista Chapala SA de CV filed a complaint against Grupo Inmobiliario del Lago, AC (GIL) and the Mexican Association of Real Estate Professionals, Section Chapala (AMPI Chapala), for possible absolute and relative monopolistic practices. The complainant alleged the existence of an agreement between real estate agents associated with GIL for charging equal fees in the provision of professional services in the real estate market in the region of the state of Jalisco. In addition, it stated that AMPI Chapala denied membership to estate agents who were not associated with GIL. In the course of the investigation, a real estate agent presented a leniency application to the CFC (the first since the establishment of this procedure in 2006). The information obtained from this applicant, together with that gathered during the investigation, allowed the CFC to demonstrate: (1) the existence of operational rules for GIL partners, through which the real estate agents fixed commissions on the sale prices of real estate; (2) the existence of a 'commissary' that monitored the compliance of the operational rules by the partners, and that was responsible for issuing fines or taking disciplinary action when violations to the rules occurred; (3) cooperation of AMPI Chapala to implement the agreement through conditioning the admission or membership renewal to their affiliates; and (4) the elimination of the competition which resulted in higher prices for consumers. In December 2009, the CFC resolved to sanction both economic agents with a total fine of $1 934 446 (one million nine hundred and thirty-four thousand four hundred and forty-six dollars).

In terms of cartel prosecution, another important amendment to the FLEC has been the strengthening of the CFC's enforcement capacity by establishing a leniency programme aimed at detecting and fighting collusive agreements that fix prices, reduce output, segment markets, or facilitate bid rigging.

The leniency programme protects the first economic agent that: (1) provides evidence to prove the existence of an absolute monopolistic practice; (2) cooperates completely and continuously with the Commission during the course of the investigation and the defence of the case; and (3) undertakes necessary actions to end its participation in the cartel. The leniency programme also considers a reduction in fines for those agents that are not the first to come forward, as long as they contribute information towards the investigation.

Mergers and Acquisitions

For the purpose of the FLEC, a merger is understood to consist of acquiring the control of a corporation, or any other action through which corporations, associations, stocks, equity interest, trusts and assets in general are combined among competitors, suppliers, customers or any other economic agents. The CFC can prohibit a merger or acquisition if the resulting economic agent would be able to fix prices unilaterally, limit supply, or facilitate any of the monopolistic practices considered in the FLEC.

Article 16 of the FLEC prohibits mergers whose objective or effect is to reduce, distort or hinder competition. Article 17 requires the CFC, in assessing mergers, to consider whether the merging parties would be enabled to fix prices unilaterally, substantially restrict competitors' access to the market, or engage in unlawful monopolistic conduct. Article 18 adds the requirement that, in analysing mergers, the Commission must identify the relevant market and determine whether the merged entity is likely to possess market power.

The 2006 amendments to the FLEC focused on increasing notification thresholds, implementing a fast track for mergers that do not put the competition process at risk, and modifying the waiting period before a merger may take place.

Article 20 of the FLEC provides the criteria for three alternative reporting thresholds and establishes that a pre-closing filing is required if any of the following three thresholds is met: when the value of the transaction exceeds $1121 million Mexican pesos (approximately US$89 million); when the transaction giving rise to the concentration involves the accumulation of 35 per cent or more of the assets or shares of stock of an economic agent, whose assets or annual sales in Mexico exceed $1121 million Mexican pesos (approximately US$89 million); when the transaction giving rise to the concentration involves the accumulation in Mexico of assets or capital stock in excess of $523 million Mexican pesos (approximately US$41 million) and the economic agents involved (buyer and seller) in the concentration have assets or volume of annual sales, jointly or individually (worldwide), that exceed $2991 million Mexican pesos (approximately US$237 million).

While the review of mandatory merger notifications consumes significant CFC resources, it is one of the most important aspects of competition enforcement in Mexico, and merger control has proven to be one of the most successful areas of enforcement of the FLEC. An important challenge for the CFC, and for many young authorities, has been to increase the efficiency of its operations and streamline the analysis of mergers so that resources can be concentrated on the handling of complicated cases. In order to accomplish this, the CFC has found that a fast-track procedure for the analysis mergers unlikely to cause competitive harm has been of the utmost importance.

One of the most important merger decisions of the CFC was in 2007, when the Commission rejected the merger of Aeromexico and Mexicana[12] – the two major Mexican trunk airlines. During the merger investigation, the Commission analysed two key issues: (1) the entrance of competition to the market by low cost carriers (LCCs) since 2004; and (2) the increased importance of barriers-to-entry airport facilities, because in 2005 the ministry of communications and transport declared Mexico City International Airport 'saturated', meaning that in peak hours there was full capacity for take-off and landing. Regarding the competition from LCC, the CFC considered it insufficient to prevent the exercise of market power by the merged firms. With respect to take-off and landing slots, the CFC found that Aeromexico and Mexicana combined had approximately 60 per cent of the slots in Mexico City, and approximately 50 per cent in the other two major cities.[13] Thus, given the low competition from LCCs and the fact that there were no slots for new competitors, the Commission did not approve the merger.

More generally, important lessons from the CFC's experience include that imposing conditions in merger approvals is challenging, and establishing behavioural remedies in particular can be very difficult to implement and should be avoided if possible. Another lesson has been that the dissolution of assets once the merger has been concluded (ex-post) presents enormous challenges.

COMPETITION ADVOCACY

Competition advocacy and outreach efforts are fundamental for communicating the benefits that competition brings to consumers and for promoting the legal framework for the defence of their rights. Moreover, international experience has proven that one of the best ways for a competition agency to be proactive is to enhance competition advocacy. Mexico is not the exception to this experience, as the CFC has conducted several activities related to the promotion of a competitive environment for economic activities by: (1) issuing opinions; and (2) creating and strengthening its relationships with other governmental entities. The FLEC explicitly vests the CFC with authority to engage in these advocacy activities as established in Article 24.

In Mexico, the evolution of a competition culture has been the product of advocacy efforts carried out by the Commission over its 17 years of operation. Since 1994, the CFC has implemented countless activities to promote the understanding of competition as a key tool for promoting productive and allocative efficiency, and for ensuring that the principles of competition prevail in all sectors of the economy, but especially in those subject to regulation.

Nevertheless, the impact and effectiveness of early advocacy efforts were still limited, which led to the CFC exploring the possibility of improving its legal instruments for preventing and eliminating anti-competitive behaviour, by seeking amendments to the FLEC, in 2006.

During the discussion of the FLEC's bill, direct lobbying efforts with Congress were conducted by the Commission on many fronts. An active media strategy was developed to generate awareness and win over allies in favour of the amendments to the law.

Even though the reform faced some strong resistance by business – with important lobbing powers – in April 2006, Congress voted unanimously to pass the amendments. These included: the increases of monetary and non-monetary sanctions for anticompetitive behaviour, having as a last resort the divestiture of assets; granting the CFC with powers to investigate restraints to local trade; allowing for the inclusion of competition principles in rule-making and public design; and strengthening the compulsory nature of the CFC's opinions on government actions in regulated sectors.

The implementation of the last two amendments has been of great importance in strengthening the CFC's competition advocacy strategy. The amendments were included to expand and strengthen the CFC's advocacy powers, recognising the importance given to the laws and secondary regulations that oversee the activities of economic agents, as well as the programmes and actions of federal, state and municipal authorities.

Promotion of Competition in Regulated Sectors

The FLEC empowers the CFC to issue opinions on legislative bills, and technical regulations, as well as any public policies or administrative acts which may affect competition. The Commission also has the authority to issue opinions on secondary regulations and legislative proposals to Congress. This mandate has been an essential tool for creating and promoting a competition culture among government bodies and institutions, and for advocating for the inclusion of competition criteria in public policies, including new laws and regulations.

The Commission regularly issues opinions and general recommendations on key sectors of the Mexican economy, and the Commission has been instrumental in influencing the design of public policies and ensuring that policies incorporate competition principles as appropriate.

Through its opinions, the CFC has specifically sought to: (1) enhance efficiency and competition in the private pension system; (2) promote a more competitive structure of the retail banking system; (3) facilitate technological convergence and promote a more competitive environment in telecommunications; (4) develop a pro-competitive regulatory framework to facilitate access to audiovisual content; (5) minimise regulatory inefficiencies in the supply of airport services; (6) reduce barriers to entry in the gasoline retail sales and transport and distribution of liquefied petroleum gas markets; and (7) remove barriers to international trade.

Despite many successes, much work remains to be done, especially in Mexico's key regulated sectors such as telecommunications, energy, transportation and financial services.

Of course, the success of the CFC's opinions is attributable to the fact that the CFC has an autonomous decision-making process. Because of public confidence in the impartiality of CFC decisions, publishing CFC opinions and integrating them into the public debate has allowed the Commission to make progress with sectoral regulators who might otherwise be less inclined to follow competition recommendations in a less transparent environment.

The CFC continues to encourage the adoption of competition principles in regulated sectors such as the autonomy and the horizontal accountability of sectoral regulators in order to promote efficiency and competitiveness. Additionally, the CFC continues to promote a culture of competition.

One important initiative is the CFC's experience with the OECD on the implementation of a competition assessment 'toolkit', whose main objective is to issue recommendations on how to strengthen competition in key sectors of the economy.

Since 2007, the ministry of the economy, the CFC, and the competition division of the OECD have been implementing the toolkit. The outcomes produced so far include a significant number of proposals for pro-competitive reforms to the regulatory framework, aimed at removing distortions to the efficient functioning of markets that are key for economic performance and the welfare of the population.

This work involved the development of a series of market studies carried out by several well-known academics and was coordinated by the CFC's directorate-general for economic studies. Based on these studies, the work also involved the formulation of concrete proposals for pro-competitive reform as well as the provision of technical support to other areas of the federal government and Congress for the implementation of the reforms. To date, the markets that have been assessed through this project are:[14]

- Foreign trade: It proposed the simplification of customs procedures and tariff structure. These recommendations led to an ambitious programme of deductibility by the ministry of economy in December 2008. The proposals on customs have been partly taken on board by the Mexican treasury.
- Telecommunications: The CFC is working with the Ministry of Communications and Transport to ensure the inclusion of the recommendations in the determination of interconnection rates in telephony services. Implementation of these recommendations will render benefits for consumers estimated at ten billion dollars a year. In addition, recommendations on the allocation of radio spectrum were included in the terms of spectrum auction that was carried out in the first half of 2010.
- Technical standards: The application of the method for assessing the competitive effects of regulation facilitated the identification of problems in 15 per cent of a sample of 120 Mexican standards.
- Pharmaceutical market: The study provided recommendations aimed at accelerating the adoption of generic drugs that could generate benefits for consumers amounting to US$2.8 billion a year.
- State regulation: Based on the successful experience in Australia, the study provides recommendations for the implementation of pro-competitive reforms to state regulatory frameworks.
- Competition and income distribution: The study calculates the effect of the lack of competition in consumers' income. The results are currently being analysed in the Ministry of Social Development.
- Banking sector: In 2009, Congress passed a reform to the Mexican banking system. The reform incorporated the CFC's recommendations developed within the framework of the Competition assessment toolkit. These recommendations aimed to increase competition and improve market performance without compromising market penetration and to decrease concentration and price levels. More specifically, these recommendations promoted: (1) increased transparency: To facilitate customer mobility by requiring banks to provide an information package about customer accounts; to allow banks to act on behalf of switching customers;

and to establish standards on the customer switching process; (2) access to essential infrastructure: To guarantee competitive access by establishing minimum standards to access the underlying switch networks; (3) to promote competitive interchange fees: To make transparent the Bank of Mexico's role in setting the interchange fee and to promote the efficient growth of the market; and (4) to eliminate excessive requirements for banking through branches.

Interaction with Key Audiences

Since the creation of the CFC, improved communication with the Mexican judiciary has been a priority. To this end, since 2006, the CFC has been developing a series of training programmes on competition matters for magistrates, judges and their staff. These programmes have been of great value to the CFC because they have strengthened the formal relationship between the Commission and the judiciary, and have also provided an excellent opportunity for promoting competition policy among local and federal government officials, consumers, the business community, academic institutions, and the media.[15]

In addition, the CFC interacts with other public authorities on an ongoing basis, at the federal, state and municipal level, to ensure the full application of the FLEC and competition principles. In particular, the Commission works jointly with the Office of the Federal Attorney for Consumer Protection (PROFECO) to protect and guarantee consumer rights.

In 2008, the Commission signed a cooperation agreement with PROFECO, which has helped both institutions to detect monopolistic practices and strengthen the promotion of competition advocacy and consumer protection across the national territory. This institutional agreement includes reciprocal training activities between both agencies and also considers the promotion of competition/consumer culture inside the country. These activities are also part of a programme between the Commission and the Inter American Development Bank, which is aimed at ensuring market access for small and medium-sized enterprises through competition policy.

Despite the progress made in the 17 years that the FLEC has been in force, the effectiveness of competition policy has been undermined by legislative loopholes, which have hindered the direct resolution of problems of lack of competition in the market and the incorporation of adequate competition provisions in regulation and public policies. For this reason, the CFC has engaged in constant communication with the

Mexican Congress to emphasise the importance of competition principles for the economic development of the country. The reforms to the competition law that were approved in 2006 are the direct result of these efforts.

The 2006 reform process required 9 months of analysis during which the CFC learned the importance of telling a credible story. That is, in order to push such an ambitious project forward, the case had to be made by explaining very clearly what the benefits of the reforms would be for the average citizen. Again, the CFC's active media strategy was a key mechanism for creating awareness and gathering allies in favour of the amendments to the law. The CFC also conducted many advocacy events which included conferences in academic institutions, meetings with industry chambers and discussing the issue in international competition fora.

In this sense, it was very important to convey a sense of urgency in the accomplishment of the reform and to situate it very clearly within the wider public policy priorities. Moreover, the CFC recognised the impact of using public pressure effectively in order to generate support for the reform. This was a particularly tricky process, not just for competition policy reform, but also because the timing for public or media pressure had to be very carefully decided.

The CFC acknowledged that for legislative reforms such as these, it was essential to identify potential 'promoters' within Congress – that is, one or more legislators who could make the case to their peers, gain their confidence, and maintain the support throughout the difficult process of internal negotiations. The key component was to ensure that the cause could become a personal crusade for an influential member of Congress. It was important to note that the promoter did not necessarily have to be a member of the legislative leadership, but could be someone with a particular defacto influence in the area of interest. In order to do this, the CFC developed a strong legislative intelligence that provided an accurate mapping of the internal workings of the legislature.

SECOND-GENERATION AMENDMENTS TO THE FLEC

The Mexican economy was not immune to the economic recession that began in 2008 and has been affected severely by a combination of several adverse factors, such as decreasing national competitiveness and low competition in several markets, especially those that are highly concentrated.

Recognizing the vital importance of a sound competition policy and competitiveness to economic growth and stability, in April 2010 the President of Mexico, Felipe Calderón Hinojosa, submitted a bill to reform competition legislation to Congress. The bill would give the CFC additional powers, make it easier for firms to comply with the law, and increase legal certainty. Following a productive and intense debate, it was approved unanimously by Congress in April 2011.

The amendments raise the expected cost of violating the law, easing compliance and providing additional legal certainty.

To improve deterrence, the amendments provide for: (1) higher fines; (2) criminal sanctions for hardcore cartel violations; (3) dawn raids; and (4) interim measures. Specifically, fines were raised up to 10 per cent of the annual domestic revenues of a firm for cartel activity and 8 per cent for abuse-of-dominance. For criminal conduct, the 2011 reforms amended the Mexican Federal Criminal Code to establish sanctions ranging from 3 to 10 years of prison for firms' officers who take part in cartels. Regarding on-site searches, before the amendments the CFC had to provide notice to companies under investigation and could search only for information previously requested from the firms. The amendments authorise dawn raids without previous notice. The amendments also empower the CFC to order interim measures to stop the alleged conduct or suspend consummation of the merger while the investigation is under way.

To ease compliance with the competition law, the 2011 amendments introduce for oral hearings, providing the parties under investigation the opportunity to present their case to the CFC's commissioners and officers. The amendments also allow the CFC to enter into settlements with parties, which can provide swift and efficient resolution to an investigation. Also in the area of easing compliance with the law, notification requirements for mergers that pose no danger to competition, such as corporate restructuring, were eliminated, and the simplified notification process was clarified.

Finally, the amendments also provide for increased transparency and predictability through measures such as additional guidelines, and eventually specialised courts for competition issues. A separate reform in 2011 introduced class actions.

At the time of writing this chapter, the CFC is busy implementing these new amendments.

CONCLUDING REMARKS

For decades, the Mexican economy was characterised by strong protectionism and heavy government intervention. By the beginning of the 1980s, the Mexican government began to introduce economic reforms that moved away from its traditional state-led development strategy. During the 1990s, the government pushed for trade liberalisation, privatised hundreds of state-owned commercial enterprises, and introduced certain deregulation measures.

Although the market-oriented reforms of the 1990s brought many benefits to the Mexican economy, in some specific instances, these same reforms yielded less impressive results in terms of making Mexico more competitive. The most notable example is the privatisation of the telecommunications sector, which merely replaced a public monopoly with a private one.

Thus, as removing trade barriers could not assure competition if private barriers sprang up instead, and import liberalisation could not ensure rivalry in non-tradable sectors, a key element in the government's economic reform was the introduction of a general competition law and an independent enforcement agency. Thus Mexico's competition policy was introduced in 1993 as part of a decade-long reform initiative to end central government control and protection of domestic economic activity, and to develop a market-based economy.

The central objective of the FLEC is economic efficiency, interpreted as the maximisation of consumer welfare. It implements the Constitution by prohibiting and sanctioning the practices by which monopoly power might be obtained or strengthened. Under the FLEC, practices are classified as either 'absolute' (Article 9) or 'relative' (Article 10). Also, it prohibits mergers whose objective or effect is to reduce, distort or hinder competition (Article 16).

Through important amendments to the FLEC in 2006 and then in 2011, the CFC has over time increased its enforcement tools, powers and effectiveness. With nearly 2 decades of enforcement experience bringing cases to stop anticompetitive unilateral conduct and cartels and to prevent anticompetitive mergers, these enforcement actions have allowed the Commission to build a level of expertise that is on par with more mature agencies around the globe, and more generally to become a world-class enforcement agency. CFC enforcement actions have brought about innumerable benefits to the Mexican economy and to the individual consumers, in the form of better quality and lower-priced goods and services.

Complementing these enforcement actions has been a sustained focus on competition advocacy and outreach. The CFC has had some of its most important impacts on the Mexican economy and for Mexican consumers through successful advocacy activities, with notable changes in sectors as diverse as private pensions, airport services, and international trade, among others.

In 2012, the Commission stands poised to continue these good efforts, and contribute to the increasing competitiveness and growth of the Mexican economy and the wellbeing of Mexican consumers.

NOTES

1. The Spanish acronym is LFCE.
2. This is the Spanish acronym.
3. See Katz, Isaac (1999).
4. See Chong, Alberto and Lopez-de-Silanes, Florencio (2004).
5. Ibid.
6. The decision to substitute public monopolies with private ones could also be result of compromises with powerful business interests allied to the government.
7. COFEMER is its Spanish acronym.
8. Although since the early 2000s there have been proposals to reform and liberalise some of these sectors – notably oil – the changes to the status quo have been marginal and, unfortunately, the debate continues to focus on historical and ideological arguments.
9. This new criterion aimed at prioritising those cases with a bigger impact on consumers' welfare and where the likelihood of success is higher.
10. Other important changes introduced by the 2006 amendments include increasing maximum fines for violation of the FLEC, allowing the CFC to order divestiture of assets as a last resort, and granting the CFC limited powers to conduct on-site verifications for evidence-gathering.
11. 'Amparo': A very powerful provision unique to Mexican law that is an order for protection against acts by authorities. There is no adequate translation for this term into English.
12. Even though Mexicana and Aeromexico started as private enterprises, by 1980 the government owned the majority of shares in both companies. At the end of the 1980s these companies were privatised when they served approximately 90 per cent of the market. By the mid-1990s these companies faced difficult financial conditions and the purchase of Mexicana by Aeromexico was approved by the Federal Government. In 1995 the major shareholders of this single company (including BBVA Bancomer, Banamex, Scotiabank Inverlat and Santander Serfin) created the International Corporation of Aviation (Cintra for its acronym in Spanish) in order to restructure the financial assets of the corporation and avoid bankruptcy. However, the Mexican financial crisis of 1995 forced the government to take control of more than 60 per cent of Cintra. This situation lasted until 2005 when the companies were privatised.
13. Monterrey and Guadalajara.
14. http://www.oecd.org/document/34/0,3343,en_2649_40381664_44948578_1_1_1_1,00.html.

15. Part of the success of the training programs for the members of the judiciary resulted from the fact that these programmes were conducted not by staff from the Commission but by judges and magistrates from more experienced jurisdictions.

BIBLIOGRAPHY

Chemtob, S.M. (2007). The Role of Competition Agencies in Regulated Sectors, Department Of Justice (DOJ). 5th International Symposium on Competition Policy and Law, Institute of Law, Chinese Academy of Social Sciences. Beijing, China.

Chong, Alberto and Lopez-de-Silanes, Florencio (2004). Privatisation in Mexico. Inter American Development Bank.

Competition Advocacy in Mexico (2008). 35th Annual Conference on International Antirust Law and Policy. Fordham University School of Law, September.

2004 Competition Law and Policy in Mexico, an OECD Peer Review. Report financed by the Inter-American Development Bank.

Contribution submitted by Mexico under Session III of the OECD's Global Forum on Competition held on 19 and 20 February 2009.

Estrada, Ernesto (2008). Competition Policy in Mexico, *The Online Magazine for Global Competition Policy* (GCP), Release One.

Improving Relationships Between Competition Policy and Sectoral Regulation (2007). Latin American Competition Forum 4th Annual Meeting, Mexico's Contribution. Mexico.

Industrial Policy and Competition Law and Policy in Mexico (2006). 33rd Annual Conference on International Antitrust Law and Policy. Fordham University School of Law, September.

Katz, Isaac (1999). *La Constitución y el Desarrollo Economic de México*. México: Cal y Areana.

Mexican Federal Competition Commission (CFC), Development of Competition Policy (2006).

The 6th Annual International Competition Network (ICN) Conference, Moscow, Panel Discussion, Development and Competition Policy – Comments by Eduardo Pérez Motta (2007).

Stewart, T., Clarke, J. and Joekes, S. (2007). *Competition Law in Action: Experiences from Developing Countries*. Canada: International Development Research Centre (IDRC).

2. The evolution of the Hungarian competition regime: 2 decades of dynamic change and continuity

*Mobilis in mobili**

Csaba Kovács and Andreas P. Reindl[1]

INTRODUCTION

In the 2 decades since the fall of the communist regime in 1989–1990, Hungary has developed what many consider one of the more successful 'new' competition regimes. Our essay examines factors that contributed to this development, the interdependence between the competition regime and Hungary's economic development, long considered a success story among emerging market economies, and developments that might threaten the success achieved to date.

Our discussion begins with a chronological overview of events that we organise into three periods: the transition years after the fall of the communist regime (approximately 1990–1998); the period during which EU accession emerged as a dominant force (approximately 1999–2004); and the 'contemporary' period following EU accession (approximately 2005–2010). Even though each period can be characterised by a particular set of domestic and international events, there are no sharp dividing lines between them: developments overlapped and certain more recent events could not have happened without earlier efforts.

The second section takes a more analytical approach and looks at features that have consistently played a prominent role in the Hungarian competition regime, including the enabling environment, the GVH[2] as an institution, and its advocacy and enforcement activities. In this section we also develop our main points about factors that most critically contributed to success: the GVH's ability to carefully identify the right opportunities – created by both the international and domestic environments – to promote competition policy and enforcement; the openness to learn from good practices developed and applied in other jurisdictions; and continuity in the Hungarian competition regime, including continuity in leadership and in the GVH's capacity-building efforts. Our story of competition law and policy in Hungary focuses on the Hungarian Competition Authority, the GVH, which has been at the centre of developments and has been driving the dynamics of the entire field in Hungary.

We conclude with some thoughts on future developments and challenges, highlighting the fact that, despite all the relative success, past achievements can quickly be undermined by adverse political and institutional developments.

CHRONOLOGICAL OVERVIEW

The Historical Context: Pre-transition Economic Reforms

The late 1980s and early 1990s can be considered the formative period of Hungary's competition regime. These were the years of change from socialism to democracy and the rule of law, as well as the beginning of the transition to a market economy. They shaped future constraints and opportunities. The way transition unfolded, however, cannot be understood without taking into account preceding reforms of socialist economic governance. These earlier events contributed to the path of competition policy, enforcement and institutions, and influenced the mindset of those involved in the formation of competition policy.

By the late 1980s the economy of Hungary was no longer a classical communist, command economy. The failure of the purer command economy pursued in earlier years to deliver benefits to society had already for a while encouraged Hungary to experiment with a limited use of the profit motive and market mechanism as economic tools. State-owned enterprises (SOEs) remained dominant, but economic entities with different ownership structures, both 'collective' ownership forms and individual entrepreneurs, had been allowed to emerge. This was especially true after 1968, a milestone year of reforms.

The principal idea of these reforms had been to replace the direct form of bureaucratic coordination with an indirect one: economic agents would not be told what to do but would follow their own interests, although factors determining those interests continued to be determined by central planning. In other words, planning would remain but goals would be realised mainly by creating incentives. Various regulations were adopted with carefully-adjusted parameters to determine pay-offs – often called 'motivators' or 'regulatory parameters'. Elements trying to imitate market economies started to appear. The tension between the logic of a planned economy and that of a market economy was one of the driving forces of further developments – during periods of regression and of reform alike.

Welfare and increasing living standards among the whole population received greater attention. This phenomenon can be traced back as far as 1956, when the uprising against the communist regime could be crushed only by Russian troops and subsequent governments understood that a greater focus on living standards was key for the acceptance of the regime. This contributed to the establishment of generous and extensive welfare systems, like 'free' universal healthcare or extended child care. It also entailed the modernisation of consumer habits and a sophistication of demand. The modernisation of households and modernisation of Hungarian society as a whole narrowed the life-style gap between Hungary and the West. Imported western goods appeared in shops. This was a move against the idea of socialist self-reliance, and Hungary was labelled as the happiest barrack in the 'Camp' (that is, the Eastern Bloc).

The focus on increased living standards favoured reforms. The performance of the Hungarian economy did not support standards of living pursued for political reasons, and the gap was financed through foreign loans made possible by a softer domestic political line. As a consequence of increased imports and the need to repay the loans in foreign hard currency, Hungarian firms were encouraged to export to the West and sometimes were even subsidised to do so. Interactions with western counterparts and a presence in western markets educated those firms. As the gap between economic performance and consumption and welfare spending continued to increase, decision-makers had to rely more on good relationships and trade with the West and its continued financial support. Hungary joined the IMF and the World Bank in 1982. During the 1980s, international organisations gained effective power in shaping economic policy and the regulatory framework in Hungary. Their assistance was needed due to Hungary's growing macroeconomic problems; in turn, they required liberalisation and structural changes, which implied further reforms.

Autonomous decision-making by economic entities became more accepted, by granting individual entrepreneurs certain opportunities to expand, and by gradually giving a substantial amount of autonomy to SOE managers, based on the idea that they be allowed to replicate the behaviour of private firms in market economies.

In the second half of the 1980s new forms of entrepreneurship emerged within existing structures, including 'side-divisions' of agricultural cooperatives and 'economic communities' within SOEs. Side-divisions of cooperatives were allowed to engage in complementary activities, which sometimes involved market niches with huge expansion opportunities that transformed the income as well as the operational structure of those cooperatives. 'Economic communities' were usually small self-organised groups of employees within a firm to whom certain activities could be 'outsourced'. Sometimes they also supplied outside customers. They used the assets and the premises of the same firm (for free or almost free), and their members carried out their activity outside of the original working hours under a different, more favourable legal framework than their host firms, especially in terms of taxation. The effects of this experiment were ambiguous. On the one hand, economic communities mobilised people for extra work and found better means of operation in various ways, including technical improvements and reacting to business opportunities. On the other hand, a large part of their advantages and expansion were based on the favourable regulation rather than on superior efficiency, and their existence within an SOE distorted incentives. For example, members of economic communities tended to take care of their work in the community at the expense of their original responsibilities toward the host SOE.

But while these pockets of capitalism emerged, they continued to exist in a socialist country with a strong sense of paternalism towards individuals and firms. Firms often were required to take on 'social responsibilities', and economic security was always supposed to be maintained. Reforms were not supposed to question the system, but to improve its performance.

By the end of the 1980s the 'Hungarian model', which had sought to provide greater economic freedom and prosperity in return for acceptance of the political regime, ceased to work. The tools serving it proved to be unsustainable and the international environment was changing dramatically.

In the cautious process toward market liberalisation, price regulation emerged as an area of special relevance in the development of future competition policy. Reforms brought gradual price liberalisation through various measures. Prices of an increasing number of products and services became unregulated or less directly regulated, moving away from the originally extensive system of price regulation where almost all prices were set by various authorities and prices were not truly cost-oriented. In many cases regulation no longer set an exact price, but a price range within which forces of supply and demand were supposed to determine price levels.

Although prices were never allowed to play a role similar to that in a capitalist economy, additional reforms moved the system in that direction. The majority of the regulated prices were intended to be cost-based.

Price-setting later began to rely on real market economies, like using world market prices or foreign market prices as proxy. All these factors were supposed to move the system more closely toward the outcome in a competitive market economy.

As price regulations became increasingly liberal, concerns emerged about uncontrollable price levels and price movements. This became even more worrying in light of the emphasis on improving standards of living and the paternalistic character of Hungarian politics. Changing economic trends was not an option. This was the context in which competition policy was discovered within the Price Office as a potential tool to keep prices at bay. The Price Office was a powerful, well-resourced, relatively professional and progressive institution at the frontline of economic reforms. And it had proven to be significantly less prone to regulatory capture that elsewhere, at institutions with closer industry and political ties, could lead to resistance against reforms.

The Price Office's perspective was not limited to the technicalities of price-setting, but included the broader significance of price regulation mechanisms as a key aspect of market reforms. A team within the Price Office with direct involvement of top-level management played a major role in exploring competition policy and preparing a competition-based regulatory framework for Hungary. Later, the competition authority was set up using largely the facilities and employees of the former Price Office. The majority of its leaders were well-experienced former Price Office executives. This substantive and institutional link between price regulation and competition policy in Hungary had an imprint in the 'DNA' of the competition policy in Hungary. It was helpful in several ways, but it brought certain controversies as well. To move from price regulation towards competition policy was a natural step in the development of reforms, but it was also a step into a new era that required a different mindset and skills.

As preparatory works for a competition regime were under way, socio-economic developments accelerated in Hungary as well as internationally, culminating in the 1989–1990 system change. This helped the preparation and introduction of competition legislation and institutional set-up in several ways. Obviously, competition policy fitted better in the market economy Hungary wanted to build. Contributions from the IMF and the World Bank were also instrumental. The World Bank sponsored Price Office research into Western competition policy regimes, and the two institutions insisted that Hungary set up a competition system as a pre-condition for loans.[3]

The Transition Period

Socio-economic and policy context

1989 and 1990 were exceptional years in Hungary. System change, an evolutionary process with a settlement negotiated between the communist party and the newly-emerged opposition parties and movements, had a long-lasting and substantial impact on institutions and policy-making. Concepts of division of power and checks and balances found increasing support. Many politicians and society in general started to accept the notion that policy-making should be governed by expertise, and that independent institutions that could not be co-opted by a political agenda could have an important role to play. Several institutions were designed to be independent from direct government influence in the coming years.

There was also strong scepticism about the state and a – perhaps somewhat naïve – trust in how smoothly markets and their self-correcting mechanisms work. This favoured switching to market economy, entrepreneurism and privatisation.

The prevailing climate helped to finalise the draft competition legislation without political interference and to design its institutional framework based on an independent authority. It also helped the Price Office to prepare for the administration of the future competition law. The draft law had been completely prepared just before the system change, but – somewhat symbolically – it was the new, legitimate government which formally submitted it to the new, democratically-elected parliament for adoption in 1990.

The new Competition Act[4] was adopted as fully fledged competition legislation. Its substance and institutional framework resembled legislation in European market economies. The Act covered agreements and abuse of dominance as well as a merger control regime based on a mandatory preliminary notification system. It established an independent competition authority, the GVH, with relatively strong information-gathering powers, the ability to impose fines, and a basically adequate procedural framework. Within the GVH, the Competition Council, which had the role of adopting decisions, was established as an institution independent of the GVH president. Inevitably, the legislation had many imperfections and some peculiarities, but it was more than suitable to launch Hungarian competition policy onto a reasonable trajectory.

The very same climate, however, also imposed severe constraints on the new competition authority. The decade-long experience of the all-powerful state and authorities that exercised their powers and interpreted the law arbitrarily brought strong support for the rule of law. The rule of law was thought to require that law-enforcement authorities have extremely limited powers, with no real discretion. This way of thinking brought the danger of turning authorities into toothless and unreasonably rigid bodies in the name of legal certainty. This attitude was complemented by the Hungarian tradition of regulating everything to a much higher level than in most other jurisdictions, for example through detailed parliamentary act instead of government regulation. Combined with the rapid pace of adopting new legislation, this led to many overly descriptive laws that could limit the flexibility and effectiveness of government institutions.

In addition, when the GVH was established and throughout the first years of operation, the macroeconomic problems – debt, inflation and recession – became very serious. They caused budget cuts, affecting the GVH's budget as well. Maximisation of short-term state revenues became a priority; this could lead to conflicts with competition policy especially in the context of privatisation as governments sought to maximise revenues by selling monopolist firms to investors, rather than breaking them up prior to a sale.

Economic crisis, which was in part a consequence of structural rearrangements, and quick and fundamental changes with far-reaching consequences, such as the widespread although gradual import liberalisation and privatisation, made transition turbulent.[5] Stakes were high and uncertainties were substantial. The sheer scale and depth of the regulatory changes implied by transition required very fast legislative processes in important areas such as corporate law, bankruptcy law or financial issues that were largely unknown, even after Hungary's experience with economic reforms. Improvisation had advantages under these circumstances, although it frequently led to inconsistent or unintended results which in turn entailed further corrective legislation. All this created an atmosphere of regulatory instability and strengthened the turbulent nature of transition.

Public enthusiasm for independent institutions had reached its peak around the time the GVH was established; it soon started to fade. But a certain degree of respect for independence was been built into the political culture and remained effective. Economic policy was preoccupied with macroeconomic crisis management, while protectionist instincts were kept low by several factors. The room to manoeuvre in trade policy was limited by international commitments, macroeconomic problems did not allow for generous subsidies, and various interest groups were not able to impose pressure on politics to protect them. Some of these circumstances were not only favourable for competition; they also helped the GVH to maintain a – beneficial – low profile. They contributed to the perception that the GVH was not involved in the 'big issues', even if in principle it administered a fundamental piece of legislation. They also decreased political interest regarding the activity of the GVH. As a consequence, competition policy was not subject to strong political pressure, while the institutional independence and reputation of the GVH protected it against occasional attempts to exercise political influence. Of course, the same perception probably did not help to improve the poor budgetary position of the GVH, as it was regarded as an unimportant factor in practical matters.

Despite its 'low profile' approach, some of the GVH's activities addressed issues of great importance for 'big' economic policy developments and political interests. The most important of these was privatisation. This area is illustrative of the GVH's attitude and its caution to avoid open conflict that could undermine its effectiveness. Privatisation in Hungary was connected to a large extent to foreign direct investment (FDI). FDI was considered crucial for attracting new capital, technology and business methods to Hungarian SOEs which had often lost or were losing competitiveness; to find owners with business experience (rather than ordinary people who had become owners overnight through a voucher-based privatisation process); and to generate substantial revenues for the state budget.

Privatisation was complex and economically and politically controversial for several reasons, as it involved much more than simply finding potential buyers and negotiating deals with them. The structure of Hungarian industry was highly concentrated with dominant SOEs which were often integrated either horizontally or vertically or both. The process of privatisation therefore offered an opportunity to de-concentrate the economy. Moreover, the need to optimise the process by identifying valuable property and creating potentially attractive combinations inevitably implied some structural reorganisation at firm level (many times the equivalent of industry level due to monopoly) and even some industrial planning. Industrial planning approaches, however, could get excessive, and the goal of maximising privatisation revenue brought the danger of neglecting competition policy considerations as buyers were willing to pay a price premium for firms that were protected from competition.

Thus privatisation had a very significant pro-competitive potential, but also entailed very significant risk of anticompetitive outcomes. The position of the GVH on these trade-offs was clearly articulated. Nevertheless, the GVH did not try to use its strongest weapon – it sent a clear signal that it would not rely on merger control law to block privatisation deals by interpreting the merger control provisions as not covering acquisitions by foreign buyers who were otherwise not present in Hungary.[6] Instead it tried to influence the privatisation process by competition advocacy and agreed with the privatisation agency that it would be thoroughly informed and able to present its advice and concerns at weekly directors' meetings. This gave the GVH an opportunity to influence the process at an early stage, which proved to be useful. It provided a lower profile and a more modest opportunity to intervene. But it was also more realistic and therefore more effective, compared to more heavy-handed intervention that would have tried to use merger review to block complex and hard-negotiated privatisation deals ex-post without offering alternative buyers. This arrangement helped to avoid strong conflicts with both economic policy and politics, while maintaining professional integrity and offering the ability to promote competition.[7]

International contribution

International support for the development of a competition policy in Hungary existed from the very beginning. It included political as well as financial support from the IMF and the World Bank to establish an effective competition policy regime. Within a very short time, the US Department of Justice (DOJ) and the US Federal Trade Commission (FTC), the OECD, and the European Commission offered the GVH (and other Central and Eastern European competition agencies) technical assistance in various forms.[8]

Technical assistance was new for the donors themselves. International technical assistance in competition policy, nowadays so prevalent, did not exist before, at any significant scale. Indeed, it was 'invented' to support the transition of Central and Eastern Europe toward a market economy. Thus, competition authorities of the region served as laboratories for experimenting with technical assistance ideas and methods, while donors were learning by doing. Donors did not coordinate much with each other, at least not in a way observable to the GVH. Programmes offered by various donors were diverse, although there were some overlaps between certain programmes in terms of experts.

The two US authorities were pragmatic in several ways. They joined forces, used USAID money, and sent their personnel to share their experience and approach to competition policy. Their principal form of contribution was the assignment of long-term experts to the recipient authority. Resident advisors were supposed to operate at the battlefield of case work (even if they were not involved in 'exchange of fire'), to be practically useful, and to demonstrate skills and approaches in the agency's day-to-day work. The same number of GVH personnel was invited to study the work of US authorities. This was complemented by short-term visits to Hungary and seminars in Vienna for competition officials from transition economies. US technical assistance ended for

Central European competition authorities, including the GVH, in 1996 as the region was declared 'sufficiently developed'.[9]

The OECD mobilised competition officials of its member countries, accompanied by its own know-how in designing, organising and managing professional events. The so-called 'Vienna seminars', hosted by the Joint Vienna Institute (today held in Budapest), have the longest continuity of technical assistance in the region. They were built around the discussion of cases from participating jurisdictions and aimed to distribute best practices through dialogue. GVH participation in OECD outreach activity as a recipient ended when Hungary joined the OECD in 1996.

The contribution of the European Commission was unique and from the start determined by the EU accession context. When Hungary became an associated member in 1991, EU competition law became the centre of gravity for all competition policy developments, as accession required the 'approximation' of Hungarian competition law to that of the EU. Programmes of the European Commission did not just involve technical assistance, but various exercises to facilitate preparation for accession and accession negotiations. Indeed they did overlap with the preparations and negotiations and therefore will be discussed in the context of the next period.

Technical assistance and other contributions became the principal source of professional knowledge for the GVH and a vital link to enforcement practices elsewhere. They provided outlook and benchmarking, keeping the GVH under a kind of constant soft intellectual pressure to think about how to adapt to international practices or good reasons to deviate from them. As a newly-established institution designed with the desired mandate and structure after extended research and discussions, the GVH concentrated on utilising its existing capacities and tools rather than re-organising or expanding them. Nevertheless, precisely because of the experience of being newly-established in a new field, the spirit of an authority 'in the making' could be sensed. This, together with the already prevailing 'mainstream orientation' contributed to openness towards using all available sources – technical assistance, trainings, and translations of literature – to learn about experiences and good practices in other jurisdictions. Differences between actual GVH practices and knowledge existing elsewhere stimulated a sparkling professional atmosphere.

Except for the EU contribution, which operated in a distinct context, the programmes did not have much direct and immediate material effect on the GVH's operations. One major reason was probably the limited absorption capacity of the GVH. It resulted from language constraints and the need to also pay attention to domestic processes and procedural technicalities, not only the broader concepts and doctrinal issues. Impact was probably also limited because certain skills and practices transmitted by technical assistance were not readily applicable in the Hungarian transition environment due to its turbulent nature and other characteristics limiting the opportunities of the GVH. Even without strong visible effects in the short run, however, the programmes did influence the thinking of young GVH officials, and contributed to developments in the following periods.

Early enforcement efforts

From the outset, the GVH pursued a mainstream competition policy approach rather than trying to develop a special competition policy for transition economies or small economies. Nevertheless, the first competition act included several peculiar elements. They reflected transition characteristics and institutional and socio-economic heritage, including certain misperceptions about markets and competition policy.

Awareness of potential shortcomings in legislation partly explains the presence of a 'general clause' in the law – a prohibition of unfair practices of any kind, even those that were not specified by other provisions. It covered a not-clearly-defined range of conduct, as the term 'unfair' had a broader meaning for the purposes of the competition law.[10] This provision made it possible to fill gaps that may have existed for any reason, but also created the possibility of an arbitrarily extensive use. Although the GVH exercised self-discipline to minimise harm from an overly extensive interpretation, in some cases the general clause was applied too broadly. This was certainly true for the advertisers' cases where some producers of cigarettes and alcoholic drinks used advertisements which were prohibited by law. The GVH found their behaviour 'unfair' under the general clause, as it provided unfair competitive advantage compared to those firms that abided by the law. By the same logic, the media companies that published these advertisements were condemned as well.

A mandatory price-increase notification system was also part of the GVH portfolio. It was not classic price regulation; instead it was, in principle, a tool to prevent excessive pricing of certain dominant firms. This form of price control relied on competition law terminology and procedural framework. Listed producers needed to obtain a preliminary GVH approval in order to be able to increase the price of certain of their products and they had to justify their case on an ad hoc basis by showing that it would not constitute an abuse of their dominant position. The GVH was not supposed to calculate and impose the 'right prices', but to check the applicants' claims. This regime represented a break-away from the price office heritage, but nevertheless reflected a fundamental attitude of price regulation. A government regulation contained a list of producer–product pairs covered by this provision of the Price Act.[11] This list was not a 'dominant firm register' – another special instrument applied in certain transition economies, but not in Hungary – as it listed only a few dominant firms and certain of their products. But one can see similarities between the two concepts.[12]

The basic economic 'units' for the purposes of the law – following the default in Hungarian economic law – were legal entities. As a result, firms under joint ownership were regarded as competitors, even though in EU competition law they would have been regarded as belonging to the same 'economic entity'. Thus, coordination between them fell under the prohibition of horizontal agreement restricting competition. Some interpreted this arrangement as a solution to reach collusion between SOEs without special rules on SOEs (since any discrimination based on ownership was regarded by many as unconstitutional). Nevertheless, it created growing controversies as the share of private ownership increased.

GVH procedures also had their share of peculiarities. Competition law enforcement relied on administrative procedures, but the procedures were designed to incorporate judicial, adversarial elements. The Competition Council was set up as an independent decision-making body within the GVH; it held trials to hear all sides (that is, the party under investigations, the complainant, and the case handler) and each side's reaction to the others' claims in a courtroom-like setting.

However, the most important feature of the competition legislation was the strong position of complainants at the expense of GVH's case selection discretion. This aspect originated from the desire to prevent the misuse of discretion of authorities. Common in transition economies in the region, in Hungary this feature took an extreme form: complaints were legally labelled as 'notifications', which by law initiated formal proceedings; complainants became fully-fledged parties to the investigation. As a consequence, the GVH had to investigate every single complaint in a formal proceeding, and complainants had the right to appeal against unfavourable final decisions of the GVH. In principle, the GVH could also initiate cases ex officio, but such cases were rare since resources were occupied with investigations of complaints. Enforcement was thus complaints-driven, and the GVH was effectively prevented from case selection and setting its own enforcement priorities.

All this contributed to the large share of consumer protection cases[13] and abuse-of-dominance cases. Most abuse-of-dominance cases involved allegations of exploitation – often excessive-pricing complaints, another frequent feature in transition economies – although the GVH was not much familiar with the notion of distinguishing between exploitative and exclusionary abuses during most of the transition period.

Cases dealing with agreements were less frequent, especially vertical restraints cases. The first competition act treated vertical restraints as a potential abuse-of-dominance issue rather than agreements restricting competition; the provision dealing with agreements covered only agreements between competitors.[14] This approach was more consistent with competition economics than approaches adopted later, where the same basic prohibition covers both vertical and horizontal agreements. The initial approach was not necessarily the consequence of a deeper understanding of economic concepts, however. During most of the period, the substantive and analytical distinction between the various types of agreements was greatly unexplored; 'cartel' in the Hungarian terminology referred to every agreement capable of restricting competition, including hardcore cartels, joint ventures and various types of vertical restraints alike. Despite these misconceptions, the majority of restrictive agreement cases did in fact deal with 'real' cartels, although not secret ones. Most cases concerned naïve and/or legacy cartels among firms for whom coordination of pricing or shipment had been part of their normal course of business or had even been mandatory before economic transition. Although these cases did not require significant cartel detection skills, they sometimes contained joint-venture-like elements, requiring careful legal assessment and carefully-developed convincing arguments before the appeals court.[15]

The low number of infringement decisions was in part also the result of a deliberate policy. The GVH understood principles of competition law well – for example, the importance of entry and efficiency in the analysis was very well recognised from the outset. But it did not yet have the skills for a sophisticated case analysis. Certain analytical and investigative techniques learned during technical assistance programmes could in any event not be applied in many cases because the GVH could not obtain required data and documents. Firms did not keep those data and documents (in the absence of business methods and the way of operation which would have produced them), and the interaction between the GVH and parties and their counsel was not highly developed. Moreover, during economic transition many markets and industrial structures were fundamentally moving targets to a much greater extent than in a mature market economy. All these reasons – together with the intention to build reputation with strong cases that were capable of surviving an appeal – led to a very cautious attitude towards intervention in general.

Even though most of the privatisation transactions escaped merger control until 1997, merger cases were numerous as the mandatory notification system started to produce merger cases 'automatically'. Only one case led to a prohibition until 1998,[16] reflecting the cautious attitude toward interventions discussed above. Merger review nevertheless was indispensable for gaining experience and developing skills in every respect, as a precondition for further achievements. A ground-breaking decision occurred only in 1998, when the GVH blocked the acquisition of JÁSZ-TEL, a local telecommunications operator, by MATÁV, the incumbent former monopolist in this newly-liberalised market.[17] Although the target operated as a local monopoly and was therefore not a direct competitor of the incumbent, it was the owner of the local loop and thus regarded as a gateway for new entry to other markets where the incumbent was dominant. The GVH wanted to prevent pre-emptive acquisitions by the incumbent. The theory of harm was sophisticated in this case and reflected the latest thinking in the field. It was fertilised by EU competition policy and the understanding of the nature of market opening as well as of telecommunications. These characteristics link the case to the next period.

The EU Accession Period

Socio-economic and policy context

By the late 1990s, Hungary had achieved major goals of economic and political transition. Private sector activity accounted for 85 per cent of economic output in 1998, up from 15 per cent in 1989. Trade was liberalised. Macroeconomic indicators were on the path of further improving due to painful stabilisation during transition and more responsible economic policy. The country continued to attract more FDI than other countries in the region which supported export oriented industries in particular. 'First generation' regulatory systems had accompanied privatisation in telecommunications and energy, but a new generation of regulations was anticipated. The OECD, while recognising the continuing challenges Hungary would face, characterised the country as being in the OECD mainstream. Hungary seemed to be the 'best student' among transition economies, and the Hungarian way of managing transition seemed to be legitimised by its many accomplishments.

Despite impressive results from economic transition, many structural reforms still lay ahead, including the liberalisation of network industries. Privatisation had left incumbents in powerful positions in these sectors, and regulation was not effective in ensuring either that potentially competitive segments were opened up, or that effective competition developed after formal market opening. For example, much of electricity production and distribution had been privatised. But the former monopolist remained state-owned, controlled the transmission network by ownership and most of the production by long-term contract, and operated as a single wholesale buyer of electricity. The marketplace therefore continued to have great similarities to a monopoly. Competition was not very effective in telecommunications either where the former monopolist retained control over much of the fixed-line network and controlled third-party access. In the postal and transport sectors, reforms and privatisation were lagging behind and there was no effective competition. Thus, further efforts to create competitive markets were needed.

The political environment facilitated further regulatory reforms. EU membership emerged as the key factor shaping the enabling environment. Hungary had been an associated member since 1991, and in 1994 submitted its application to become a full member. EU membership, which became increasingly realistic both economically and politically, was an undisputed aim and an absolute priority of successive governments. Readying the legislative and regulatory system for EU membership determined the government's agenda over subsequent years. Preparing for EU membership involved all aspects of life and the entire regulatory system of Hungary, and reinforced in particular a focus on market-oriented reforms.

Other factors contributed to a reform-minded environment. Transition and macroeconomic issues no longer required as much attention, while the reform mindset which had characterised the transition period did not disappear. For example, there were permanently plans about the modernisation of the civil service. Moreover, successive governments appeared to recognise that macroeconomic success could be sustained only by continued structural reforms and by further increasing competitiveness, which in turn implied reforms too. Indeed, the need for competitiveness-enhancing economic policy was emphasised. Previous success had increased people's confidence in professional policy-making. It also strengthened self-confidence among policy-makers. Reforms therefore could be part of an organic development from a transition economy into a modern and mature market economy.

External support for Hungary's pro-market agenda remained vital and influential. The OECD advocated regulatory reform, which the EU also required. But both institutions went further and also offered know-how as well as political legitimacy. This was true especially for the EU, as the Community *acquis communautaire* provided specific goals that had to be implemented over a given time-period as a condition to become a member. In most cases, Community rules were more competition-friendly than the domestic status quo. For example, in the electricity sector, the market had to be liberalised for large industrial users until 2004, and various functions of vertically-integrated operators had to be separated.

One should not overlook, however, that the political situation was far from perfect to meet the challenges facing Hungary at that time. The new reform agenda required a systematic and sophisticated approach, and predictability in policy-making. During the transition period, constant improvisation had proven to be quite effective. That approach was reinforced as economic results created positive feedback, perhaps misleading decision-makers into believing that the same approach is a general formula of success. But improvisation was not adequate for designing complex regulations. In many areas, policy-makers lacked sufficient expertise in the economics of special areas, in particular the roles of competition and potential market failures. The need to carefully design complex regulation and the value of commitment were not sufficiently recognised.

The government's actions supported the impression that reforms were driven to a great extent by a desire to stand out among the candidate countries and meet external expectations, and not always by a conviction that pro-competitive reforms were in Hungary's own best interests. In regulated industries, for example, EU directives were implemented in a timely manner and without much internal opposition. But the eagerness to meet EU expectations led to a largely formal fulfilment of EU requirements; the substantive merits of regulatory reform, including consumer benefits, were rarely understood. Whenever EU directives allowed a range of implementation options to liberalise network industries, Hungary consistently chose the least competitive alternative. Similarly, useful inputs from the OECD's regulatory reform project were in most cases not welcome because of their recognised benefits, but in order to obtain the 'OECD certificate' in the pursuit of EU membership.

The pace of the legislative process increased even further. This was partly justified by tight EU deadlines. But in most cases it was the result of the nature of the political process which tended to make decisions at the last minute, leaving very little time for careful exploration of alternatives and drafting. It became more widely accepted that politics and politicians rather than experts or bureaucracy should ultimately control decision-making concerning regulated sectors, even detailed rule-making. Speedy regulation continued to produce the same side-effects as during transition, with inconsistent provisions and sometimes unintended outcomes that required further intervention and did not allow much impact assessment. This was not perceived as a major problem, as fulfilling the EU criteria was taken primarily as a necessary as well as a relatively mechanical exercise, even if it had its own challenges given the large volume of required legislation.

The domestic and international environments shaped the major topics, opportunities, and constraints of GVH competition advocacy. GVH competition advocacy efforts became more pro-active, intensive and systematic. For example, the GVH had actively advocated for better regulation in telecommunications since their privatisation in the mid-1990s. Similarly, it had earlier warned against plans to privatise the incumbent electricity 'national champion' without effective de-monopolisation and proper regulation. Now the GVH became involved in working groups and committees dealing with liberalisation, with a strong presence in particular in telecommunications and the energy sector, especially electricity. It also organised events and published bulletins promoting its positions.[18] Renewed efforts were also made regarding other 'natural monopolies' such as the railways and postal services.

EU policies, and to some extent OECD best practices, continued to inform much of the GVH's efforts. But while past advocacy efforts had focused on raising awareness of the existence and interpretation of EU law, they now began to emphasise the proper interpretation of context, details and purposes. This reflected the fact that the GVH understood better than other parts of the administration certain key issues in regulatory reform.

Regulation of supermarket buying power emerged as a relatively new topic of competition advocacy and quickly became an important area for the GVH. The GVH supported the status quo, and argued against government restraints on the competitive strategies of newly-established and more efficient firms that would have benefited more traditional competitors and domestic suppliers who were losing their bargaining power. The situation was unique also because, as regulatory measures were considered, the GVH was urged to stop the 'anticompetitive' practices of large-scale retailers. This forced the GVH to carefully map out the issue for itself, and to explain repeatedly the difference between asymmetric bargaining power and a dominant position for the purposes of competition law, the benefits of competition among modern retail outlets, and the underlying reasons for complaints such as lack of modernisation in agriculture and traditional retail.[19] This issue reappeared in waves and the push for regulatory (or GVH) intervention to fight 'abuses of buyer power' seemed to be increasingly serious. During this period, however, it ultimately never received sufficient political support, probably due to fears that the EU would not look kindly at intervention.

The GVH responded to these pressures primarily by investing in research programmes, rather than by initiating cases or drafting regulations. This response should not exclusively be seen as a tactic to show activity without causing harm (even though delaying tactics were one motivating factor). It was a genuine effort to explore all relevant issues. This approach also gave the GVH an edge in professional discussions. At the same time, research programmes prepared the GVH for effective enforcement, as they enabled it to identify and remedy anticompetitive practices or anticompetitive mergers in future.

International contribution

EU competition law, which had always been an important reference point, also became the principal driver of developments in competition law and enforcement.

Interactions with the Commission, which had begun right after the GVH had started to operate and had increased ever since, reached their peak in the period prior to accession. The European Commission had established various programmes for the competition authorities of candidate countries to facilitate preparation for accession and accession negotiations. Several GVH officials visited the Commission's Directorate General for Competition (DG Comp) either as participants in intensive courses in EU competition law or as 'stagiere official' assigned to a case handler unit for a 'learning by doing' experience. The GVH was eager to utilise opportunities, and to expand them where possible. For example, it sponsored further additional young GVH officials to work temporarily at DG Comp, and invited DG Comp officials to participate in its professional events. DG Comp also organised 'annual meetings with associated countries' from 1995 – an event consisting of high-level conferences, enforcement-oriented expert-level workshops, and semi-formal negotiations. Other technical assistance programmes were outsourced. The Commission also devoted substantial resources to finance the setting-up, replacing, and upgrading of GVH IT systems.

Naturally, the GVH was heavily involved in the negotiation of the competition chapter of the accession, and connected exercises such as the 'screening' of the Hungarian competition law. The intensity of EU involvement increased on various fronts: from 2002, competition authorities of the associated countries – including the GVH – were invited to participate in the process that led to EU competition law procedural reform, decentralising enforcement and establishing the European Competition Network (ECN).

Even though the GVH was on its way to becoming a 'regular' player in the European competition environment, it remained 'multicultural' and critical, and open to good practices promoted elsewhere. The GVH managed to continue to benefit from US technical assistance, even though such programmes had ended for the region in 1996. For example, the GVH hosted professional programmes of the US authorities for Balkan countries from 2001 in which its own personnel were able to participate. Around these programmes, satellite programmes within the GVH could be organised at a negligible marginal cost for US authorities. Using the same low-cost approach, economists and attorneys travelling between the US and countries in South-East and Eastern Europe were invited to spend extra time in Budapest for presentations and consultations in the GVH. This could not have happened in the absence of links, mutual trust, and respect established in previous programmes during the years of transition. The same contacts also prepared the scene for future cooperation.

The GVH's involvement in OECD activities also intensified. Since Hungary had joined the OECD in 1996 the GVH participated in the meetings of the OECD Competition Committee. Initially the OECD and its Competition Committee had almost exclusively served as a source of knowledge. But gradually Hungary became more fully involved in the substantive work of the Committee as the number and quality of submissions to Committee roundtable discussions increased. Also, the GVH became a regular contributor to technical assistance programmes organised by the OECD for the competition authorities of non-member countries, especially in the case of South-East and Eastern European countries. In addition, the GVH arranged a 'secondment' programme with the OECD Competition Division which allowed GVH officials to participate in the work of the Division as resident fellows in order to learn about international best practices.

An important step was the involvement of the GVH in the OECD's regulatory reform review of Hungary in 1999. Aimed more broadly at improving regulatory quality, the project included a review of competition law enforcement and institutions and of two regulated sectors which had been a priority for the GVH, namely telecommunications and electricity. The report concluded with a positive assessment and confirmed that Hungarian competition law and policy was well within the OECD mainstream, which was a significant achievement for a young competition regime.[20] The report also adopted several recommendations to further improve competition law enforcement – including greater focus on horizontal agreements and exclusionary conduct, more effective merger review procedures – and renewed advocacy efforts in areas such as liberal professions.

Many of the OECD report's recommendations provided further impetus for efforts that strengthened competition law enforcement and policy over the ensuing decade. The timing of the report and its recommendations proved to be significant: the review happened after the initial, quite successful period in Hungarian competition law, during which the competition authority had already implemented several concrete and constructive steps to establish a respectable competition regime along the lines of some of the leading jurisdictions. At the same time, a new incoming leadership was ready to make further adjustments and changes and was very open to the whole exercise and receptive to the Report's recommendations. And the pending EU accession process required the legislator to make further changes to competition law and enforcement in any event.

Enforcement

Prospective EU membership also had a significant impact on competition law enforcement, although less on the adoption of new basic rules. After a major revision in 1996, Hungarian competition legislation already followed EU standards in many aspects. The 1996 Competition Act[21] – still in force, although amended several times – represented closer convergence with EU norms, and had eliminated several (although not all) peculiarities discussed above. Substantive and procedural improvement went hand in hand with the 'approximation' to EU provisions. An important exception from the trend of EU-inspired improvements was the treatment of vertical restraints: Hungary originally had a more relaxed treatment of vertical agreements, consistent with principles of competition economics; but accession required adoption of the form-based EU-style block exemption system for vertical agreements in order to harmonise the Hungarian system to European rules. Paradoxically, as Hungary adopted the then-applicable EU regime, the EU started its own reforms in an attempt to align its regime dealing with vertical restraints with principles of competition economics. So Hungary re-adjusted its law to fall in line with the new EU approach which manifested itself in the new vertical restraints group exemption regulation.[22]

In addition to 'approximation' of laws, the Commission expected from competition authorities of candidate countries a decent enforcement record to demonstrate preparedness for the EU 'club'. This, again, was in line with what the GVH wanted to achieve. Conditions for a reasonably more activist attitude were better after the dust of transition had settled, rules were improved, and the GVH had accumulated experience, better understanding, and more experienced personnel. Within the GVH, the impression took hold that cartels were widespread though undetected, and that other anticompetitive practices could be identified with more sophisticated analysis and procedures. This coincided with the intuition that the risk of decisions representing false positives had been lessened and with it the risk of negative consequences which such decisions would entail.

It was widely recognised within the GVH that significant efforts were needed to become a more mature competition authority with greater sophistication and effectiveness; these included the ability to identify cases where intervention is justified as well as the ability to defend novel types of decisions before court on appeal. A major way of accomplishing this goal was engaging in capacity-building projects, often involving organisational changes to set up more effective institutions within the GVH. The first development of this kind was the establishment of the Infocommunications Unit in 1999 to handle cases in telecommunications and converging areas. This unit concentrated a large portion of the brightest young case handlers and was led by an ambitious young head, who had been the case handler in the above-mentioned *JÁSZ-TEL/MATÁV* merger decision. It represented fresh, new thinking and skills in an increasingly important area which was very difficult to understand and handle properly for the GVH. The creation of the new unit manifested a move from the transition period to the EU accession period where market opening constituted a major part of the policy agenda and thus of the activity of the GVH.

A further move was the creation of the cartel unit in 2001. The goal was not only to have a unit that was dedicated to fighting cartels and not distracted by other tasks, but to have people with experience and skills that were adequate for cartel detection. This might seem to be trivial today. But at that time it was a leap in the understanding not only of the nature of various kinds of agreements, but also of the distinct enforcement style and personal background of enforcement officials required to take effective action on cartels as well as of the analytical problems this area would entail. The ideas for such a unit had already been developing within the GVH, inspired in part by looking toward the US DOJ Antitrust Division and DG Comp. The wave of international and European anti-cartel enforcement reinforced these ideas by providing examples to follow as well as know-how to refer to. The adoption of the latest techniques used in cartel prosecution, like IT forensics, was an example of internationally-inspired reforms. The Cartel Unit proved to be extremely successful. Within a relatively short time, several large cartels were uncovered and fined severely.[23]

The substantial increase of the amount of fines imposed by the GVH after 2001 must be seen as a significant development of this period. Between 2001 and 2003 the amount of fines imposed increased almost ten times, and between 2003 and 2005 another three and a half times (disregarding 2004 as an outlier). Fines have remained high, although volatile. The trend toward higher fines can be explained by the increased anti-cartel enforcement, due to the seriousness of the infringement and the size of affected markets. It also coincided with changes in the Competition Council's attitude towards fines: while during transition the Competition Council had used sanctions mostly as an indication that wrongdoing had occurred, after 10 years of the existence of the competition law in Hungary it found it more appropriate to impose sanctions that hurt.

Another important step towards becoming a more sophisticated authority was heavy investment into competition-economics training for case handlers, on top of the existing basic competition-policy course. Almost all case handlers participated in the course and passed a basic exam. While actual impact was less spectacular than attendance statistics, the effects of the courses must be considered in the light of their aim, which was to show the logic of economic analysis rather than transforming case handlers into industrial organisation economists.

Third, the GVH experimented with guidelines in the form of notices in order to increase legal certainty and transparency, to ensure greater consistency in its own operations, and to explore certain new aspects of enforcement. Notices and draft notices addressed various issues, such as the calculation of fines and the criteria of distinguishing between complex and non-complex mergers. There was also work on guidelines on merger remedies, dealing with both substantive and procedural aspects. These guidelines proved to be controversial for many reasons – they provoked debates about substance, their legal status, and especially about their impact on legal certainty. This latter aspect had also to do with the fact that the guidelines were prospective in many respects, reflecting policy intentions rather than merely distilling established practice.

The structure of cases changed, as anti-cartel activity gained momentum. Nevertheless, enforcement remained basically complaints-driven. Exploitative abuse cases, mainly involving excessive-pricing allegations, still represented a large portion of all cases; exclusionary cases remained virtually non-existent. During this period a big share of excessive-pricing cases was related to cable television services provided by local monopolies that were not the subject of price regulation.[24] The GVH continuously advocated for sectoral regulation. However, policy-makers were not open to the idea, partly because the sector was decentralised. The GVH experimented with various methods to deal with these cases as effectively and efficiently as possible without becoming a true price regulator. However, in spite of some progress, the fundamental contradiction between the nature of the conduct and the analytical and remedial toolkit of the GVH could not be reconciled.

The Contemporary Period

Socio-economic and policy context

By the mid-2000s, Hungary had become a mature market economy and was confronted with essentially the same issues as other, developed market economies: dealing with long-term macro-economic stability, including the development of more sustainable solutions for healthcare and social security; injecting more competition into previously closed sectors such as postal and rail transport, and dealing with opposition by entrenched interests.

Hungary's policy agenda continued to be shaped primarily by the relevant EU policies. The nature of EU influence changed, however, as Hungary's enthusiasm to implement EU policies was losing steam. Prior to accession, the political threat of slowing down or blocking the accession process in cases of non-compliance had been highly effective in ensuring proper implementation of EU laws; Hungary's obligation as an EU Member State to implement EU policies was a less powerful motivator. In addition, Hungary was now able to influence the design of EU policies by participating in the preparation of legislative acts and by exercising its voting rights. Relationships with EU institutions changed as well: before accession, EU affairs almost exclusively meant interactions with the Commission; after accession the European Council and the European Parliament began to play important roles. EU relationships, which used to be almost exclusively administrative and professional, became more political. Public support of EU membership declined.

As a result, policy-making in Hungary changed. EU-related considerations became less powerful in shaping substantive policies, even though formally they were inevitably part of the legislative process. During the accession period the attitude towards EU policies and their implementation had focused on fulfilling formal criteria rather than substantive adoption; after accession even the attitude toward formal compliance became more relaxed. Second, the nature of domestic policy-making became more political and less professional – the influence of interest groups and instances of regulatory capture increased, as stakeholders felt less constrained by respect for EU policies. EU-related considerations became less effective in deterring those who sought anticompetitive or protectionist measures, which was illustrated by increased calls for the regulation of large-scale retailers and certain regulatory measures that were eventually adopted.

As EU policies typically had promoted a pro-competitive agenda, their decreasing influence implied that domestic policies were becoming less competition-friendly. Particularly affected were certain network industries, namely the energy sector, postal services, and transport (especially railways). For instance, in 2006, the government integrated MAVIR, the state-owned electricity system operator, into the MVM group, the state-owned former monopoly still controlling most of production and wholesale. MAVIR remained a separate legal entity, but its independence was significantly weakened. The GVH intensively advocated against this move and subsequently recommended re-separation several times but without success. Liberalisation of postal services was not regarded as urgent, and a 'derogation' from full market opening was negotiated. In addition, strict regulation prevented new entry into the 'competitive' segment which triggered an EU infringement procedure in 2009. Another example was the liquidation of the independent railway regulator in 2008. This had been established 2 years earlier and had aggressively pursued competition and consumer welfare goals in the sector, trying to create a level playing field for all actors. It was eliminated overnight and without explanation. In this case the GVH did not even have an opportunity for advocacy.

Another important development was the return of macroeconomic difficulties. This was not simply the impact of the global recession towards the end of the 2000s. Problems in Hungary had emerged earlier and were related to economic fundamentals and policy, especially the overwhelming economic role of state. Hungary had lost its edge in attracting FDI as well as its relative position in competitiveness; its economic growth has been lagging behind that in other former transition economies in the region which had joined the EU at the same time.[25] The Government delayed and later dropped its 2008 target date for introducing the Euro, the common European currency, which would have required Hungary to meet demanding economic criteria. In 2008 it had to turn to the IMF for financial support. One can interpret these developments as symptoms of the lack of regulatory and structural reforms and insufficient reliance on markets and competition. Policy-makers, however, either did not reach the same conclusion or were not capable of moving in the direction of competition-oriented reforms.

The only, although significant, development contrary to these trends was a wave of ambitious structural reforms launched by the government under Prime Minister Ferenc Gyurcsány in 2006–2007, which targeted mainly electricity and certain parts of the healthcare sector. The proposed reforms were inspired partly by the idea of using competition and market mechanisms to get a better outcome for society. In spite of the strong commitment by the prime minister and his political allies, the reform suffered from serious shortcomings. They were met with fierce industry resistance, and were badly managed politically. Even the party of the Prime Minister did not fully support all reforms. Attempts to overcome opposition by pushing through reforms without negotiation led to a vicious circle of ever-intensifying industry resistance, political opposition, weakening public support, and in turn more aggressive reform strategies. Developments culminated in a referendum in 2008, which essentially rejected the reforms. All this further undermined the already-weakened legitimacy of the government which imposed austerity measures although it had promised otherwise.

The reforms in healthcare suffered in addition from a lack of attention to the microeconomic aspects of the industry. The reforms were motivated primarily by the need to address public spending and were approached mainly as a macroeconomic issue. Financial measures were easy to introduce and understand, and more easily captured the attention of decision-makers. Insufficient resources, intellectual capacity, attention and time were allocated to understand how healthcare markets and industries work. Thus, decision-makers lacked sound knowledge on the economics of healthcare and hence were unable to identify and tackle phenomena like market failure, regulatory failure, unexpected motivations of market participants, and unintended outcomes. As the government sought to introduce more competition in 'hardcore' areas of healthcare services like hospitals and health insurance, the GVH became the institution that warned policy-makers of the dangers of naïve expectations of the benefits of competition.

Likewise, repeated attempts to reform the banking sector proved largely ineffectual. Although publicly motivated by a desire to strengthen competition and consumer protection, government measures were in fact driven primarily by a desire to fulfil populist instincts without actually hurting the politically powerful sector. The political attention towards consumer protection and competition in the bank sector was triggered by consumer outcry about the proliferation of unilateral contractual changes by banks. Ultimately, however, these developments could not be remedied without really hurting the profit made by the sector. At the same time, the government relied on banks to decrease budget deficit, by imposing a special, 'luxury' tax on bank profits.[26]

The only really successful reform of this period was the liberalisation of pharmacies, a hitherto largely closed industry protected by restrictive regulations. The GVH had started to advocate pharmacy liberalisation by publishing a sector analysis in 2003.[27] Later it incorporated in its advocacy efforts international sources such as an OFT report on pharmacies, the Europe-wide advocacy of DG Comp, and OECD sources on liberal professions. All this greatly influenced subsequent reform in 2006, which was strengthened by the direct involvement of the GVH in designing the liberalisation process. The reform sought to introduce competition by removing certain administrative barriers to entry. This turned out to be a realistic objective which could be achieved by relatively simple means and without a big risk of failure. The reform produced a positive outcome in almost all respects. Within a relatively short period of time, entry occurred and many consumers benefited from greater choice and better service. Efficiency-driven structural changes started to emerge, such as the formation of pharmacy chains. Concerns that less populated areas might suffer from less reliable supply did not materialise.[28]

GVH competition advocacy evolved organically, reflecting changes both in the political environment and developments within the GVH. On the one hand there was continuity – advocacy was regarded as important and maintained a focus on key areas such as network industries, especially electricity and telecommunications, and the retail sector. On the other hand, there were changes – new topics emerged in particular in connection with EU competition policy developments and domestic reform initiatives, and advocacy became more sophisticated, focused, aggressive and pro-active.

Although EU influence on advocacy topics remained strong, the GVH increasingly relied on EU positions more as a source of inspiration than as ready-made 'ammunition'. In other words, the GVH increasingly adopted analytical approaches and techniques reflected in EU documents instead of simply copying results. The same applied to best practices developed elsewhere, such as by the OECD and some EU Member States; an example is the market studies carried out by the Office of Fair Trading which became more relevant for the maturing Hungarian market economy and inspired similar work by the GVH.

In some areas the GVH's advocacy efforts reached new levels and led to the GVH's deeper involvement in reform efforts. In electricity, the GVH undertook a sector inquiry from 2004 to 2006 in order to understand why competition did not appear to emerge after formal market opening.[29] The findings of the inquiry reinforced and refined the position represented by the GVH; they also contributed to the opening of a formal proceeding investigating the use and allocation of cross-border transmission capacities.[30] GVH advocacy improved due to several additional factors: First, the same issues were discussed by international fora, like the OECD. Second, the EU intensified its activity in the field: it launched its own sector inquiry in 2005 which lasted for 2 years,[31] opened formal proceedings (some of which involved Hungary directly), issued a new, more pro-competitive directive,[32] and generally made the topic a high-profile issue. Third, the GVH had learned to more effectively utilise synergies between advocacy and enforcement, as well as between international engagement and domestic operation. And, fourth, activities were also facilitated by the ECN, which provided information and created personal links, and by the active engagement of the GVH in EU affairs. For example, the GVH provided not only information but also human resources for DG Comp to investigate certain practices in the Hungarian electricity sector.

The strength and visibility of the GVH advocacy played a key role when Prime Minister Gyurcsány chose electricity as one area for pro-competitive reforms. The announcement of the prime minister was made in 2007 at the GVH's international conference for stakeholders, and the GVH was invited to a special high-level committee, set up by the Prime Minister, to supervise energy issues. Although the GVH did not achieve its objectives – not even through the Prime Minister's reforms, which ultimately failed – it kept the issue alive and probably prevented further worsening.

In the retail sector, the GVH had been on the defensive for several years, trying to prevent the introduction of less competition-friendly regulations. In 2006, as a result of relentless waves of political pressure to limit the commercial freedom of supermarket chains and to address buyer-power allegations, a change of tactics occurred. The GVH no longer found it plausible to maintain its previous practice, which had relied on competition-based explanations and research to prevent government interference in markets. Instead, it decided to offer a regulatory solution of its own, hoping that it would be less harmful than alternatives as it would imitate to some extent competition policy principles and be administered by the GVH. Inspired by the structure of the EU telecommunications regulatory framework's concept of significant market power (SMP), the proposal set up simple criteria, based on size and market share to determine SMP in retail; SMP retailers would be prohibited from certain practices like sales below cost. This approach aimed at leaving the concepts underlying abuse-of-dominance provision intact, while applying measures that included competition law vocabulary. With that approach, there was a chance of avoiding at least blatantly anticompetitive outcomes. Still, it also brought the danger of indirectly distorting competition policy concepts and creating a conflict of missions within the GVH – a risk the GVH management believed had to be accepted in the given political situation.

The attitude and style of GVH competition advocacy changed as it became more ambitious, more aggressive, and more direct in seeking outcomes that would make a real difference. As a consequence, the GVH sometimes overreached, either in the sense of over-estimating political opportunities or in terms of resources and expertise. This manifested itself, for example, in concurrent fights at too many advocacy fronts, and in wars that could not be won. In communication battles with banks or the electricity incumbent, for example, the GVH was simply outgunned in the media. At the same time, the changes of political climate were reflected in certain types of compromise that were previously unknown, such as the one related to supermarkets. These developments also demonstrated that advocacy – even by an ambitious authority that keeps an edge professionally – cannot substitute sound policy-making by other parts of the administration.

International contribution

The GVH's international relations became more incorporated into daily activities. They increasingly occurred at the level of case handlers, rather than being considered special, stand-alone projects with a somewhat more abstract character, in the sole responsibility of 'specialists'. These changes occurred primarily as EU technical assistance was transformed into cooperation within the ECN.

At the same time, the GVH became an active participant in providing technical assistance. It has hosted the OECD regional competition training centre since 2005, which focuses its activities on South-East Europe and Eastern Europe, and contributes to its professional activities. For years, the GVH was also the driving force behind the activities of the Central European Competition Initiative, an informal and workshop-oriented regional cooperation forum, which sought to emphasise contacts at a case handler level. Launched in 2003, the forum today involves the competition authorities of Austria, the Czech Republic, Poland, Slovakia and Slovenia.

Cooperation with US antitrust agencies, in particular with the Federal Trade Commission, was renewed from 2008. The GVH benefited from 'advanced technical assistance', whereby interactions have developed from basic technical assistance towards a more professional dialogue and cooperation between equal partners.

The result of these developments was an increased presence of the GVH in the international arena, especially at various European organisations and at the OECD. On several occasions the GVH hosted events for these organisations. International events organised by the GVH were seen as valuable opportunities for GVH staff and for stakeholders alike to hear about international best practices and latest competition policy developments.

It is difficult to assess the impact of all of these developments. As international affairs have been incorporated into daily activities they have affected many developments implicitly and in a less visible form. Nevertheless, certain visible instances of adopting international best practices can be mentioned. The most important was the creation of the Chief Economist Section in 2006; it is a separate unit within the GVH dedicated to supporting enforcement with sophisticated economic analysis, especially in complex cases, although it may occasionally also support other activities. This step was encouraged by a broader European trend. It improved significantly the overall quality of the enforcement activity of the GVH. The Chief Economist Section did not only have a direct impact on case work in terms of technical and empirical analysis, and of identifying proper theories of harm and doctrines; it also created an additional channel for international best practices in general.[33]

Another development was the founding of the Competition Culture Centre in 2005, with the mission to support the development of competition culture in Hungary, including competition policy research and development. The Centre is financed by a small portion of the fines imposed by the GVH, which ensure its financial stability. This was not a copy of a widespread international practice, but was inspired by examples of competition culture promoting efforts of other competition authorities, such as the research fund of the Konkurrensverket, the Swedish competition authority.

Sector inquiries were not a new instrument, but should be mentioned here as they became more embedded in an international context than in previous periods.[34] This was especially so in the case of the sector inquiry into consumer switching between banks regarding current accounts and mortgage loans in 2007–2009.[35] The topic was widely discussed at the OECD and the ECN, and addressed in an EU sector inquiry.[36] The GVH thinking on the issue was originally triggered by case experience, but developed hand-in-hand with international developments.

New activities were inspired to a great extent by international developments, such as managing relationships with stakeholders. However, ambition to keep up with many 'must have' international developments and activities, sometimes without proper selection, implied overstretching resources and moving beyond realistic absorption capacity.

Enforcement

The GVH's enforcement activities increasingly resembled those of the more experienced and advanced competition agencies in terms of prioritising high impact cases, sophisticated analysis, and facing challenges as market participants react to the competition authority's previous success and adapt.

Changes in the legal framework for enforcement activities continued. Certain statutory reforms could be seen more as fine-tuning the system than substantial reforms, but they were nevertheless important improvements. These included the introduction of a 'substantial lessening of competition' test in merger review, strengthening of the GVH's investigative powers, provisions on fines the GVH could impose, and refining the instrument of sector inquiries.[37] The only major change was to relax the legal obligation on the GVH to investigate all complaints thoroughly in order to increase the GVH's ability to set enforcement priorities. Although this was a significant step for Hungary, it still did not provide the degree of discretion that is available in some other developed competition law regimes.

The GVH's capability to deal with complex cases by conducting sophisticated economic and legal analysis increased substantially during the period. In addition to the establishment of the Chief Economist Section, this period also saw a breakthrough in terms of case management skills. Sophisticated procedural solutions as well as informal hearings were used in an effective and fair way.[38] This not only improved operational efficiency, but contributed to better substantive results by allowing the GVH to rely more (and more effectively) on 'hybrid' remedies like undertakings of the parties. These developments led to a change in the outcome of merger cases. Although the GVH blocked only one merger completely during the period, the proportion of cases increased in which various behavioural and structural merger remedies were accepted to address competition concerns.

The profile of investigated cases continued to change. The number of investigations into exploitative abuses decreased, and the number of infringement decisions dropped dramatically. Exclusionary abuse cases did not fill the gap even though the GVH was actively seeking them. Instead, many exclusionary abuse cases turned out to be a major challenge. Allegations and complaints of exclusionary conduct which indicated sound cases were infrequent and concentrated in regulated industries post market opening. Therefore they tended to uncover regulatory problems rather than pure competition law infringements, moving cases from pure enforcement interventions toward advocacy. Moreover, these cases kept raising questions about the scope of the regulated conduct defence. Links to politics created additional problems, particularly in the energy sector. Other industries, such as rail and (to a lesser extent) postal services, gave rise to a *déjà vu* experience, as the state of affairs sometimes resembled those experienced in other industries during the transition years. For example, when investigating a denial of access by the incumbent railways company to feeding tracks which were connected to its network from the sites of major industrial customers, it turned out that even the ownership rights in these and related assets were greatly unclear due to lack of proper registries.[39]

All this limited the ability of the GVH to prove infringement, to identify a clear-cut theory of harm, or even to establish jurisdiction. The GVH's enforcement record suffered. At the same time, however, legal and economic understanding and analysis of exclusionary abuses deepened and links between advocacy and enforcement evolved; a more comprehensive approach was adopted, under which the Infocommunications Unit was strengthened and transformed into a Unit of Network Industries from 2008.

Cartel enforcement remained aggressive and the GVH uncovered and prosecuted cartels in various areas, but in recent times especially it also faced new challenges. The reasons are not entirely clear. It appears that cartel members were increasingly aware of the teeth of the GVH, and became more sophisticated. They avoided creating evidence of their activity or hid it in areas less accessible to GVH IT forensics, such as on mobile platforms. There are some indications of active state involvement in arranging bid-rigging, transforming many (potential) cases from a classic cartel enforcement scenario into a situation that is difficult to detect and address with the competition law toolkit. The ratio of unsuccessful dawn raids increased. Enhanced information-gathering opportunities were considered a major new tool aimed at facilitating cartel detection, but at least so far they failed to bear fruit. For instance, leniency policy has not attracted many applicants. The criminalisation of bid-rigging in public procurement may prove to be counterproductive. By increasing the stakes it may discourage certain potential whistleblowers and leniency applicants. It may also blur the dividing line between competences of the police and those of the GVH. Again, the reasons are not fully explored and are certainly complex, involving factors both inside and outside the GVH.

FACTORS THAT HAVE SHAPED THE HUNGARIAN COMPETITION REGIME OVER THE YEARS

In this section, we seek to highlight the most significant factors that have shaped competition law and policy in Hungary since 1990. These are features that emerged already during transition and in our view continue to best explain the achievements of the Hungarian competition regime. We begin with 'external' factors – issues that tend to be less influenced by the GVH – and move toward 'internal' factors – areas where the GVH could exercise a greater degree of influence. Our discussion seeks to highlight the interdependence of these factors and the interaction between them.

The Domestic Environment

The domestic environment is full of paradoxes and controversies. As we described earlier, the introduction of competition policy in Hungary was preceded by economic reforms that started in 1968 and accelerated at the end of the 1980s. They aimed at improving economic performance by experimenting with incentives based on profit motives, and economic governance increasingly tried to imitate certain elements of market economies. When transition occurred, Hungary already had some experience with markets and there was openness towards switching to Western type capitalism. At the same time, however, real understanding of markets was as rare as real markets themselves. Reforms imitated market processes imperfectly and often distorted them. A belief in paternalism continued to exist as well as naïve expectations and misconceptions about the operation of markets and of 'fair' competition.

The broader domestic context has reflected these conflicting trends. During and after the system-change, paternalism, notions of 'fair competition', and misconceptions about markets were largely overshadowed by strong pro-reform efforts, but they proved to be resilient and became more influential in the longer run. These phenomena facilitated transition, but hampered progress after EU membership commenced in 2004. The inclination for improvisation, weaknesses in principle-based policy-making, rushed law-making without proper regulatory impact assessment, and the increasing political influence strengthened the effects of the resurgent scepticism in markets.

All this explains the overall trend toward a decreasingly competition-friendly domestic environment. Hungary was often nudged by international influence, and in particular by EU requirements, towards more pro-competitive solutions. Once an EU member, however, Hungary has been able to behave somewhat more independently and to pursue its own policy goals.

Not only did public support of EU membership decline; research showed an alarming disconnect between the concept of a competitive market economy and the dominant mindset among the Hungarian population. A 2009 study using international survey data found that, unlike other Central European countries, Hungary was closer to countries in the Balkans and Eastern Europe than to the West when measuring the attitude of the general population toward a market economy.[40] This result is strikingly different from the prevailing impression in the 1980s and 1990s when Hungary was regarded by many observers – and, with some pride, by its own population – as more 'western' than most of its peers in Central and Eastern Europe.

Still, the worsening environment did not necessarily translate into immediate visible consequences. The GVH was able to fight and sometimes win increasingly uphill advocacy battles. The development of competition legislation remained almost exclusively on a non-political, 'professional track', and the GVH kept its integrity and strong pro-enforcement attitude. Indeed, one of the most persistent characteristics of the domestic environment has been the relative lack of political interference with the GVH and its activities. In part this may have been the result of a perception of the GVH as an unimportant expert body with a good reputation. Perhaps later this was more frequently based on a misunderstanding of the GVH's mission, a lack of knowledge of the GVH's exact tasks, and on the notion that competition law should ensure 'fair' competition. This attitude allowed even the protectionist-minded politicians to consider the GVH a 'friend', although it also raised dangerous expectations towards the GVH.

While much of the domestic pro-competition attitude was weakening, at least legal thinking and legal culture became more conducive to competition enforcement. Legal reasoning remained rigid, but experience in competition cases, the influence of EU law, and the emergence of new generation of lawyers often with an international outlook moved the system slowly in a direction that was more supportive of administering competition law effectively, flexibly, and efficiently. This phenomenon helped, for example, to ease gradually the straightjacket of the complaints-driven enforcement agenda.

The domestic environment offered two major waves of opportunities for pro-competitive reforms, and the GVH managed to effectively exploit both. At the outset, the 'founding fathers' put the institutional framework on the right track by securing critical attributes like the mainstream orientation, independence of the GVH, its decent size,[41] its activity portfolio, and its relative recognition in economic policy during transition. Some of these achievements probably could not have been replicated later in the same way and at the same low cost. The GVH did not miss the next grand opportunity either – the process to join the EU. As a well-prepared proponent and representative of a key EU policy, it managed to develop further legislation, to 'borrow' strength in advocacy, and to gain resources.

Other opportunities were used as well. When the new government in 1998 emphasised the notion of the 'strong state', the GVH quickly presented itself as a representative of the 'strong state' protecting consumers against special interests. The new president at the time was able to build on mutual trust with the new government. The Government's ambitions to expand investment in neighbouring countries were used when the GVH asked for financial support for the international training centre jointly established with the OECD in 2005. When Prime Minister Gyurcsány launched his reforms in 2006–2007, the GVH tried not only to achieve competitive gain but also to strengthen its position by being a strong (although not uncritical), politically neutral and professional supporter of the competition-related reforms. It was engaged with the Government in various ways, by providing input, participating in committees, and by 'lending' staff to the Ministry of Healthcare.

The International Environment

International influence proved to be a major, continuous, and mostly supportive factor in a variety of ways, including providing opportunities, inspiration, and benchmarks. It had an impact not only on competition policy in a narrow sense, but also on competition in general.

Some of this influence came through 'hard power', in particular when the IMF and the World Bank insisted in the early years on the introduction of decent competition legislation. Commitments towards international organisations were critical also in liberalising foreign trade, which transformed the competitive landscape in Hungary – the single most important factor in shaping the conditions of competition during transition. Similar, strict external requirements played a role in the process of aligning Hungarian with EU competition law and in implementing pro-competitive EU directives. Finally, EU membership brought formal obligations in competition law, primarily as a consequence of the procedural reform of EU competition law enforcement. It also put Hungary irreversibly on the train of EU regulatory reforms, although, paradoxically, EU influence lost some of its steam after accession.

'Soft' external influence has been crucial in different ways and has had long-lasting effects. It gave access to and provided understanding of good practices applied elsewhere, and it transmitted peer pressure. Technical assistance, received primarily from the EU, the United States and the OECD was a major influence. Another was cooperation within international organisations, primarily within the ECN, the OECD and the ICN. The line between technical assistance and cooperation increasingly became blurred: EU technical assistance was integrated with accession preparation and negotiations; in the first years of regular OECD membership, participating in OECD work was for the GVH similar to receiving technical assistance and not unlike the period from 1991 to 1996 when Hungary had been an observer, whereas over time became a more active contributing member in committee work and outreach activities.

It was a mix of opportunities, the right attitude, and timely international developments that made international contacts so fruitful. As positive and as enabling as the broader international environment was, it was up to the GVH to recognise opportunities and to translate this potential ultimately into achievements in enforcement and advocacy. Indeed, one of the factors of the relative success of competition policy in Hungary was the open-mindedness, willingness and ability of the GVH to do so.

There are several explanations for the GVH's openness to foreign practices and experiences. First, the GVH sought to follow a mainstream line, rather than something unique. Second, competition policy was a new area with no original home-based experience. Third, earlier research sponsored by the IMF and the World Bank had shown the usefulness of an international outlook. Consequently, early on there was a sense within the GVH that contacts with foreign counterparts and organisations would offer useful benchmarks and as well as an opportunity to learn about best practices.

Things did not happen automatically, though. A legalistic way of thinking was strong even within the GVH, emphasising that the application of law has to do basically with the black letter of the law (of Hungary); along the same lines, foreign examples could be considered intellectually interesting but not very relevant. Nevertheless, a critical mass of the staff and management understood competition policy as an area where analysis and a sensible purpose are needed for the proper application of the rules and for their further development, implying a greater openness towards foreign experience. These perspectives were in turn reinforced by the effect of being among 'friends', as competition authorities usually understand each other, while they might feel more 'lonely' within their respective domestic administrations.

How the GVH wanted to gain and utilise knowledge from foreign sources was also significant. One key element was that the GVH preferred first-hand information as it revealed more directly context, policy considerations, and surprising details. Publicly-available information was considered valuable but not a good substitute. In other words, it wanted to see the kitchen at work rather than only read the recipe or see the nicely-arranged meal. Soon the GVH realised that insights that were gained more effectively through dialogue than through a one-way flow of information provide superior insight in several ways. They are not only richer, and bring fewer misunderstandings due to being more interactive, but they also provide a more up-to-date and honest state of affairs. The ambition of real understanding – including understanding of the underlying logic – and the already-mentioned ambition to incorporate and adapt best practices, rather than simply copying practices or analytical outcomes, mutually reinforced one another.

The GVH tended to be proactive and adaptive even when receiving assistance. Its visitors to foreign sister authorities had to have a 'research plan', and when initially long-term-assigned US experts could not contribute as originally intended, due to language and (perceived) procedural constraints, they were quickly transformed into 'resident professors', holding regular presentations and consultations on various competition policy issues.

The GVH was intent on projecting an image of professional competence abroad. This, however, required the ability to follow the policy dialogue and speak the language of international competition law. Consequently, many of the very best members of the authority became involved in international relationships. As a result, international relations tended to be internally considered not as pure 'diplomacy', where shortcomings are to be hidden, but primarily as dealing with substantive issues with foreign institutions and as an opportunity to improve domestic law enforcement and policy.

The intention to become part of the international mainstream was accompanied with a mix of humility and critical attitude. This may seem inconsistent, but is in fact consistent with the approach of adopting rather than copying. However, the balance sometimes shifted toward more critical thinking, especially before EU accession.

In such cases the GVH 'processed', decomposed and attempted to redesign foreign models with the aim to adopt them with improvement (that is, adopt them only in part, and replace some elements with its own ideas). The implementation of the EU block exemption regulations and designing the leniency policy illustrate this approach. It was fundamentally different from translating ready-made and proven legal texts of the

EU, which was the approach followed, for example, by many candidate countries and by Italy when they adopted their competition laws.

The results of these exercises were not necessarily better than the originals, though sometimes the model provided by the EU was not perfect either. Besides, simple translation had advantages, other than simplified law-making: when Italy introduced modern competition legislation it 'cut and pasted' the whole body of established EU case law into its national law by basically translating the relevant EU provisions, thus advancing competition law in one step. On the other hand, the 'do it yourself' attitude of the GVH had positive effects in terms stimulating thorough discussion and thinking, which ultimately facilitated better understanding and development.

The GVH as a Competition Policy and Enforcement Institution

For a better understanding of the nature of the development of Hungary's competition regime, we highlight two institutional aspects of broader significance: the GVH's unique enforcement structure, and its role among other institutional stakeholders in competition policy and enforcement. Discussing institutional aspects of the GVH also provides the context to explore the importance of continuity in the development of the Hungarian competition regime.

An important institutional peculiarity has been the position of the Competition Council, the decision-making body of the GVH. On the one hand, it has been part of the GVH, and its decisions have been the decisions of the GVH. On the other hand, it has been independent even within the GVH (which has been an independent authority itself) and from the GVH President in applying the law. This hybrid institutional setting – different both from models with a separate authority and a separate council and from models with a single authority with integrated leadership and decision-making, although sometimes collective – brought benefits as well as risks.

First, it provided a double check on case work, which improved quality, certainly in the first decade. However, it also led to significant inefficiencies in procedures as independence too often was used in practice as an excuse for a lack of coordination. The GVH was supposed to act as a single authority with a single voice, and decisions and procedures were regulated as one piece. At the same time, procedures were divided and easily took different directions at different stages, resulting in a duplication of efforts and thus a waste of time and resources. The application of certain more sophisticated procedural tools, like pre-notification consultations or commitments to grant leniency, had also been a challenge as parties did not know whether the position of the case handler would in turn be shared by the Council. Similar, although less worrying, inconsistencies emerged in the relationship between advocacy and enforcement. In addition, the independence of Council members led to inconsistencies even within the Council, and complicated its efforts to provide legal certainty through guidelines.

Second, the position of the council reinforced the concept of independence of decision-making as final enforcement decisions were protected by a 'double layer' of independence – that of the GVH with respect to other institutions and that of the Competition Council within the GVH. This had been one of the main reasons why the 'founding fathers' preferred this model. At the same time, the model brought the risk of creating the image of an ivory tower. In fact, in particular during the early years, some ivory-tower thinking could be observed in the Council.

This institutional setting remained essentially unchanged, even though it was gradually refined over time. For example, a legislative amendment allowed the Council's upfront involvement in dealing with leniency applicants. This setting required the development of informal ways of coordination and a change of attitudes, which started to happen very slowly and painfully.

From an inter-institutional perspective, the GVH has been the engine of broader developments in competition law enforcement and policy in Hungary. This remained so even after it joined the EU, as DG Comp cases with a Hungarian component concerned only a handful cases and firms. Being the centre of expertise in the field, the GVH assumed responsibility for the development of competition law expertise among the bar, the courts and academia. In 1992 it co-founded and has since sponsored the operation of the Hungarian Association of Competition Law (the Hungarian branch of the LIDC),[42] which quickly became the main platform of dialogue between practitioners, scholars and the GVH on enforcement-related issues.

Preparations to join the EU increased both legal and economic academic interest in competition policy, one of the most powerful EU policies at the time. A subsequent step was the establishment of the Competition Culture Centre, which supported higher education and academic research both in competition law and economics, not only by sponsoring research and education but also by other means such as organising events.

Courts were initially extremely reluctant to have any contact with the GVH or even with international organisations. Presumably this attitude was in part due to obvious conflict-of-interest considerations, and due to their conviction – embedded in Hungarian legal traditions – that, to apply competition law, courts had only to read the letter of the legislation. EU membership and preparations for it slowly led to changes: EU competition law, complex and accompanied with an extended body of case law, was to be directly applicable before national courts, requiring preparations. From that point, the GVH became able to contribute to the education of judges in competition law, by indirect means, like supporting seminars on EU competition law.[43]

The value of continuity has emerged throughout our story of competition law and policy in Hungary. It becomes particularly apparent when describing the GVH as an institution. Continuity includes continuity in leadership, senior management and staff; but also, more broadly, continuity in professionalism, attitude and enforcement philosophy. Continuity proved to be an important factor in the evolution of legislation as well as in the development of the GVH and its activities. It made the accumulation of experience possible, which resulted in an organic way of development and contributed significantly to the achievements by connecting several developments over time as well as across activities.

Personal continuity was reflected at different levels of the hierarchy. During the first 18 years, the GVH had only two presidents and two vice presidents over the case handlers; two vice presidents chairing the Competition Council served for 16 years combined within the same period. Some of them had already participated heavily in the preparations leading to the 1990 Competition Act and the establishment of the GVH.

Senior management was also characterised by little fluctuation, and new appointments reflected a tendency to promote in-house based on merits. Average turnover at the staff level was below 10 per cent over the first 20 years. Decent salaries – relative to the average of the administration, although not relative to regulatory authorities – certainly had an impact, at least during the second decade. Committed job applicants who were attracted by the high professional standards and the positive character of the field were often appreciated. Mutual commitment was strengthened by 'relation specific investments' on both sides. Loyalty remained strong despite the fact that very limited career paths were available in the GVH, a small organisation with a flat structure.

Continuity was a foundational principle not only in this strictly institutional sense, but also in other respects, including building reputation, competition culture, and a body of professional knowledge. The second president, Zoltán Nagy, for example, emphasised continuity as one of his 'leitmotivs.' He wanted to – and could – build on his predecessor's achievements, and expressed a personal preference for evolution over revolution. Continuity in these aspects, however, has not implied rigidity that prevented the adjustments and dynamic transformative changes described earlier, nor did it undermine the attitude that competition law is a work in progress and subject to continuing changes. All this helped to develop a GVH 'corporate identity' around the idea of an independent authority pursuing professional excellence with a strong international outlook, which seeks to avoid becoming a bureaucratic 'evil'.

The impact of continuity as a principle of the organisation should not be underestimated, even if it worked mostly 'behind the scenes'. For example, we have described earlier the creation of the Cartel Unit and the Chief Economist Section as key steps to boost cartel enforcement and a leap in economic analysis, respectively. These were the visible organisational reforms, but they were the results of gradual and long-term processes in which experience and institutional memory was accumulated, and strategic projects that were translated into a change of the organisation. In turn, the new organisations contributed to continuity as without them any momentum would have been exhausted, management attention would have declined, and forces of regression would have gained the upper hand.

Continuity also played a major, enabling role in other respects which we described elsewhere. For example, continuity helped the GVH to build personal relations and familiarity with international institutions. Greater familiarity with international players and institutions made efforts to benefit from international relations more effective and fruitful. In an inter-institutional perspective, continuity of the GVH's position was crucial to the development of expertise among other stakeholders. And advocacy efforts would have been less credible had the approaches and goals of the GVH materially changed over time.

Advocacy

Competition advocacy has always been a cornerstone of GVH activity. It played an important role in shaping the competitive landscape as well as in the GVH's development. Although always intended to follow mainstream approaches, it was special in several particular ways at the beginning of the GVH's existence. Competition advocacy proved to be an area where the GVH was able to make a difference with reasonable confidence almost from day one. This made it possible to get practice, to raise awareness, and to build its reputation – although with obvious limits – without being irresponsibly ambitious in visible enforcement.

One important attribute of advocacy efforts, and one explanation for their relative success, was the flexibility in the GVH's approach, which existed especially during transition. On the one hand, the GVH followed a kind of 'competition policy imperialism'. Competition is such an integrated and indispensable feature of a market economy, the reasoning went, that competition policy considerations must always be kept in mind when laying down the foundations of Hungary's market economy; moreover, the initial design of the economic system would determine the fundamental conditions of future competition. The first president of the GVH, Ferenc Vissi, often said that 'everything is competition policy [in economic policy] during transition'.[44] This implied that the competition authority had to have a voice on issues that otherwise might not be the subject of competition advocacy. For example, the GVH formulated opinions on issues like corporate law, civil law provisions governing non-profit organisations, and tax law.

On the other hand, the GVH had a very modest attitude by offering an escape for the targets of its advocacy efforts: it emphasised that competition advocacy captures only one aspect of a usually complex problem where other considerations can legitimately prevail; either those responsible for the policy in question or political decision-makers should have the final word. This was expressed in several ways, from 'this is our contribution to the discussion but it is up to you', to 'explain your reasons', to 'demonstrate the net positive effects' – depending on the GVH's confidence, competence and influence.

This double-sided approach provided both strength and flexibility: the GVH could be aggressive in terms of representing competition policy considerations, without becoming counterproductively irritating. Over time, the GVH concentrated increasingly on issues with a direct link to the conditions of competition. It also became more demanding when seeking explanations for how its views were integrated into policy discussions.

Despite the GVH's efforts to maintain a sense of modesty and an understanding of 'Realpolitik', bureaucratic in-fighting could occur, often resulting from the professional character of GVH advocacy, the fact that the GVH lacked real power, the ways of policy-making, and increasing differences in substantive objectives. An inter-institutional battle could be triggered by efforts of the GVH to defend competition against anti-competitive proposals or by proposals for progressive changes hurting special interest. Therefore advocacy overall did not work without conflicts. These conflicts became stronger over time, as the substantive differences became larger, and major players in Hungarian policy involved the GVH less. Fighting quickly became a struggle characterised by lack of transparency, information and mutual trust. Consequently

GVH advocacy gradually became more aggressive even in issues close to political interests, such as liberalisation of certain network industries.

An unusual feature in the advocacy toolkit has been the provision allowing the GVH to challenge anticompetitive administrative measures before court. This power has been interpreted by foreign observers often as both an unorthodox and mighty weapon providing the GVH with teeth in advocacy. In fact, it was not designed to condemn and overrule regulations, unlike apparently similar provisions in some other former transition economies where a broad range of administrative activities are the subject of competition law enforcement and administrative agencies can even be fined by the competition authority. Although the provision was used several times by the GVH both as a threat and in court proceedings – an illustrative example is the licensing practices of municipalities discriminating against non-locals – and therefore proved to be useful, it did not provide particular strength for competition advocacy.

It appeared that during transition, advocacy could potentially achieve more than enforcement. Decisions to de-monopolise or deregulate had far-reaching consequences on future conditions of competition and were much more significant than individual decisions affecting the behaviour of individual firms. Although there was never a straightforward 'advocacy first' approach, competition advocacy thus had a far easier start than enforcement, and initially played a greater role, not only in substance, but also in building reputation.[45] This asymmetry faded away only slowly, as more sophisticated enforcement gained momentum.

In addition, strong emphasis on advocacy fitted very well with the personal attitudes, background and skills of officials at the newly-established GVH, who had previously worked in the forefront of economic reforms in the Price Office. These attitudes were mutually reinforced by the perception of top economic policy-makers, in which the GVH and its senior officials, known from the Price Office, were considered worth being consulted because they supposedly represented important viewpoints. The president of the GVH was a member of the 'economic cabinet' (the weekly meeting of economic ministers) between 1991 and 2002; the vice president was a permanent invitee at the weekly meetings of the state under secretariats preparing for the cabinet meeting between 1998 and 2002. These channels provided an overview of policy-making and additional fora to advocate. Their evolution and eventual elimination says much about a changing domestic environment.

Advocacy had certain characteristics in common with enforcement. For example, advocacy was dealing frequently with pricing issues. Not only access-type 'wholesale' price regulations were subject to advocacy, but for long also 'retail' price regulation in various regulated industries as well as for services to be used on a mandatory basis, especially if the service-provider was a monopoly, including the fees of certain administrative services. Similarly to enforcement, this was a legacy of the price office experience, and the GVH tried not to behave as a price regulator.

Not only was enforcement complaints-driven; advocacy also had its own straightjacket. Paradoxically it stemmed from a provision of the Competition Act designed to strengthen advocacy, which required that the GVH be consulted on each proposal potentially affecting the conditions of competition or prices. The unintentional consequence of this provision was a flood of proposals of minor importance, while consultation on the more important proposals was often 'forgotten', and a greatly self-imposed moral or tactical burden placed on the GVH to respond. Dealing with such proposals especially under the circumstances of a fast-track legislative process was neither efficient nor often effective, and was especially prone to escalating the fight with other institutions. It often required resources that could have been used in other ways. Nevertheless, this burden in many ways was less severe than that of law enforcement. It has been further relaxed over time, allowing priority-setting in GVH competition advocacy.

Advocacy – often inspired by international outlook – became more mature and sophisticated over time. While often limited to represent principles at the beginning, it produced several well-elaborated proposals built on thorough and sometimes empirical analysis, based either on a sector inquiry, enforcement or research.

Enforcement and advocacy were handled through different organisational settings throughout most of the time. The centre of advocacy work and thinking was formed around the Competition Policy Section, the President and/or one of the Vice Presidents, even though case handlers always took part in advocacy as well. The Competition Council was rarely involved and typically only in an enforcement context. For example, sometimes an advocacy warning was included in a formal written decision, opining that proper regulation could offer (or could have offered) a more adequate remedy than enforcement. The institutional setting of enforcement was almost the opposite, relying primarily on case handlers and the Competition Council. As a consequence, enforcement and advocacy evolved distinctly in several ways. Controversies over directions existed from time to time, and insufficient coordination sometimes prevented the ideal combination of enforcement and advocacy. But convergence could be ensured in the long run as case handlers became more deeply involved in advocacy.

An area in which synergies between advocacy and enforcement (as well as between the GVH's domestic initiatives and international supporting developments) were clearly understood and utilised was the GVH's effort to fight against anticompetitive arrangements in liberal professions. Starting in the late 1990s, an increasing number of liberal professions sought to organise themselves as 'chambers', preferably with the statutory right to limit competition among their members, to discipline their members, and with mandatory membership. Efforts to obtain statutory powers that would protect them from competition enforcement extended even to professions where such traditions had never existed before in Hungary. While open to the possibility of market failure justifications, the GVH recognised that most restrictions were clearly disproportionate by any standards. A first wave of cases ensued in 1998–1999 with subjects like auditors, veterinarians, pharmacists, physicians, real estate agents, architects, and various associations dealing with agricultural products. In parallel with enforcement, the GVH was engaged in competition advocacy, encouraging associations to change their ethical codes, and urging regulators to narrow down statutory exemptions for the associations of liberal professions or to abstain from expanding them.

Although the GVH's initial actions against restrictive self-regulation of liberal professions started primarily as a domestic initiative in response to complaints, US ideas and OECD work provided intellectual support from the outset. An EU advocacy campaign around 2005 targeting liberal professions, which was closely related to OECD work, provided a further boost and definite directions for all GVH activities.[46] By that time, the GVH had become mature enough to properly absorb and utilise these external sources. Analysis and remedies became more refined. For example, in the late 1990s there had been reluctance even within the GVH to consider that legal professions were engaged in economic activities and that their codes of conduct could be potentially anticompetitive. But now a new wave of enforcement included cases involving bar associations trying to limit advertisement, price competition or new entry.[47] A major advocacy effort was made in relation to pharmacists as discussed earlier. Liberal professions have remained a lively area of GVH activity to date both in advocacy and enforcement.

Enforcement

Hungarian competition legislation, its institutional framework, and enforcement practice alike pursued mainstream objectives from the outset. Indeed, the 1990 Competition Act was a fully-fledged competition law that followed European patterns regarding both substance and investigative powers. Already, in its early years, the GVH had a fairly good understanding of basic issues, such as the importance of economics or market entry, and eschewed rigid and static structuralism. A remarkably good intuition and a healthy dose of common sense of some in key positions – occasionally reinventing best practices independently – prevented many potential mistakes. Nevertheless, development was needed both in terms of legal framework and in terms of skills in order to be able to carry out sophisticated analysis, to make procedures effective, and to overcome existing constraints and misconceptions.

The most severe of those constraints were the complaints-driven character of operation and other procedural imperfections, such as: the very short deadlines; the lack of certain investigative and analytical skills at the GVH; and the lack of benchmarks. Much of this originated in the combination of legal tradition, pre-transition legacy (including unintended but implicitly surviving Price Office legacy within the GVH), and the turbulence of transition.

Enforcement was busy from day one, but it was neither proactive nor activist. The duty to deal with complaints imposed a straightjacket which initially prevented (and later greatly reduced) case selection, prioritisation, and consequently the launching of ex-officio cases based on agency discretion. When legislative requirements were relaxed, a similar complaints-driven process was to some extent self-imposed by the GVH. Attitudes changed only slowly. Reluctance towards activism, however, was in part intentional and had certain benefits. Being aware of shortcomings, the GVH was a cautious enforcer during transition and sought to avoid causing harm by undue interventions. Thus, the initial period provided ample opportunities to learn and develop institutional and individual experience without an ambitious agenda that might have led to major mistakes and failures that could ultimately undermine the GVH's credibility.

Enforcement started to gain momentum at the 'right time' in the late 1990s, facilitated by a confluence of factors; conditions improved in terms of accumulated practice, skills and understanding, and better legal framework – reducing the dangers of a more activist practice. Greater self-confidence and ambition to make a difference developed at the same time as EU expectations built up. Around the same time, efforts to intensify contacts and cooperation between competition authorities were seen increasingly as a means to improve the effectiveness of competition law enforcement (rather than primarily as a conflict-avoidance mechanism). Within the EU in particular, these trends were manifested by the establishment of the ECN. As a result of better, 'positive' cooperation, best practice became both more available and more applicable in daily practice, affecting various areas from regulated industries to the financial sector, from cartel enforcement to economic analysis.

By 2009–2010, the GVH had become a mature authority with the ability to deal with sophisticated cases with challenges in substantive analysis and procedural questions. Enforcement practice today closely follows international best practice and continues to evolve with it.

Reviews and amendments of the competition act have been a constant phenomenon in the Hungarian competition regime and have contributed to more effective enforcement. After adopting the 1990 Competition Act, review and redrafting led to a technically new Competition Act in 1996 which was subsequently amended several times. A major amendment was adopted in 2000 with the principal goal of 'approximation' to EU competition law, but which was also heavily influenced by the OECD recommendations of the regulatory reform review.[48] Another major amendment occurred in 2005, which resulted from a comprehensive review of the procedural framework for domestic and EU-related reasons alike and had far-reaching material consequences.[49] Other amendments may appear minor as changes became less and less radical, but they were nevertheless important refinements and adjustments which sometimes followed international trends. These included the switch from a 'dominance test' to a 'substantial lessening of competition' test in merger review, introducing professional disqualification of corporate executives of those firms involved in cartels,[50] a refined procedural framework, as well as stronger investigative powers.[51]

There are several different explanations for Hungary's legislative activism. It partly stems from Hungarian legal tradition – not unique in the region and historically influenced by Germany – that legal rules must be detailed, often covering issues which elsewhere are dealt by guidelines. For example, one of the latest amendments of the Hungarian Competition Act moved the details of cartel leniency policy from a notice into the act in the name of legal certainty. Another reason was the formative experience of drafting of the first modern competition statute. This had been a complex and successful exercise, which contributed to continuing thinking about reforms in competition law. Despite being responsible to apply the law, it became almost habitual for the GVH to regard legislation in a *de lege ferenda* manner, in other words to view the legislative framework as evolutionary. The fact that legislative changes did not stop after EU accession may also indicate that the willingness and efforts to approach the mainstream and adapt to evolving international good practice and benchmarks have been genuine and not driven merely by the desire to become a member of good standing in the EU 'club'.

Hungarian competition acts have also included certain consumer protection provisions enforced by the GVH. They concern, primarily, consumer deception, making the GVH portfolio resemble those of the OFT in United Kingdom and the FTC in the United States, although the GVH's consumer protection remit has been narrower both in substantive scope and available tools. Consumer protection is beyond the scope of this chapter. This is more so as consumer protection and antitrust developed autonomously from each other for most of the time, even if consumer protection by the GVH was often referred to not as genuine consumer protection but as protecting competition in another way. The idea of exploring true synergies and complementarities between the two areas emerged only recently, reinforced by dealing with issues such as consumer switching.

Nevertheless, two effects of consumer protection activity on antitrust enforcement must be mentioned. First, until the Consumer Protection Unit was established in 2004 the same case handler units were involved in the enforcement in both areas. This organisation took substantial resources away from antitrust, given the strong influence of complaints and that most of them concerned consumer protection allegations. But consumer protection enforcement had a positive influence on antitrust enforcement as well. It provided the image of an authority being on the people's side, providing a decent enforcement record for the GVH and also credibility in its efforts to communicate complex antitrust positions and to carefully develop some activism in antitrust enforcement during the transition. It also helped antitrust enforcement in its early years by testing the shared procedural framework and thereby contributed to the accumulation of those skills that are beneficial for consumer protection enforcement.

CONCLUSION

This chapter has described how a successful competition regime could be established in Hungary, built around a competition authority that has gained domestic and international respect. Hungarian conditions and developments were to some extent similar to those of other transition economies in Central and Eastern Europe, but also distinct in many ways. Even before Hungary became a 'transition economy', it had a head start as it had already implemented elements of a market economy with some recognition of competitive principles. Geopolitical and domestic policy developments since the early 1990s shaped an enabling environment that was unusually positive for the creation of a competition regime and a pro-competitive regulatory policy.

Our story of the Hungarian competition regime has identified a limited number of key conditions that substantially contributed to the development of a mature and respected competition system in a relatively short period of time: international pressure, obligations and opportunities to cooperate with foreign counterparts; a domestic environment supportive of competition policy, or at least accepting of it as an important component of the economy; the dedication and quality of the GVH's leaders and its staff, including their openness to international assistance and cooperation and their willingness to learn and adapt in order to become a respected, mainstream competition authority that excels at its tasks. We have also identified continuity as a key condition that has permeated institutional and substantive aspects of Hungarian competition law and policy. Despite shortcomings, the enabling environment and good luck provided significant opportunities, and the GVH was able to make use of that potential to a large degree.

Overall, one could be optimistic about the future of the GVH. The GVH's 'DNA' and its basic attitudes, such as openness toward international cooperation and the sense that persistent efforts are needed to keep professional standards, appear to be deeply embedded and proven to work under various and changing circumstances. But complications exist that could undermine success. Most significant are changes in the domestic enabling environment, which has worsened since the early 2000s. The GVH has become an island in an increasingly incompatible environment in terms of values and objectives – professional excellence and international best practice as opposed to politicised and improvised policy-making; competition and consumer welfare, based on the concept of the liberal market economy as opposed to protectionism, paternalism, over-regulation and rent seeking. It has been able to remain an island because political interference has continued to be almost absent – but around it things have changed.

The emerging divergence between the domestic environment and the mission of the GVH brings a sense of fragility. Ironically, the accelerated pace of development and change at the GVH in recent years also raises questions about the sustainability of its achievements. The benefits of overstretching resources cannot be permanent, and, as in any institution that goes through a period of increasingly rapid and perhaps overly ambitious change, there is the risk of losing focus and coherence. This could in turn make the GVH less robust in resisting pressures that emerge from a changing domestic environment, even if the original intention might have been just the opposite: to resist external pressures.[52]

Many of the key contributing factors identified in our story are not immune to change. In fact, in some instances change may be perilously close. Lack of political interference is easy to end, as it is basically a question of political will. Recent developments such as the abrupt elimination of the railways regulator suggest that the political acceptance of the notion of truly autonomous regulators has greatly eroded. Interference can occur in less conflicting ways, such as by budget cuts or through making the 'right' appointments of top GVH managers. Personal continuity can be undermined also by internal developments such as a change in the GVH's human resources policy, changing personnel sufficiently to erode the attitude and institutional experience of the entire authority.

Even if GVH values are embedded in GVH culture, they need to be nurtured by leadership and internal decisions. They are therefore more resilient, but can ultimately be affected by change as well. If there is a confluence of too many changes, even the professional culture, esteem and integrity of the GVH may be altered.

The fragility of the GVH's capabilities brings a 'systemic risk', due to the fact that the GVH is the institutional driving force of the development of the whole field. However developed competition policy is in Hungary, other participants – such as the courts or law firms – are probably not yet sufficiently strong and integrated among all stakeholders to compensate if the GVH, for any reason, should fail to maintain its achievements and progress.

Thus, our story of the Hungarian competition law and policy ends on a cautious note: that future success depends on continued efforts and commitment, leadership, and a set of external factors. The achievements of the past will quickly wear off if these necessary ingredients become less effective. Regaining strength and credibility would require enormous time and effort once past achievements are lost.

NOTES

* *Mobilis in mobili* was the motto of the *Nautilus*, Captain Nemo's submarine in Jules Verne's novels *Twenty Thousand Leagues Under the Sea* (1870) and *The Mysterious Island* (1874). We translate it, slightly adapted for our purposes, as 'changing in a changing environment'.
1. This chapter reflects the personal views of the authors and does not represent the views of the institutions they are affiliated with.
2. Gazdasági Versenyhivatal (GVH) – the Hungarian Competition Authority.
3. Preparatory works, as well as their institutional and political context, are discussed in more detail in GVH (2010b), pp. 19–20, 32–34, 41–43, 75.
4. Act No LXXXVI of 1990 on the Prohibition of Unfair Market Practices.

5. The crisis was severe: GDP in real terms dropped by 15 per cent between 1990 and 1993, and returned to its 1990 level only in 1999. Comparisons are even more striking with 1987, the peak year before the changes. The retail price index remained above 115 per cent until 1998, was 135 per cent in 1991 and 128 per cent in 1995.
6. Only conduct of entities carrying out economic activity in Hungary was considered to fall within the scope of the 1990 Competition Act, and mere acquisitions were not regarded as economic activity for the purposes of the Act.
7. Voszka (2003, pp. 73–84) discusses this strategy, with some criticism, as part of a broader analysis of privatisation and de-monopolisation during transition in Hungary.
8. GVH (2010c), pp. 227, 229.
9. The beginnings of US technical assistance in Central Europe as well as its main instruments and evolution are discussed in more detail from a provider's viewpoint in US FTC (2008), and in US FTC – US DOJ (2002).
10. Competition acts in Hungary have been covering not only antitrust rules but also certain consumer protection regulations as well as unfair business practices (called unfair competition) regulations, although it has not been the task of the GVH to enforce the whole range of rules. The 'general clause' was the first substantive provision of the act ahead of and covering all chapters regulating particular types of conducts.
11. For example, vegetable oil, margarine, certain paper products, sugar, and their major producers were involved. The list changed over time as items were gradually eliminated until 1996 when the last product was taken off the list.
12. Similarities and differences between controversies concerning price control and competition policy in transition economies are discussed in Pittman (1998), pp. 211–216, as part of a broader comparative analysis of Central and Eastern European competition regimes.
13. The Competition Act also included certain consumer protection provisions enforced by the GVH. Consumer protection is beyond the scope of this chapter, but its impact on antitrust enforcement is briefly discussed later.
14. The only exception was resale price maintenance which was treated in the same way as horizontal agreements.
15. An example is the Budapest meat joint venture case (vj-49/1991). It concerned a company which was jointly established by major Hungarian meat producers to organise proper meat supply for the capital city. On the one hand this arrangement served investment into better logistics by setting up a network of modern storage capacities around Budapest; on the other hand it coordinated prices and shipments as well. Owners used to be part of the same meat producer conglomerate, and they considered joint operation natural and efficient. The GVH found that the arrangement was anticompetitive. But parties challenged the decision and the appeal court ruled against the GVH. The jointly-owned company was a 'joint venture', a distinct category of entities recognised by Hungarian corporate law. 'Joint ventures' under corporate law had the function of achieving objectives jointly determined by their founders. The appeal court decided that the Competition Act cannot prohibit the very operation of such legitimate entities. Finally, the Supreme Court overturned the decision of the appeal court, declaring that even if 'joint ventures' are legitimate corporate entities, and even if their function is to achieve joint objectives, those objectives cannot contradict other laws and thus 'joint ventures' are not allowed to restrict competition between their founders disproportionately. The process was surrounded by legalistic debates, like whether the competition law is *lex specialis* and the corporate law is *lex generalis* or vice versa.
16. It was the merger of Junior and Gasztrolánc, the two market leaders in student catering in Budapest with a combined share of 66 per cent, while competitors were far smaller (vj-172/1994).

17. *JÁSZ-TEL / MATÁV* (vj-107/1998).
18. The first two of these bulletins discussed telecoms and electricity ('Key Issues of Telecommunications Market Liberalisation: The Competition Policy Position of the Hungarian Competition Authority', Competition Office Bulletin No 1, Budapest, July 1999, and 'Key Issues of Electricity Market Liberalisation: The Competition Policy Position of the Hungarian Competition Authority', Competition Office Bulletin No 2, Budapest, July 1999.).
19. One of the first manifestations of these efforts was the third 'Competition Office Bulletin' ('Large Scale Retail Trade and Competition: The Competition Policy Position of the Hungarian Competition Authority', Competition Office Bulletin No 3, Budapest, August 2000.).
20. OECD (2000), p. 51.
21. Act No LVII of 1996 on the Prohibition of Unfair and Restrictive Market Practices.
22. Commission Regulation (EC) No 2790/1999 of 22 December 1999 on the application of Article 81(3) of the Treaty to categories of vertical agreements and concerted practices, O.J. L 336/21 (1999). See also OECD (2005), pp. 4–5, observing that Hungary's initial, more lenient approach to vertical restraints was more in line with contemporary competition economics than with the European system Hungary was required to adopt.
23. Two of these cartels involved bid-rigging cartels in connection with construction projects, like the motorway construction cartel (vj-27/2003), and a major road-repair tender in Budapest (vj-138/2002). Construction cartels remained an active area with similar large-scale cases in the coming years, together with large IT tenders such as the upgrading of the computer network of universities (vj-162/2004), and of the corporate IT system of the Paks nuclear power plant (vj-97/2006). The combined amount of fines in these particular four cases was more than 8800 million HUF (more than €43 million / US$57 million, inflation-adjusted at 2010 exchange rates). See also OECD (2005), p. 11, commenting on the successful creation of a cartel unit.
24. OECD (2005), pp. 5–6, comments on the large number of cable-television excessive-pricing cases and recommends regulatory solutions to pricing problems in this sector.
25. For example, in the IMD World Competitiveness Yearbook Hungary was ranked 27th in 2000, 34th in 2004 and 42nd in 2010. In the World Economic Forum Global Competitiveness Report Hungary was ranked 35th in 2005 and 52nd in 2010. During the same period Poland and the Czech Republic moved ahead of these lists and had better scores than Hungary in 2010. Slovakia first moved ahead of Hungary although the trend was later reversed.
26. How these problems emerged, as well as some of the attempts to treat them by regulatory measures, are discussed in more detail in GVH (2010a).
27. 'The Competition Policy Position of the Hungarian Competition Authority on the Key Issues of Transparency of Subsidy System Regulation and Pharmacy Market Liberalisation', Competition Office Bulletin No 6, Budapest, July 2003.
28. GKI-EKI (2010).
29. 'A Gazdasági Versenyhivatal jelentése a magyar villamosenergia piacon lefolytatott ágazati vizsgálatról', GVH, Budapest, 2006. május 15.
30. *MAVIR crossborder capacities* (vj-52/2009).
31. 'Inquiry pursuant to Article 17 of Regulation (EC) No 1/2003 into the European Gas and Electricity Sectors', Communication from the Commission, COM(2006) 851 final, Brussels, 10 January 2007, and 'DG Competition Report on Energy Sector Inquiry', SEC(2006) 1724, Brussels, 10 January 2007 (the full technical report).
32. Directive 2009/72/EC of the European Parliament and of the Council of 13 July 2009 concerning common rules for the internal market in electricity and repealing Directive 2003/54/EC, O.J. L 211 14/08/2009.

33. The activity and contributions of the Chief Economist Section are discussed in more detail in GVH (2011).
34. The practice of the GVH concerning sector inquiries is discussed in more detail in GVH (2008).
35. 'Váltás egyes lakossági és kisvállalati pénzügyi termékek esetében', Ágazati vizsgálat, Végleges jelentés, GVH, Budapest, 2009, február 5.
36. 'Sector Inquiry under Art 17 of Regulation 1/2003 on Retail Banking', Communication from the Commission, COM(2007) 33 final, Brussels, 31 January 2007, and Commission Staff Working Document accompanying the Communication from the Commission, SEC(2007) 16, Brussels, 31 January 2007 (the full technical report).
37. The considerations to change the test in merger control are discussed in more detail in GVH (2009a).
38. Procedural issues, including informal hearings, are discussed in more detail in GVH (2010d).
39. Nevertheless, in this case (vj-22/2005) the GVH was able to clarify the state of affairs for its legal assessment of alleged denial of access and other practices. It concluded that MÁV, the incumbent railways company, unduly restricted competition at the critical time of market opening. The GVH imposed a record fine of 1000 million HUF (more than €4.5 million / almost US$ 6 million, inflation-adjusted at 2010 exchange rates), which was partly the result of the size of the affected commerce.
40. The study, by the TÁRKI Social Research Institute, used the World Values Survey in 2009 and – among others – dealt with values which are either indicative of the acceptance of markets or instrumental in their proper functioning (or both), such as attitudes towards inequalities, state vs individual responsibilities, the economic role of the state, trust and social capital, or entrepreneurialism and risk (TÁRKI (2009)).
41. A study found that the GVH was a better resourced and larger institution than its regional counterparts in relative terms (Fingleton, Fox, Neven, Seabright (1996), pp. 89–92).
42. Ligue Internationale du Droit de la Concurrence – International League of Competition Law.
43. GVH efforts to promote competition culture and to reach out to courts are discussed in more detail in GVH (2009b), pp. 7–8, 13.
44. He also wrote in 1991 that 'In this particular period of time competition policy can be, and should be, implemented through economic policy as a whole. In other words the entire economic policy fulfils the criteria of being competition policy in the course of transition into market economy' (translated from the Hungarian original by the authors) (Vissi (1991), pp. 19–20).
45. According to 'advocacy first', competition authorities in new competition regimes should limit themselves to competition advocacy and only later engage in enforcement (within which they should start by dealing with mergers and cartels and only then should deal with vertical restraints and abuse of dominance). It is not about replacing the mainstream substantive framework, but about the process to reach a state where the mainstream framework is properly utilised. The 'advocacy first' approach is briefly described, and in part criticised as overly simplified, in ICN (2002), pp. 34–37. The ICN Report cites Kovacic (1997) in support of the 'advocacy first' concept.

    As our discussion shows, Hungarian experience suggests that some criticism is fair, but that the underlying idea has a substantial merit. On the one hand, a pure 'advocacy first' approach probably would have been neither more effective nor even feasible under Hungarian conditions. Advocacy did not always prove a safer area than enforcement in terms of complexity and sensitivity. Early imperfections in enforcement could be corrected in the longer term and provide opportunity to gain experience. On the other hand, however, institutional factors identified by Kovacic (1997) for transitional economies – such as the scarcity of resources and indigenous substantive expertise, frail academic infrastructure and weak consumer groups, the lack of information networks and weak availability of relevant business records, inadequate limits of administrative discretion and unrealistic expectations about competition policy – sometimes critically shaped the challenges and opportunities the GVH has encountered. Moreover, GVH strategies to a great extent have been characterised by features like gradualism and capacity-building, which resembled at several points the approach advocated by Kovacic (1997).

46. This campaign was based on a comprehensive report on liberal professions. ('Report on Competition in Professional Services', Communication from the Commission, COM(2004) 83 final, Brussels, 9 February 2004.)
47. Some of the cases involving bar associations are discussed in more detail in GVH (2007). Advocacy addressed very visibly another legal profession, the Notaries, in 2005 ('Recommendation of the Gazdasági Versenyhivatal concerning the Review of the Regulation of the Notarial Services', GVH, Budapest, 27 May 2005).
48. Act No CXXXVIII of 2000 on the Amendment of Act LVII of 1996 on the Prohibition of Unfair and Restrictive Market Practices.
49. Act No LXVIII of 2005 on the Amendment of Act LVII of 1996 on the Prohibition of Unfair and Restrictive Market Practices.
50. This provision was later found to be unconstitutional. The Constitutional Court did not reject the whole idea of professional disqualification, but found that its procedural context in the concrete case did not meet the criteria of fair procedure, as disqualification would have been automatic without proving, or even investigating, personal involvement (19/2009 (II. 25.) AB határozat).
51. Sárai, Szoboszlay (2012) provides a more detailed overview of legislative developments until 2007, including laws from 1923, 1931 and 1984 that we do not cover here in the absence of their impact after 1990.
52. A speech of the second president of the GVH suggests that overstretching resources in its second decade was to some extent a side effect of the desperate desire of top management to show significant achievements and excellence, and to demonstrate international reputation in part to protect the GVH and its mission from pressure (GVH (2009c), pp. 2–3).

    These efforts involved increasingly sophisticated activities and initiatives. However, they failed to change the prevailing attitude toward assessing the GVH's performance. Political stakeholders continued to consider quantitative parameters as principal indicators of good performance – such as the numbers of cases, complaints handled, interventions and fines. They neglected the quality aspect, as they failed to recognise the complexity of proving cartel cases, controversies about abuse-of-dominance allegations, and the value of everyday merger control, even if its intervention rate is necessarily 'low'. A decrease in quantitatively-measured output was a concern also for GVH leaders. Thus, a focus on quantity persisted, which interferes with efforts to improve the quality of the GVH's performance.
53. Annual reports by the GVH are not listed here.

REFERENCES[53]

Fingleton, Fox, Neven, Seabright (1996)
John Fingleton, Eleanor Fox, Damien Neven, Paul Seabright: *Competition Policy and the Transformation of Central Europe*, Centre for Economic Policy Research (CEPR), London.

GKI-EKI (2010)
A patikaliberalizáció hatása a gyógyszerfogyasztókra, GKI-EKI Egészségügykutató Intézet Kft., Budapest.

GVH (2007)
Hungary
In: *Competitive Restrictions in Legal Professions 2007*, OECD Policy Roundtables, OECD, Paris, DAF/COMP(2007)39.

GVH (2008)
Hungary
In: *Market Studies 2008*, OECD Policy Roundtables, OECD, Paris, DAF/COMP(2008)34.

GVH (2009a)
Hungary
In: *Standard for Merger Review 2009*, Policy Roundtables, OECD, Paris, DAF/COMP(2009)21.

GVH (2009b)
Contribution from Hungary to the Roundtable on Challenges Facing Young Competition Authorities, OECD Global Forum on Competition, 19–20 February, DAF/COMP/GF/WD(2009)47.

GVH (2009c)
Key Elements of Strategy to Overcome Challenges in Transition: The Hungarian Experience, speech by Mr. Zoltán Nagy, president of the GVH in the Roundtable on Challenges Facing Young Competition Authorities, OECD Global Forum on Competition, 19–20 February, DAF/COMP/GF/WD(2009)18.

GVH (2010a)
Hungary
In: *Competition, Concentration and Stability in the Banking Sector 2010*, Policy Roundtables, OECD, Paris, DAF/COMP(2010)9.

GVH (2010b)
Tiszta verseny – Interjúk a Gazdasági Versenyhivatal 20 évéről, Ed: József Péter Martin, Gazdasági Versenyhivatal Versenykultúra Központ, Budapest.

GVH (2010c)
A Gazdasági Versenyhivatal 20 éve – az országgyülési beszámolók tükrében, Eds: Andrea Belényi, József Péter Martin, Márta Nagy, Gazdasági Versenyhivatal Versenykultúra Központ, Budapest.

GVH (2010d)
Hungary
In: *Procedural Fairness: Transparency Issues in Civil and Administrative Enforcement Proceedings 2010*, Policy Roundtables, OECD, Paris, DAF/COMP(2010)11.

GVH (2011)
Hungary
In: *Economic Evidence in Merger Analysis 2011*, Policy Roundtables, OECD, Paris, DAF/COMP(2011)23.

ICN (2002)
Advocacy and Competition Policy: Report Prepared by the Advocacy Working Group, ICN's Conference, Naples, Italy.

Kovacic (1997)
William E. Kovacic: Getting Started: Creating New Competition Policy Institutions in Transition Economies, *Brooklyn Journal of International Law*, 23 (2), 403.

OECD (2000)
OECD Reviews of Regulatory Reform: Regulatory Reform in Hungary 2000, OECD, Paris.

OECD (2005)
Hungary – Report on Competition Law and Institutions
In: *OECD Country Studies, Hungary – Update Report 2004*, OECD, Paris, DAF/COMP(2005)7.

Pittman (1998)
Russell Pittman: Competition Law in Central and Eastern Europe: Five Years Later, *The Antitrust Bulletin*, 43 (1), Spring, 179–228.

Sárai, Szoboszlay (2012)
József Sárai, Gábor Szoboszlay: The Development of the Hungarian Competition Law – from the Outset (1991) until 2007
In: *Evolution of Competition Laws and their Enforcement – A Political Economy Perspective*, Ed.: Pradeep Mehta, Routledge, New York, Oxon.

TÁRKI (2009)
TÁRKI European Social Report 2009, TÁRKI Social Research Institute, Budapest.

US FTC (2008)
Opening Remarks of Chair Deborah Platt Majoras, International Technical Assistance Roundtable, February 6, US FTC – US DOJ.

US FTC – US DOJ (2002)
The United States Experience in Competition Law Technical Assistance: A Ten Year Perspective, Note by the US Federal Trade Commission and the US Department of Justice, Antitrust Division for the OECD Global Forum on Competition, Session II, 14-15 February, CCNM/GF/COM/WD(2002)20.

Vissi (1991)
Ferenc Vissi: A versenypolitika
In: *Verseny- és árszabályozás – A versenytörvény és az ártörvény magyarázatokkal*, Ed.: Ferenc Vissi, Unió Könyvkiadó, Budapest.

Voszka (2003)
Éva Voszka: *Versenyteremtés – alkuval*, Akadémiai Kiadó, Budapest.

3. Pigeon-holed by precedent: form versus substance in the application of South African competition law

Janice Bleazard*

INTRODUCTION

South Africa's competition law regime was launched in 1998, with the passing of the Competition Act, No. 89 of 1998. The Competition Act established three institutions, each independent of the executive and of one another: the Competition Commission, which investigates and prosecutes anti-competitive conduct;[1] the Competition Tribunal, an administrative decision-making body, composed of lay persons with expertise in the field;[2] and the Competition Appeal Court, a special division of the High Court dedicated to hearing appeals from the Tribunal.[3] From the very first, South Africa's competition authorities have enjoyed considerable political backing, as the ANC-led government recognised competition law and policy as instruments for remedying the oppressive distortions of the apartheid economy.[4] Competition law and policy were introduced not simply to pursue the traditional functions of promoting market efficiency and consumer welfare. In addition, they were viewed as a means of remedying the excessive concentration of economic power in the hands of the state and a whites-only elite; promoting the participation in the economy of small and medium-sized enterprises, especially if owned by historically-disadvantaged persons; promoting employment; and dissolving state-owned monopolies and market oligopolies.[5]

The government reaffirmed its commitment to using competition law and policy to advance public interest objectives, with the release of its new macro-economic strategy framework, *The New Growth Path*, in November 2010.[6] The strategy framework places the creation of decent and sustainable employment, and the promotion of a more inclusive economy, at the front and centre of the country's economic agenda. It aims ambitiously to create 5 million new jobs by 2020, narrowing the official unemployment rate from 25 percent to 15 percent.[7] Recognising that anti-competitive conduct 'ultimately implies lower output, investment and employment', the strategy document prioritises promoting competitiveness in key sectors (specifically, infrastructure, the agricultural value chain, the mining value chain, manufacturing, the green economy and tourism) in order to encourage broad-based growth in the private sector and, ultimately, job-creation.[8]

The Commission and the Tribunal have worked energetically to fulfil their broad mandates, focusing their attention increasingly on tackling abuse of dominance and cartel activity. The Competition Commission spent its first 5 years focused on institution-building, advocacy and merger-regulation, with considerable success.[9] In 2004, however, the Commission shifted its attention to enforcing the prohibitions against anti-competitive conduct. To facilitate its enforcement work, the Commission introduced a highly successful Corporate Leniency Policy (CLP)[10] – a policy that has attracted considerable media attention and garnered widespread public support. The Commission's anti-cartel enforcement work under the CLP has also attracted international recognition: in February 2011, the Global Competition Review named the Commission 'Agency of the Year' in the Asia-Pacific, Middle East and Africa regions, and proclaimed it to be 'a beacon to all other authorities in Africa'.[11]

Similar to the CLP pioneered in the United States,[12] South Africa's policy induces firms to disclose cartel activity by offering immunity from prosecution – or, more precisely, immunity from being subjected to adjudication before the Tribunal and the imposition of any fine[13] – to the first firm to expose the cartel and to admit to participating in it. The immunity granted is conditional on the firm ceasing any cartel activity; its 'complete and truthful disclosure of all information regarding any cartel conduct' (which includes cartel conduct in other industries); and its 'full and expeditious cooperation until proceedings are completed'.[14] Despite a sluggish start, the CLP has become an essential part of the Commission's enforcement work. As awareness of its operation and effectiveness spread through the business community, and following the policy's refinement in 2008,[15] the Commission experienced a steep rise in the number of leniency applications.[16] Under the CLP, the Commission has exposed cartel activity in several key sectors and industries, including health and pharmaceuticals, automobile and tyre manufacturing, food and agro-processing, airlines, construction and infrastructure, and telecommunications.[17] A major breakthrough was achieved in 2007, with the exposure of a national bread cartel, and the imposition of a record-breaking R98.7 million fine on a large bread company, Tiger Brands. In

2009, the Commission went on to fine another member of the bread cartel, Pioneer Foods, 10 per cent of its annual turnover, which approximated R196 million. And, a year later, the Commission imposed a novel, mixed-structural remedy on Pioneer Foods for collusion in the wheat, maize, eggs and poultry market. Valued at R1.05 billion, the settlement agreement required Pioneer Foods to pay R445 million in penalties; R250 million into the National Revenue Fund; and R250 million to a new agro-processing competitiveness fund to be administered by the Industrial Development Corporation Fund.[18] In addition, the settlement agreement required Pioneer Foods to reduce the sale price of its bread and flour products by R160 million, and to increase its planned expenditure of R1.2 billion over the next 2 years by a further R150 million.[19]

The alarming degree of collusion, market-sharing and bid-rigging exposed by the Commission provoked public outrage, and prompted government to boost the Commission's enforcement powers. Parliament undertook a review of the Competition Act in 2007, and the Competition Amendment Bill was promulgated by the Department of Trade and Industry in May 2008. The Bill was signed into law by President Jacob Zuma on 28 August 2009, but the President did not proclaim the date on which the new Competition Amendment Act, No. 1 of 2009, is to come into force. The Competition Amendment Act promises to expand the competition authorities' powers in novel ways.[20]

Despite enjoying broad-based support, the Commission and the Tribunal have found their enforcement work increasingly stymied in the courtroom, where legal formalism has prevailed in the application of competition law. In a recent line of cases – *Woodlands Dairy,*[21] *Netstar*[22] and *Yara*[23] – the Competition Appeal Court (CAC) and the Supreme Court of Appeal (SCA) have upheld technical, procedural challenges to circumscribe the investigatory powers of the Commission and curtail the jurisdiction of the Tribunal. These cases, since followed by the Tribunal in *South African Breweries (SAB)*,[24] have generated a profound tension in South Africa's competition enforcement regime. Procedural minutiae have been successfully exploited by well-resourced respondents to frustrate access to justice, and to prevent the furtherance of the substantive legal and economic policy commitments underpinning the law. In short, form has got the better of substance in the courts' application of competition law.

The courts' formalistic approach is inimical to the constitutionally-inspired project of 'transformative adjudication', which is characterised by substantive, normative and purposive legal reasoning. As Deputy Chief Justice Dikgang Moseneke has explained, transformative adjudication in South Africa marks a crucial departure from the 'homogenous, conservative and predictable' apartheid-era legal culture – one that was 'informed by inflexible legal positivism predicated upon parliamentary sovereignty', and strictly rule-based adjudication where the 'the material context or the social aftermath of the application of the rule was deemed irrelevant'.[25] Transformative adjudication demands, instead, judicial reasoning that is informed by the political and social context, and which is responsive to substantive considerations – legal and extra-legal – in the application of the law. As one academic commentator puts it,

> The mode of reasoning that transformative adjudication requires allows for formal reasoning, but not formalism. Under this approach judges are allowed and may at times be required to decide cases narrowly with reference to concepts and the text of legal rules for example, but not in an abstract formalistic manner. Reference to form should not result in adjudication that is 'based on abstract and rigid constructs and reasoning… unresponsive to the political and social context and power relations in society'.[26]

The importance of transformative adjudication is all the more apparent in competition law, a branch of law that is so fundamentally informed by economic substance. The institutional design of the Tribunal is particularly telling in this regard. Although it is an adjudicative body, the Tribunal is intended to function as an administrative body, and not as a court. The Tribunal is staffed by economists and laypersons, not judges,[27] whose powers under the Competition Act include: the power to determine 'any matter of procedure' for a hearing (subject to the Tribunal's rules of procedure);[28] to 'condone any technical irregularities arising in any of its proceedings';[29] and to exercise quasi-investigative powers – that is, to summons persons to appear before it or to produce evidence.[30] The Competition Act provides that the Tribunal 'may conduct its hearings informally or in an inquisitorial manner', and requires that the Tribunal 'must conduct its hearings in public, as expeditiously as possible, and in accordance with the principles of natural justice'.[31] The informal and inquisitorial nature of the Tribunal's hearings is manifestly designed to enable the Tribunal to focus its expertise on unpacking highly complex economic enquiries, without inflexible legal complexities rendering its task even more complex, if not impossible. Moreover, the nature of its proceedings is intended to facilitate access to justice by expediting proceedings and reducing the costs involved.

THE CONSTRAINTS OF LEGAL FORMALISM

The multi-faceted objectives of South Africa's competition regime pose particular challenges for the competition authorities, who are required to balance competing public interest considerations in developing a pro-competition culture. At the same time, the authorities must interpret the scope of their own powers and mandate, which is inevitably informed by how they approach the purposes set out in section 2 of the Competition Act.[32] In two early enforcement cases, *Nationwide Poles* v *Sasol Oil*[33] and *Harmony Gold* v *Mittal Steel*,[34] the Tribunal and the CAC adopted strikingly different approaches in respect of these matters. In both cases, the CAC overruled the Tribunal to insist on a more formalistic interpretation of the provisions of the Competition Act, and a more restrained role for the competition authorities. These cases were early indications of the tensions between the activism of the Commission and the Tribunal on the one hand, and the deeply-engrained culture of procedural legality shared by the judges of appeal. I examine them briefly before turning to recent jurisprudential developments, because they illustrate clearly the relationship between legal form and substance: specifically, how the procedural formalism of the CAC and SCA informs their more conservative interpretation of the substantive provisions of competition law.

Early Signs of Tension: Interpreting Abuse of Dominance

In *Nationwide Poles* v *Sasol Oil,* the Tribunal and the CAC were required to interpret section 9(1)(a) of the Competition Act to determine whether an action by a dominant (and formerly state-owned) firm amounted to price discrimination. Section 9(1)(a) prohibits price discrimination 'if it is likely to have the effect of substantially preventing or lessening competition'. The Tribunal interpreted this as a low threshold, requiring the complainant to show only that the price discrimination had competitive *relevance*, and not that it caused competitive *harm* to actual consumer welfare.[35] The Tribunal explained the basis for its interpretation as follows:

> It is our view that the proscription of price discrimination reflects the legislature's concern to maintain accessible, competitively structured markets, markets which accommodate new entrants and which enable them to compete effectively against larger and well-established incumbents. This set of concerns points directly to problems confronting small and medium sized enterprises (SMEs) which, in the absence of a 'level playing field', or, what is the same thing, in the presence of discrimination, may well find it difficult to

enter new markets and even more difficult to thrive, to compete effectively 'on the merits'.[36]

The Tribunal thus adopted a purposive interpretation of section 9(1)(a), which emphasised the Competition Act's objective of promoting market access for SMEs and formerly-excluded market participants. It observed that the traditional mantra of 'protect competition, not competitors', took for granted the existence of competitors operating within a competitive market structure.[37] Since these conditions were lacking in South Africa's economy, the Tribunal deemed it both appropriate and necessary to adopt a more intrusive stance, directed at *promoting* a competitive market structure and, indeed, at protecting new competitors as they entered the market. The CAC took a very different position, however, and one more akin to the traditional, 'hands-off' approach to competition law. The CAC insisted that 'competition law does *not* protect the competitor, it protects competition', and that proof of prejudice suffered by one competitor was simply insufficient to meet the standard set under section 9(1).[38] It stipulated further that, policy concerns notwithstanding,

> section 9(1)(a) must be interpreted in terms of the words employed by the legislature to give effect to its purpose. The wording of section 9(1)(a) may be open textured but a court is still required to engage with the text and justify the meaning. … [T]here is nothing in the text of section 9 which shows that the purpose of the section was to protect small enterprises as opposed to protecting the competitive process or, in the words of the Tribunal, 'the underlying competitive structure of the market'.

Turning to the second case of *Harmony Gold* v *Mittal Steel*, the issue confronting the Tribunal and the CAC was whether the former state-owned steel-producing giant, Mittal, had charged an 'excessive price' on its domestic sales of flat steel products, in violation of section 8(a) of the Competition Act.[39] The Tribunal found in favour of the complainants, and imposed the then-largest administrative penalty totalling R691.8 million on Mittal. The method of the Tribunal was again informed by a purposive interpretation of its mandate – in this case emphasising its responsibility 'to promote and defend competitive market structures'[40] – and a readiness to depart from traditional doctrine. The Tribunal resisted following the approach set out by the European Court of Justice in *United Brands*,[41] which asks whether the higher price 'bears no reasonable relation to the economic value of that good or service'. Eschewing this 'price regulation approach', the Tribunal instead based its determination on a structural analysis of the market. It reasoned that Mittal's super-dominance in the flat-steel market, and the absence of any competitive structure, allowed it to 'engage in conduct designed to take advantage of – to "abuse" – those structural opportunities by imposing excessive prices on its customers'.[42] The CAC rejected the Tribunal's structural-economic approach, and insisted that the wording of section 8(a), which borrowed directly from *United Brands*, required 'a detailed exercise in comparative costing' as set out in that case.[43] The CAC thus again reined in the Tribunal by appealing to the provisions of the Competition Act, emphasising that the policy objectives and economic principles underpinning the statute could not be separated from the text itself.

In a subsequent paper addressing these cases, CAC Judge President Dennis Davis insists that he does not deny the need for purposive interpretation, nor the importance of the economic and policy considerations that the Tribunal has sought to promote.[44] Instead, he argues that his concern in these cases was to prevent breaches of the rule of law and the principle of separation of powers by ensuring the Tribunal's fidelity to the text. Yet, as these two cases illustrate, determining what the rule of law requires is inevitably a contested exercise – since the law must be interpreted, and the very concept of 'the rule of law' is associated with several, diverse values and commitments. The rule of law may require the existence of legal constraints (procedural or otherwise) on the exercise of power; certainty and predictability in the law; equality before the law; fairness; and access to justice, to name but a few.[45] As for the separation of powers, it might equally be argued that the CAC's strict reading of the Competition Act undermines the policy commitments that government seeks to advance through it, and that it is therefore the CAC rather than the Tribunal that is violating the separation of powers.

Procedural Challenges to the Commission's and Tribunal's Exercise of Power

The enforcement initiatives of the Competition Commission have been hindered by vigorous litigation over jurisdictional and procedural matters from the outset. This is hardly surprising considering the vested interests involved, the freedom with which South African big business has operated in the past, and the strong culture of legal enforcement in the country. Recently, the CAC and the SCA have decided several cases challenging the powers of the Commission and the Tribunal to investigate and hear matters arising from complaints of anti-competitive conduct. The first three cases – *Woodlands Dairy, Netstar* and *Yara* – show the appellate courts following the tendency evident in *Nationwide Poles* and *Mittal Steel* to err on the side of cautious legalism. In *South African*

Breweries (SAB), the Tribunal came out forcefully to critique the approach it was by then bound to follow.

Before turning to the cases, it is necessary to appreciate how allegations of prohibited practices like cartel conduct reach the Tribunal for a hearing. First, a *complaint* is initiated against an alleged prohibited practice – either at the instance of the Commissioner (section 49B(1)) or when a member of the public lodges a complaint with the Commission by completing the prescribed 'CC 1 Form' (section 49B(2)).[46] As the CAC observed in the early case of *Glaxo Wellcome*,[47] section 49B is notably non-prescriptive as to how a complaint may be initiated, since its object is 'to enable complaints to be lodged without the need for procedures that are too technical and/or formalistic'.[48] The CAC observed further that section 49B requires only that the complaint be directed at a 'prohibited practice'; it does not require a complainant 'to pigeonhole the conduct complained of with reference to particular sections of the Act'.[49] The CAC went on to explain, in what has become an oft-quoted dictum, what this requirement implies:

> While the complaint need not be drafted with precision or even a reference to the Act, the allegations or the conduct in the complaint must be *cognizably linked* to the particular prohibited conduct or practices. There must be *a rational or recognizable link* between the conduct referred to in a complaint and the prohibitions in the Act, otherwise it will not be possible to say what the complaint is about and what should be investigated.[50]

Second, following a complaint initiation, the Commission *must* undertake an *investigation* into the alleged prohibited practice (section 49B(3)),[51] and is empowered at any time during the investigation to summons persons for interrogation or the production of documentary evidence (section 49A).[52]

Third, once the Commission has conducted its investigation, the matter is *referred* to the Tribunal for adjudication. The Commission is given the first option to refer the matter (section 50(1)), which referral must be within 1 year after a complaint is submitted to it (section 50(2)).[53] In the event that the Commission does refer the matter, section 50(3) provides that the Commission may:

> (a) (i) refer all the particulars of the complaint as submitted by the complainant;
> (ii) refer only some of the particulars of the complaint as submitted by the complainant; or
> (iii) add particulars to the complaint as submitted by the complainant; and

(b) must issue a notice of non-referral as contemplated in subsection (2)(b) in respect of any particulars of the complaint not referred to the Competition Tribunal.

The complainant is only entitled to refer the case to the Tribunal if the Commission issues a notice of non-referral (section 51(1)),[54] or if the Commission does not refer the case within 1 year of receiving the complaint and no extended period of investigation is agreed to by the complainant (section 50(4) and (5)).[55] With this framework in mind, let us now turn to the cases.

Woodlands Dairy/Milkwood Dairy

This case centred on the question of whether a complaint initiation by the Commission in respect of alleged cartel activity must be framed against a *specific* firm before the Commission may investigate that firm and summons it in the course of its investigation. The applicants, Woodlands Dairy and Milkwood Dairy, received summonses pursuant to the Commission's investigation of anti-competitive behaviour in the milk-processing industry. The summonses required the company executives to produce documents and, in the case of Milkwood Dairy, to submit to interrogations. The summonses described the complaint informing the investigation as follows:

> The gist of the complaint initiated by the Commissioner relates to the reasonable believe (*sic*) that there exists anticompetitive behaviour in the milk industry. The alleged prohibited practices include possible collusion and/or price-fixing, possible abusive behaviour as well as restrictive vertical practices.[56]

The applicants argued that the summonses were issued in violation of sections 49A and 49B of the Competition Act,[57] as the initial complaint made no mention of them whatsoever, and accordingly no investigation had been initiated under which they could legally be summonsed. The Commission replied, first, that the initiating document constituted a 'generalised complaint initiation' which need not specify all the firms subject to investigation. Second, the Commission submitted that the section 49A(1) summons power could in any event be used without any complaint initiation, since 'the Commissioner needs to be able to investigate before deciding whether to initiate a complaint'.[58]

These arguments were first put to the Competition Tribunal, which did not decide whether a summons could be issued without a complaint initiation, or whether a 'generalised complaint' sufficed. Instead, it settled the matter by finding that the summonses issued – which described the subject of the investigation simply as 'anticompetitive behaviour in the milk industry' – were void for vagueness and over-breadth.[59] The Tribunal found that in failing to stipulate 'a prohibited practice accompanied by some particularity as to its nature', the summonses were 'not sufficient to guide the addressee to appreciate the boundaries to the request for documentation [or interrogation]'.[60] However, the Tribunal did not declare the evidence that had been obtained pursuant to the summonses inadmissible. Instead, it issued a preservation order on the basis that any breach of privacy resulting from the over-broad summonses had not been serious,[61] and it prepared to continue with the hearing. Before the hearing could proceed, however, Woodlands Dairy and Milkwood Dairy took the procedural issue on appeal as a point *in limine*.

Unlike the Tribunal, the CAC did address the issue of whether the complaint underpinning a section 49A(1) summons had to be framed against a specific entity. Adopting a substantive rather than a formalistic approach to the definition of a complaint, the Court found that 'the purposive interpretation of section 49B supports the argument that the complaint does not have to be framed against a specific entity'.[62] The CAC elaborated on this point in deciding a subsequent application for leave to appeal arising in the same matter.[63] The CAC noted the inherently collective nature of cartel activity, and determined that a complaint framed against an industry as a whole would be competent without the specification of each firm under investigation. Davis JP forcefully rejected the applicants' contrary suggestion as indicative of 'the Austinian formalism' associated with 'the kind of jurisprudence employed during apartheid', and which is 'not reflective of the purposive jurisprudence which seeks to balance the exercise of power, captured in a doctrine of proportionality which is central to the constitutional structure'.[64] With regard to the scope of the summonses, the CAC found that only the summons issued against Woodlands was void for vagueness. Pointing to an additional paragraph in the Milkwood summons, the Court held that, 'It affords a reasonably well informed person with knowledge of the Act, a fair idea of the ambit of the enquiry and the purpose of the summons'.[65] The Court accordingly ordered the Commission to return all the evidence obtained under the summons against Woodlands.

The matter did not end there, however. The applicants proceeded to take the matter on appeal to the SCA, which adopted a far stricter interpretation of the Competition Act.[66] Writing for the full bench, Harms JA rejected any suggestion that a summons could be issued without an initial complaint commencing an investigation,[67] and overruled the CAC's finding that the complaint initiation need not name the specific firms subject to the subsequent investigation. Harms JA expressed concern that, despite being administrative in nature, the procedural powers of the Commission may nevertheless lead to punitive measures and the infringement of the constitutional values of dignity and freedom and the right to privacy, a fair trial and just administrative action. As a result, the Court insisted, '[the Commission's] procedural powers must be interpreted in a manner that least impinges on these values and rights'.[68] Harms JA declared that there was 'no reason to assume that a [complaint] initiation requires less particularity or clarity than a summons', particularly since 'the scope of a summons may not be wider than the initiation' and because the Act presupposed that the complaint as initiated would be referred to the Tribunal.[69] Harms JA accordingly held that the initial complaint, like the summons that follows it, must 'survive the test of legality and intelligibility' and must *specify* the firms subject to the investigation, so that 'a suspicion against some [cannot] be used as a springboard to investigate all and sundry'.[70] Harms JA suggested that requiring the initial complaint to meet this standard need not hamper the Commission's effectiveness, since it remained open to the Commission to either *amend* the complaint during the course of its investigation or initiate a new complaint.[71]

On the facts, Harms JA found that there was no basis for any suspicion that the applicants were involved. Harms JA thus proceeded to strike down the summonses issued against both Woodlands Dairy and Milkwood Dairy, and declared invalid all evidence obtained under them. The Commission subsequently withdrew its case against the four other milk-processing companies it had named as respondents in this long-running prosecution. In a media statement, the Commission noted that its withdrawal followed the SCA's ruling, which applied equally to the other respondents. It accepted that its entire investigation into the milk-processing market was unlawful because it did not specify allegations faced by each firm, and was not based on a reasonable suspicion that all firms in the industry were engaged in such conduct.[72]

Netstar/Matrix/Tracker

This case also addressed the issue of the degree of specificity required in the initial complaint, but this time for the purposes of determining the scope of the Tribunal's jurisdiction in hearing the matter. The case concerned whether certain standards set by a motor-vehicle security association created barriers to entry that prevented competitors of members of the association from competing in the market. The Tribunal found in favour of the Commission, and declared that the respondents (Netstar, Matrix and Tracker) had contravened section 4(1)(a) of the Competition

Act 'in concluding an agreement and/or engaging in a concerted practice'.[73] The Tribunal's finding was appealed to the CAC, and sternly overruled to bring it in line with the SCA's approach in *Woodlands Dairy*.[74]

The CAC raised three main criticisms of the Tribunal's judgment. First, and echoing the concerns raised in *Harmony Gold*, the Court chastised the Tribunal for relying on an abstract, hypothetical test to determine the general impact of standards in a market, as a matter of structural-economic theory, rather than assessing the specific factual matrix before it.[75] Second, it criticised the Tribunal for simply misinterpreting the evidence, and reaching unfounded findings of fact.[76] Third, and most important for our purposes, the Court reprimanded the Tribunal for not confining itself to the *specific complaint* referred to it by the Commission, and for failing to ensure that the complaint referred to it was no broader than the complaint initially lodged with the Commission for investigation (in this case by a competitor company).

Writing for a full bench, Wallis AJA interpreted the SCA in *Woodlands* to have set the following standard by likening an initial complaint to a summons: 'that the conduct said to contravene the Act must be expressed with sufficient clarity for the party against whom the allegation is made to know what the charge is and be able to prepare to meet and rebut it'.[77] Wallis AJA recognised that the level of precision demanded in court pleadings was not required of a complaint lodged by lay persons, but that nevertheless 'broad and unspecific generalities' could not be allowed to take the place of a 'properly articulated complaint before the Tribunal to which the target of the complaint can respond'.[78] This statement may not seem particularly controversial, but it reveals how the Court failed to distinguish between the initial complaint lodged with the Commission by lay persons, on the one hand, and the referral that is made to the Tribunal on the other hand. Moreover, what the Court takes to constitute 'broad and unspecific generalities' in the referral is formalistic to the extreme. Wallis AJA criticised the Commission for referring to the Tribunal a case of prohibited cartel conduct in respect of *either* a collusive agreement *or* concerted practice (both forms of prohibited conduct cited in section 4(1)(a) of the Competition Act) when the *only* allegation made in the initial complaint was of a collusive agreement. The Court conceded that 'No doubt in many cases the same evidence may be relied upon as pointing towards either an agreement or a concerted practice', but insisted nevertheless on the 'jurisdictional and procedural reasons for a careful observance of the distinction'.[79]

Wallis AJA went on to find that the Tribunal lacked the jurisdiction to hear the case as framed, since it was confined to the scope of the initial complaint being that of an alleged collusive agreement only. As Wallis AJA put it, 'The Tribunal's jurisdiction is confined to a consideration of the complaint so referred and the terms of that complaint are likewise constrained by the complaint initiated by the Commissioner or made by some other person'.[80]

Yara/Omnia

In this case, the power of the Commission to *amend* a complaint referred to it in the course of its investigation came under scrutiny. Back in 2002 and 2003, the Commission received two complaints from Nutri-Flo, a company that produced and supplied fertilizer, alleging that another company in the industry, Sasol Chemicals, had abused its dominance by excessive and discriminatory pricing, and suggesting that it had engaged in collusion with the two respondent companies, Yara South Africa (Pty) Ltd and Omnia Fertilizer Ltd. After investigating the complaints, the Commission referred the matter to the Tribunal in 2005, seeking prosecution not only of Sasol, but also of Yara and Omnia for collusion (in contravention of section 4(1)(b) of the Competition Act).[81]

The case immediately became mired in procedural wrangling: Omnia and Sasol filed exceptions to portions of the referral relating to the section 4 contravention for lack of sufficient particularity, compelling the Commission to amend the referral twice. Then, in 2009, Sasol entered into a settlement agreement with the Commission, in which new details of its alleged collusion with Yara and Omnia emerged. The Commission sought to include these details in the prosecution by seeking yet another (a third) amendment to the complaint referral affidavit, but this time its application to amend was challenged. The respondents, Yara and Omnia, argued that the Commission sought to introduce matters not covered in Nutri-Flo's initial complaint, which was directed *only* at excessive and discriminatory pricing *by Sasol*. They argued that the Commission did not have the power to refer a different complaint – *viz.* of collusion by the respondents – to the Tribunal for prosecution.

The Tribunal found in favour of the Commission, and permitted the amendment. It reasoned that, even had Nutri-Flo only *intended* to bring a complaint against Sasol, its complaint nevertheless included allegations of collusion with Yara and Omnia, which the Commission had the discretion, and indeed the duty, to investigate. The Tribunal emphasised the responsibility of the Commission to act as 'the guardian of the public interest', and observed that:

> while third party complainants may have a grievance against a particular respondent, they are not the guardians of the public interest. They are usually

> concerned with the impact of the conduct on their own commercial interests. What may be of critical importance to the Commission, who is the guardian of the public interest, may not hold the same weight with the complainant.[82]

The Tribunal reasoned further that it is precisely because complainants generally do not have the full conspectus of facts before them at the time of lodging the complaint, that the Commission is required to investigate the complaint,[83] and is empowered under section 50(3)(a)(iii) of the Competition Act to add further particulars to a complaint submitted to it at any stage of its investigation.[84] Quoting dicta from *Glaxo Wellcome*,[85] the Tribunal held that, in referring a matter to the Tribunal for prosecution, the Commission only had to show a 'rational or recognisable link' between the conduct referred to in the complaint and the relevant prohibition in the Act.[86]

On appeal, the CAC took a stricter interpretation of the Commission's investigative and referral powers.[87] Dambuza JA also relied on a passage from *Glaxo Wellcome* to hold that 'what is intended is that the Commission consider and investigate *the particular conduct complained of by the complainant*', and that what must be referred to the Tribunal 'are the particulars of the complaint *as submitted by the complainant*'.[88] The judge's reasoning suggests that the Commission is bound to respect the *intention* of the complainant as to the particulars of the complaint it refers to the Tribunal. Thus, Dambuza JA emphasised that the Commission ought to take care in distinguishing when information is submitted to it in the form of a *complaint* (under section 49B(2)(b)) and when information is submitted by a member of the public for the purpose of merely *informing* the Commission of the conduct (section 49B(2)(a)). While the Court accepted that an affidavit attached to Nutri-Flo's complaint form contained details of alleged cartel activity on the part of Yara and Omnia, the Court found that these allegations were not *intended* to constitute a distinct *complaint* or cause of action against them, but only constituted additional *information* relating to the complaint against Sasol.[89] This intention was manifest, Dambuza JA suggested, in the fact that no mention was made of Yara and Omina in the complaint form, and that while the attached affidavit mentioned the two companies it also specifically stated that Nutri-Flo sought no relief against Yara and Omnia.

Dambuza JA also went on to find, in a significant departure from Harms JA's suggestion in *Woodlands Dairy*,[90] that the Commission is *not* empowered to *amend* a complaint. Dambuza JA noted that the Rules for the conduct of proceedings in the Competition Tribunal provide only for the amendment of a referral, not the complaint (which can only be initiated or submitted to the Commission under section 49B(1) and

49B(2)(b) respectively). Dambuza JA concluded that where, as in the present matter, information regarding additional instances of prohibited conduct came to light in the Commission's investigation, the Commission was obliged to initiate a new complaint, rather than amend an existing one.[91] Adherence to such 'proper procedure' was important, Dambuza JA reasoned, since 'the parties look to the CC 1 Form for the details of the complaint(s) against them', and are entitled to rely on it when determining whether they are true parties to the proceedings.[92] The CAC accordingly dismissed the Commission's application for amendment of the referral, and declared that no complaint was pending against Yara and Omnia.

No doubt in response to Dambuza JA's judgment, the Tribunal went to great lengths in the next matter to arise in this saga, *South African Breweries*, to explain the implications of the CAC's decision in *Yara* – not only for the work of the Commission, but also for the rights of complainants under the Competition Act.

South African Breweries (SAB)

On the force of the CAC's judgment in *Yara*, the Tribunal dismissed the *SAB* case in April 2011 for lack of jurisdiction. Specifically, the Tribunal struck down the case on the grounds that the complaint referred to it by the Commission differed from the initial complaint, which the Commission was not competent to amend. The dismissal of the *SAB* case is a profound blow to the Commission, not least because of the scale of the investigation and the seriousness of the Commission's charges. The initial complaint was lodged with the Commission by an independent beer wholesaler in 2004, and was referred by the Commission to the Tribunal in 2007. Thereafter, the Commission battled against a litany of procedural challenges. The Commission's main charge is that SAB, which has a share of between 85 and 90 per cent of the domestic beer market, discriminated against independent wholesalers by not giving them the same discount on beer that it gave to a group of 13 appointed, but independently-owned distributors. Moreover, the Commission alleges that, under its now 40-year-old distribution system, SAB carved up territories between these distributors and imposed prices on them.[93]

In the course of dismissing the case, the Tribunal took the unusual step of critiquing the very precedents that dictated its decision, and explained at length why it believed the case-law needed reconsideration by the appellate courts. The Tribunal insisted that,

> It needs to be borne in mind that disputes in the Tribunal are subject to section 34 of the Constitution of the Republic of South Africa which deals

> with access to courts. This requires that access to justice be granted to all participants – those who seek to bring a complaint and those who seek to defend themselves against a complaint. The right of access to justice by a complaint is no less compelling than the right of a respondent to a fair administrative process. But at the stage where a case is dismissed on jurisdictional grounds there is no symmetry in the consideration of the balance between the two competing rights. A right of access to justice is wholly negated if a matter cannot even proceed to trial.[94]

The Tribunal drew attention to the policy considerations underpinning the two-step complaint-and-referral procedure: namely, 'to regulate the interrelationship between the complainants' right to pursue relief *vis-à-vis* the Commission's duties as prosecutor of first instance in matters involving competition law infringements'.[95] While the Competition Act affords the Commission, as a specialist public enforcement body, a preferential right to prosecute matters under the Act, it seeks also to protect the rights of complainants to seek relief and damages in the event that the Commission fails to prosecute.[96] The function of the complaint initiation document (the CC 1 Form) in this system is thus primarily to establish *who the complainant is* in order to preserve that party's right to pursue private prosecution in the event of non-referral, as well as its right to seek interim relief, and to control the timing of the prosecution (that is, beyond the 1-year period granted the Commission to investigate and refer the matter). The complaint initiation document was not intended to function as a pleading, or even as an initiation document in legal proceedings. In the view of the Tribunal, it is akin to a complaint registered at a police station before the charge is drawn up.[97] As the Tribunal explained,

> The complaint, in and of itself, does not require a respondent to answer. There is no obligation for it to do so under the Act, and no procedure for this under the rules. It may ignore a complaint without any legal prejudice to its rights. Secondly, the initiating document may only partially find its way into the eventual referral. Whatever was disposed of, unless referred by the complainant in the event of a private referral, does not see the light of day before the Tribunal.[98]

Treating the initial complaint as the definitive statement of the cause of action thus transforms it into something it was never intended to be. Moreover, it simply presupposes the impossible. The complex economic relations and activities underpinning competition means that the complainant is often not in a position to identify the precise nature of the prohibited conduct, but only experiences the *effect* of what it suspects to be anti-competitive conduct. Further, as evidenced in *Yara*, relying on the initial complaint to determine the Tribunal's jurisdiction encourages resort to hair-splitting interpretative exercises. The CAC's preferred 'intention test' is problematic on a number of levels. It places undue weight on the ability of lay persons to articulate their complaint with lawyerly precision, and it presumes that the complainant knows precisely who is responsible for the anti-competitive effects. The intention test will invariably prolong trials, and render them more costly, as it invites respondents to question, in every case initiated by a public complaint, whether the Commission's investigation has remained true to the intention of the complainant, or has been expanded to the point at which it has become a 'new investigation'.

For justice to be done, the initial complaint cannot be treated as a pleading that dictates the terms of the referral. In the same vein, it must remain open to the Commission to *supplement* the complaint following its investigation, even where this changes the initial cause of action. While the CAC suggested in *Yara* that the Commission was not competent to *amend* a complaint – so that any supplementation meant initiating a new complaint – the Tribunal set out several reasons in *SAB* for rejecting this interpretation of the Competition Act. First, to require the Commission to initiate a new complaint undermines the logic of the two-step complaint-and-referral system described above, which seeks to protect the rights of private parties *as complainants*. Were the Commission to institute a new complaint, the Commission would effectively become the complainant in the matter, depriving the original complainant of its rights under the Competition Act. Second, the CAC's approach incentivises the Commission to take the initiative of simply instituting its own complaints, rather than pursue public complaints, and to cast these complaints as widely as possible. In other words, it encourages the very 'fishing expedition' that the courts are so anxious to guard against. Third, and most importantly, the CAC's approach ignores the powers afforded the Commission under section 50(3)(a)(iii) to 'add particulars to the complaint as submitted by the complainant'. As the Tribunal observed, on a reading of section 50(3) as a whole, the Commission's power to 'add further particulars' must involve the power to add a new cause of action. The Tribunal reasoned as follows:

> If particulars meant only detail this would not make any sense when used in relation to the rest of section 50(3). To take one example the Commission may issue a non-referral in respect of particulars (section 50(3)(b)). If this meant only detail, it makes no sense, since we know that this non-referral of particulars [of] a complaint can bring its own referral (section 51(1)). It cannot refer detail – it can only refer a cause of action or claim. Particulars

> must mean facts akin to claim. Similarly the section says the Commission may only refer 'some' of the particulars. Again, if particulars are something susceptible to referral or non-referral they must refer to something susceptible to being a claim, not mere detail.[99]

What then is the proper relationship between the initial complaint and the referral? The Tribunal attempted to articulate the relationship in *SAB*. It acknowledged that some meaning must be given to the phrase 'as submitted by the complainant' in section 50(3), but insisted that it cannot be read to require that the complaint must contain the *facta probanda* of the referred cause of action. The Tribunal struggled, however, to articulate an alternative to the *facta probanda* test. It accepted the standard of 'substantial similarity' set in *Glaxo Wellcome* as an appropriate benchmark (emphasising, though, that it must be applied with sensitivity to the limitations of the complainant's knowledge),[100] and proposed simply that the courts apply a doctrine of interpretation that reads complaints 'in an inclusive manner that allows [them] to be heard on the merits'.[101]

The precedent defining the relationship between the initial complaint and the section 49A summons is also highly problematic. Recall that, in *Woodlands Dairy*, Harms JA held that the Commission may only issue summons against firms specifically named in the complaint initiation document. In *SAB*, the Tribunal responded directly to this holding, and argued that the underlying concern over potential abuse of power by the Commission was quite simply misplaced. This was so because there is an intermediary step, before a summons is issued, that the SCA failed to take cognisance of. As the Tribunal explained,

> The Commissioner, who is required to authorise a summons in terms of section 49A of the Act, is required to apply a fresh consideration to the issue of the summons and this creates a distinct and new jurisdictional fact. The Commissioner has to decide what documents to require, from whom and for what purpose. The recipient of the summons need not even be potential respondent – simply someone believed to have the information required. The summons involves the exercise by the Commission of a policing power, albeit more limited than a search warrant, and therefore its terms need to be more strictly construed than those of a [complaint] initiation document.[102]

Distinct considerations therefore inform the Commission's initiation of a complaint and the issuance of a section 49A summons, which considerations should be subjected to *separate* judicial scrutiny. Accordingly, as the Tribunal makes plain, 'it does not follow that because the issue of a summons has as a prerequisite the initiation of a complaint that the requirements of a valid initiation document need to be the same as those for a valid summons'.[103]

All told, the decisions of the CAC and SCA in *Woodlands Dairy, Netstar* and *Yara* have made the work of the Commission and Tribunal exceedingly difficult. Following *Woodlands Dairy*, only the firms specified as suspects in the initial complaint may be summonsed in the course of the Commission's investigation. Following *Netstar*, only the specific cause of action described in the initial complaint may be referred to the Tribunal for determination. And following *Yara*, the initial complaint may not be amended in the course of the investigation, and its precise scope must be gleaned from the intention of the complainant. The immediate threat presented by *Woodlands Dairy*, *Netstar* and *Yara* is that a host of cases that the Commission has already begun to investigate without the discipline demanded by these precedents, such as *SAB*, may no longer be heard by the Tribunal.

CONCLUSION

The Commission and the Tribunal find themselves pigeon-holed by precedent. The Commission and the Tribunal are tasked under the Competition Act with large and complex mandates, and the success of their work has become a core tenet of South Africa's macro-economic policy. They enjoy the political backing of Parliament and the executive, and of a general public anxious to see economic reform and the growth of a pro-competitive business culture. However, the Commission and the Tribunal are battling against giant firms that are accustomed to operating free of the strictures of competition law, according to their own rules of practice, and in markets that they have long dominated. These firms readily resort to litigation over technical matters of jurisdiction and procedure to avoid the reach of the young competition authorities. Big business has found a sympathetic judiciary in the appellate courts, where there is an enduring culture of strict procedural legality, backed by constitutional commitments to the rule of law and an extensive Bill of Rights.

The recent rulings of the CAC and the SCA in *Woodlands Dairy*, *Netstar* and *Yara* – now followed by the Tribunal in *SAB* – have made the task of the Commission and the Tribunal considerably more difficult. In seeking to ensure procedural legality and fidelity to 'the rule of law', the appellate courts have resorted to technical line-drawing to circumscribe the investigative powers of the Commission and the jurisdiction and inquisitorial functions of the Tribunal. The promotion of a more disciplined Commission and Tribunal is clearly a laudable objective. However, there are other values and policy priorities at stake, which the courts have failed to weigh in the balance – including maximising the effectiveness, efficiency and accessibility of the Commission and the Tribunal. The courts' formalistic approach encourages vexatious litigation by well-resourced respondents, which threatens to overwhelm the Commission and the Tribunal, and to undermine the pursuit of their mandates. The resulting costs are not simply wasted litigation costs, but the costs of allowing abusive, collusive and corrupt business practices to persist in South Africa at inestimable public expense. As the extraordinary level of cartel activity uncovered under the CLP reveals, anti-competitive conduct is widespread and pervasive in the country. Indeed, in February 2011, the Commission reported that it was investigating some 65 cases of bid-rigging in the construction sector, involving more than 70 projects valued at R29 billion, and including all five of South Africa's major listed construction companies.[104] With the government's macro-economic growth strategy heavily reliant on cost-effective infrastructure and investments (set at over R250 billion a year), the cost of unchecked cartel activity could become very high indeed. The Tribunal is thus surely correct to insist in *SAB* that the recent case-law addressing the powers of the Commission and the Tribunal needs serious reconsideration if the competition regime is to achieve its objects.

POSTSCRIPT

A recent judgment by the Constitutional Court of South Africa in yet another matter addressing the powers of the Tribunal, *Senwes*,[105] indicates that the reconsideration required has got underway. The Constitutional Court endorsed a flexible approach to the Tribunal's powers, holding that if the evidence placed before the Tribunal establishes a contravention of the Competition Act, the Tribunal is competent to impose an appropriate remedy – regardless of the label that is put on the contravention when it is referred to the Tribunal. The Court held further that while the Tribunal cannot initiate a hearing, this does not mean that it cannot determine a complaint brought to its attention during the course of deciding a referral. Confining a hearing to matters raised in a referral 'would undermine the inquisitorial enquiry' which the Tribunal is authorised to conduct.

NOTES

* Special thanks to Professor Eleanor Fox at New York University for inspiration and encouragement.

1. Chapter 4, Part A of the Competition Act, No. 89 of 1998, sections 19–25.
2. Chapter 4, Part B of the Competition Act, sections 26–35.
3. Chapter 4, Part C of the Competition Act, sections 36–39.
4. Even before coming to power, the ANC identified competition policy reform as essential to redressing the apartheid economy. *See* ANC Policy Guidelines for a Democratic South Africa, 1992. The ANC-led government's first macro-economic policy, the Reconstruction and Development Policy (RDP) stipulated that:

   > A credible competition policy is crucial to the proper functioning of the economy. Objectives of this policy are to remove or reduce the distorting effects of excessive economic concentration and corporate conglomeration, collusive practices, and the abuse of economic power by firms in a dominant position. In addition, the policy will ensure that participation of efficient small-and-medium enterprises in the economy is not jeopardised by anti-competitive structures and conduct. (RDP White Paper, 1994 at para 3.8.2.)

5. Section 2 of the Competition Act sets out its objectives as follows:
   The purpose of this Act is to promote and maintain competition in the Republic in order –

   (a) to promote efficiency, adaptability and development of the economy;
   (b) to provide consumers with competitive prices and product choices;
   (c) to promote employment and advance the social and economic welfare of South Africans;
   (d) to expand opportunities for South African participation in world markets and recognise the role of foreign competition in the Republic;
   (e) to ensure that small and medium-sized enterprises have an equitable opportunity to participate in the economy; and
   (f) to promote a greater spread of ownership, in particular to increase the ownership stakes of historically disadvantaged persons.
   See further on the background to the Competition Act, D. Lewis, 'South African Competition Law: Origins, Content, and Impact' in V. Dhall (ed.), *Competition Law Today: Concepts, Issues and the Law in Practice* (Oxford: OUP, 2007) at 340.

6. *The New Growth Path: The Framework*, 23 November 2010, available at http://www.info.gov.za/aboutgovt/ programmes/newgrowthpath/index.html.
7. Statistics South Africa uses the following official definition of unemployment:

   > The unemployed are those people within the economically active population who (a) did not work during the seven days prior to the interview, (b) want to work and are available to start work within a week of the interview, and (c) have taken active steps to look for work or to start some form of self-employment in the four weeks prior to the interview.

   See Stats SA, *Concepts and Definitions for Statistics South Africa*, 2010 (version 3), available at http://www.statssa.gov.za/. The official unemployment rate of 25 per cent therefore excludes full-time students, people who are too sick to work, unpaid family workers and parents or partners who work without pay in the home. Most importantly, it excludes people who have looked for work unsuccessfully and are so discouraged that they have not sought employment in the last four weeks, and persons who cannot afford to seek employment. Searching for a job is expensive: it may require telephone calls, postage or travel from rural areas. So, while the official figure for unemployment is approximately 25 per cent, South Africa's statistics bureau recognises that the real figure is above 40 per cent.

8. *The New Growth Path* identifies eight key strategies in the area of competition policy. These are:

   (1) Competition investigations should continue to focus on areas of strategic importance, including the food sector, construction and infrastructure, other key input costs, the green economy and the IPAP [Industrial Policy Action Plan] sectors.
   (2) Law-enforcement agencies will cooperate more actively with the competition authorities to address pervasive breaches of the competition laws.
   (3) The competition authorities will review their procedures to reduce the opportunity for vexatious litigation and speed up competition probes.
   (4) More consideration should be given to mandating public interest conditions on proposed mergers, particularly in respect of employment and prices.
   (5) Competition authorities should involve trade unions more, as provided for in the Competition Act. Unions should develop their capacity to share information and insights on employment issues in mergers and acquisitions.
   (6) Government will consider draft amendments to the Competition Act to enhance the Tribunal's power to order divestiture where inherited market power permits repeated abuse and to provide mechanisms to address pricing in markets characterised by economic concentration.
   (7) The competition authorities and DFIs [Development Finance Institutions] should cooperatively identify instances where support for new market entrants is needed to secure more competitive outcomes, in order to combine competition and investment measures.
   (8) Government will develop guidelines for granting exemptions in terms of the Competition Act for cooperation between producers where it will demonstrably benefit job creation and expansion into export markets. (At 10.)

9. Mergers have been by far the busiest area of activity for the Commission. It has received and processed over 3500 merger notifications, with over 500 notifications in the merger-boom year of 2007/2008. For its part, the Tribunal has ruled on over 700 mergers (with an average of 64 decisions a year). While the merger regime instituted by the Commission and Tribunal has been generally permissive (with unconditional approval of approximately 90 per cent of mergers), the Commission has not shied away from imposing novel conditions on merging entities to advance public interest factors, such as maintenance of employment levels and Black Economic Empowerment.

   With regard to advocacy, a separate division in the Commission is devoted entirely to building public and governmental support for competition principles and compliance by private firms. The advocacy work of the Commission has been considerable, and has included the establishment of targeted forums for the public sector, trade unions and business; promoting the engagement of the media, especially by issuing regular media statements; and establishing an up-to-date and accessible website.

   For an internal review of the first 10 years of the Commission and Tribunal's activities, see Competition Commission South Africa and Competition Tribunal South Africa, *Unleashing Rivalry 1999–2009: Ten Years of enforcement by the South African Competition Authorities* (2009), available at www.comptrib.co.za/assets/Uploads/Reports/unleashing-rivalry.pdf.

10. Competition Commission, *Corporate Leniency Policy* (as amended in 2008), hereinafter 'CLP'.
11. This award followed a 3-month period of nominations and polling among the international competition law community. *See* Competition Commission, Media Release, 8 February 2011. A few months earlier, the annual Global Competitiveness Report 2010–2011 of the World Economic Forum ranked South Africa 12th out of 139 countries for the 'effectiveness of its antimonopoly policies'. *See* World Economic Forum, *Global Competitiveness Report 2010–2011* at 303, available at www3.weforum.org/ … /WEF_GlobalCompetitivenessReport_2010-11.pdf.
12. On the US Corporate Leniency Policy, see S.D. Hammond, 'Cornerstones of an effective cartel leniency programme' (2008) 2 *Competition Law International* 4.
13. CLP, above n 10, para 3.3.
14. CLP, above n 10, para 10. Although the CLP does not provide immunity to the second or third applicants, the Commission may recommend that the Competition Tribunal impose a reduced administrative fine on other members of the cartel if they cooperate.
15. Notice 628 of 2008, Government Gazette No. 31064 of 23 May 2008. The key amendments were: (1) the extension of the policy's application to leaders and instigators of a cartel; (2) the injection of greater certainty in the leniency application process by rendering it mandatory for the Commission to grant immunity when the conditions of the CLP are met; (3) the introduction of a marker procedure to encourage early disclosure (enabling a potential applicant to reserve its place in the 'immunity queue' while it collects the information necessary to make a formal application); and (4) the allowance of oral submissions, at the discretion of the Commission.
16. While the Competition Commission had received only three applications for leniency by the end of 2004, and only three in 2005 and 2006 combined, nine applications were lodged in 2007/2008, followed by 19 in 2008. (See *Unleashing Rivalry* above n 9 at 49). The Annual Report of the Competition Commission for 2009/2010 notes 'a substantial increase in the number of leniency applications, resulting in a very steep rise in the number of cartels under investigation'. An astonishing 79 leniency applications were filed in that reporting year, two-thirds of which involved the construction sector, while the Commission launched 31 new investigations that year. In 2010/2011, the Commission received 33 applications for leniency, with the decline attributable to the introduction of a concurrent fast-track settlement process for the construction sector in 2011 (discussed further above). The Commission launched 22 new investigations in 2010/2011, and established a specialised unit dedicated to investigating the large number of cartel cases emerging from the CLP. For its part, the Tribunal heard 30 cases concerning prohibited practices in 2010/2011, and imposed fines to the total value of R794 million – a considerable increase on the previous year's record of ten cases and fines to the value of R292 million. (See the Annual Reports of the Competition Commission and Competition Tribunal for 2009/2010 and 2010/2011, available on their websites: http://www.compcom.co.za and http://www.comptrib.co.za.)
17. Unsurprisingly, the CLP was not left unchallenged. In 2010, a steel and wire product manufacturer, Agriwire (Pty) Ltd, unsuccessfully sought to challenge the CLP on the basis that it unlawfully extended the Commission's powers beyond those afforded it under the Competition Act. The Court affirmed the legality of the CLP, observing that it allowed the Commission only to grant *conditional* immunity, with the Tribunal retaining 'the final authority' to determine whether to impose a fine on the party concerned. The Court reasoned that this arrangement was in line with the Competition Act, which empowers the Commission to 'negotiate and conclude consent orders' to be made by the Tribunal. *See Agriwire (Pty) Ltd and*

Another v *The Commissioner of the Competition Commission and Others*, North Gauteng High Court (5 July 2011), Case No. 7585/2010, [2011] ZAGPPHC 117 at paras 62–65. All the South African cases cited in this chapter are available at http://www.saflii.org.za.

18. Although the settlement agreement was confirmed by the Competition Tribunal, the National Treasury refused to approve payment of Pioneer Foods' fine directly into the Industrial Development Corporation Fund. Instead, the Treasury insisted that this portion of the fine be paid into the National Revenue Fund and allocated by the Treasury (in accordance with section 213 of the Constitution, section 59(4) of the Competition Act, and section 13 of the Public Finance Management Act, No. 1 of 1999). *See* A. Crotty, 'Treasury feeds Pioneer fine through IDC fund', *Independent News Online*, 25 February 2011.
19. This innovative settlement was nominated by the Global Competition Review as 'Enforcement Matter of the Year' in February 2011. Another structural settlement was reached in June 2010 with Sasol Chemical Industries, which required Sasol to divest of 5 of its 6 fertiliser blending facilities within 12 months to prevent further abuse of dominance, exclusionary conduct and price discrimination in the supply of ammonia and derivative fertiliser products. *See* Competition Commission, 'Media Release: Sasol agrees to divestiture in the fertilizer case', 5 July 2010, available at http://www.compcom.co.za/ 2010-media-releases/.
20. The Competition Amendment Act (CAA) has five main aspects, which together are aimed at strengthening the enforcement capacity of the Competition Commission, and at extending the Commission's power to scrutinise markets and anti-competitive conduct. First, the new legislation clarifies the long-vexed issue of the jurisdiction of the Commission vis-à-vis sector regulators. It provides that the Commission shares concurrent jurisdiction with other regulatory authorities, while having '*primary authority* to detect and investigate alleged prohibited practices within any industry or sector, and to review mergers' (section 3 of the CAA amending section (3)(a) of the Competition Act). Second, the CAA formalises the CLP (which has remained an internal policy of the Commission), by incorporating it into the Competition Act (section 8 of the CAA, amending section 50 of the Competition Act). Third, and perhaps most contentiously, the CAA introduces personal criminal sanctions for directors and managers who cause or knowingly acquiesce in the prohibited practices of price-fixing, market-sharing or collusive tendering. Those found guilty of such conduct are liable under the CAA to a criminal fine not exceeding R500 000, or imprisonment not exceeding 10 years, or both (section 12 of the CAA, inserting 73A of the Competition Act). Fourth, the CAA empowers the Commission to initiate and conduct 'market inquiries', which it defines as 'a formal inquiry in respect of the general state of competition in a market for particular goods or services without necessarily referring to the conduct or activities of any particular named firm' (section 6 of the CAA, inserting sections 43A to 43C of the Competition Act). And finally, section 4 of the CAA introduces unique provisions to regulate what it terms 'complex monopoly conduct'. The newly-inserted section 10A(1) of the Competition Act provides that 'complex monopoly conduct' subsists in a market if:

    (a) at least 75% of the goods or services in that market are supplied to, or by, five or fewer firms;
    (b) any two or more of the firms contemplated in paragraph (a) *conduct* their respective business affairs in *a conscious parallel manner or co-ordinated manner*, without agreement between or among themselves; and
    (c) the conduct contemplated in paragraph (b) has the *effect of substantially preventing or lessening competition* in that market,

unless a firm engaging in the conduct can prove that any technological, efficiency or other pro-competitive gain resulting from it outweighs that effect.

While complex monopoly conduct does not constitute a prohibited practice *per se*, such conduct is made subject to investigation by the Competition Commission, which may thereafter seek a declaratory order from the Tribunal requiring firms to cease engaging in complex monopoly conduct having anti-competitive effects. It is only if the firms *persist* in complex monopoly conduct in the face of a declaratory order, that they commit a prohibited practice, and are liable to be fined.

On 8 March 2013, the President proclaimed that section 6 of the CAA, concerning market inquiries, will come into force on 1 April 2013. The date of entry into force of the remainder of the provisions of the CAA is yet to be determined however.

21. *Woodlands Dairy (Pty) Ltd and Another* v *Competition Commission; Competition Commission* v *Clover Industries Limited and Others*, Competition Tribunal (17 March 2009), Case No. 103/CR/Dec06, [2009] ZACT 18; *Woodlands Dairy (Pty) Ltd and Another* v *Competition Commission*, Competition Appeal Court (26 September 2009), Case No. 88/CAC/Mar09, [2009] ZACAC 3; *Woodlands Dairy (Pty) Ltd and Another* v *Competition Commission*, Supreme Court of Appeal (13 September 2010), Case No. 105/2010, [2010] ZASCA 104; 2010 (6) SA 108 (SCA).
22. *Competition Commission and Another* v *Netstar (Pty) Ltd and Others*, Competition Tribunal (19 April 2010), Case No. 17/CR/Mar05, [2010] ZACT 29; *Netstar (Pty) Ltd and Others* v *Competition Commission South Africa and Another*, Competition Appeal Court, (15 February 2011), Case No. 99/CAC/MAY10, 98/CAC/MAY10, 97/CAC/MAY10, [2011] ZACAC 1.
23. *Competition Commission* v *Yara South Africa (Pty) Ltd and Another, In re Competition Commission* v *Sasol Chemical Industries and Others*, Competition Tribunal (24 February 2010), Case No. 31/CR/May05, [2010] ZACT 15; *Yara South Africa (Pty) Ltd* v *Competition Commission and Others, Competition Commission* v *Sasol Chemical Industries Ltd and Others, Omnia Fertilizers* v *Competition Commission*, Competition Appeal Court (14 March 2011), Case No. 93/CAC/Mar10, 94/CAC/Mar10, [2011] ZACAC 2.
24. *Competition Commission and Another* v *South African Breweries and Others*, Competition Tribunal (7 April 2011), Case No. 134/CR/DEC07, [2010] ZACT 45 ('*SAB Dismissal: Order*'); *Competition Commission and Another* v *South African Breweries and Others*, Competition Tribunal (16 September 2011), Case No. 134/CR/DEC07, [2010] ZACT 45 ('*SAB Dismissal: Reasons*')
25. D. Moseneke, 'The Fourth Bram Fischer Memorial Lecture: "Transformative Adjudication"', delivered in Johannesburg on 25 April 2004, reproduced in *South African Journal on Human Rights* (2002), 18(3) at 309.
26. G. Quinot, 'Substantive Reasoning in Administrative-Law Adjudication' (2010) 3 *Constitutional Court Review* 111 at 116.
27. Section 28(2)(b) of the Competition Act provides that the members of the Tribunal must *inter alia* 'have suitable qualifications and experience in economics, law, commerce, industry or public affairs'.
28. Section 55(1)(a).
29. Section 55(1)(b).
30. Section 54(c).
31. Section 52(2)(a) and (b).
32. Section 2 or the Competition Act is set out in note 5 above.
33. *Nationwide Poles CC* v *Sasol (Oil) Pty Ltd*, Competition Tribunal (31 March 2005), Case No. 72/CR/Dec03, [2005] ZACT 17; *Sasol (Oil) Pty Ltd* v *Nationwide Poles*

CC, Competition Appeal Court (13 December 2005), Case No. 49/CAC/Apr05, [2005] ZACAC 5.

34. *Harmony Gold Mining Company Ltd & Another and Mittal Steel South Africa Ltd and Another*, Competition Tribunal (27 March 2007), Case No. 13/CR/Feb04, [2007] ZACT 21; *Mittal Steel South Africa Limited and Others* v *Harmony Gold Mining Company Limited and Another*, Competition Appeal Court (29 May 2009), Case No. 70/CAC/Apr07, [2009] ZACAC 1.
35. *Nationwide Poles* v *Sasol (Oil)* (CT), above n 33, para 102.
36. Id at para 81.
37. Id at para 86.
38. *Sasol (Oil)* v *Nationwide Poles* (CAC), above n 33, paragraphs unnumbered in original. Emphasis added.
39. Section 8(a) of the Competition Act provides: 'It is prohibited for a dominant firm to (a) charge an excessive price to the detriment of consumers'.
40. *Harmony Gold Mining Company* v *Mittal Steel* (CT), above n 34, para 74.
41. *United Brands* v *Commission* [1978] ECR 207.
42. *Harmony Gold Mining Company* v *Mittal Steel* (CT), above n 34, para 84.
43. *Mittal Steel* v *Harmony Gold Mining Company* (CAC), above n 34, para 52.
44. D.M. Davis, 'Reflecting on the effectiveness of competition authority: prioritisation, market enquiries and impact', paper presented at the *Third Annual Competition Commission, Competition Tribunal, and Mandela Institute Conference on Competition Law, Economics and Policy in South Africa*, University of Witwatersrand, 3–4 September 2009. Available at http://www.comptrib.co.za/publications/speeches/.
45. *See generally* on the 'essential contestability' of the Rule of Law: Jeremy Waldron, 'Is the Rule of Law an essentially contested concept (in Florida)?' (2002) 21 *Law and Philosophy* 137.
46. Section 49B(1) and (2) of the Competition Act provides:

    (1) The Commissioner may initiate a complaint against an alleged prohibited practice.
    (2) Any person may –
        (a) submit information concerning an alleged prohibited practice to the Competition Commission, in any manner or form; or
        (b) submit a complaint against an alleged prohibited practice to the Competition Commission in the prescribed form.

47. *Glaxo Wellcome (Pty) Ltd* v *National Association of Pharmaceutical Wholesalers*, Competition Appeal Court (21 October 2002), Case No. 15/CAC/Feb 02, [2002] ZACAC 3.
48. Id at para 14.
49. Id at para 15. The CAC also drew attention to the wording of the prescribed complaints form, the CC 1 Form, which requires that a complainant only 'provide a concise statement of the conduct' that is the subject of the complaint.
50. Id at para 16. Emphasis added.
51. Section 49B(3) and (4) provides:

    (3) Upon initiating or receiving a complaint in terms of this section, the Commissioner must direct an inspector to investigate the complaint as quickly as practicable.
    (4) At any time during an investigation, the Commissioner may designate one or more persons to assist the inspector.

52. Section 49A regulates the issuance of summons by the Commissioner, and provides in relevant part:

(1) At any time during an investigation in terms of this Act, the Commissioner may summon any person who is believed to be able to furnish any information on the subject of the investigation, or to have possession or control of any book, document or other object that has a bearing on that subject –

(a) to appear before the Commissioner or a person authorised by the Commissioner, to be interrogated at a time and place specified in the summons; or

(b) at a time and place specified in the summons, to deliver or produce to the Commissioner, or a person authorised by the Commissioner, any book, document or other object specified in the summons.

53. Section 50(1) and (2) provides:

(1) At any time after initiating a complaint, the Competition Commission may refer the complaint to the Competition Tribunal.

(2) Within one year after a complaint was submitted to it, the Commissioner must –

(a) subject to subsection (3), refer the complaint to the Competition Tribunal, if it determines that a prohibited practice has been established; or

(b) in any other case, issue a notice of non-referral to the complainant in the prescribed form.

54. Section 51(1) provides accordingly:

(1) If the Competition Commission issues a notice of non-referral in response to a complaint, the complainant concerned may refer the matter directly to the Competition Tribunal.

55. Section 50(4) and (5) provides:

(4) In a particular case –

(a) the Competition Commission and the complainant may agree to extend the period allowed in subsection (2); or

(b) on application by the Competition Commission made before the end of the period contemplated in paragraph (a), the Competition Tribunal may extend that period.

(5) If the Competition Commission has not referred a complaint to the Competition Tribunal, or issued a notice of non-referral, within the time contemplated in subsection (2), or the extended period contemplated in subsection (4), the Commission must be regarded as having issued a notice of non-referral on the expiry of the relevant period.

56. Cited in *Woodlands Dairy* (CT), above n 21, para 20.
57. Sections 49A and 49B are set out in relevant part in notes 51 and 52 above.
58. *Woodlands Dairy* (CT), above n 21, para 9.
59. Id at para 15.
60. *Woodlands Dairy* (CAC), above n 21, paras 68, 74.
61. Id at para 95.
62. Id at para 36.
63. *Woodlands Dairy (Pty) Ltd and Another* v *Competition Commission*, Competition Appeal Court (7 December 2009), Case No. 88/CAC/Mar09, [2009] ZACAC 3.
64. Id.
65. *Woodlands Dairy* (CAC), above n 21, para 52.

66. *Woodlands Dairy* (SCA), above n 21. The applicants challenged the CAC's approach to the 2005 summonses, as well as a subsequent complaint initiated by the Commission against them in 2006. I discuss the judgment only in respect of the 2005 summonses.
67. Harms JA reasoned as follows at para 20:

> I do not accept the submission on behalf of the commission that these far-reaching invasive powers may be used by the commissioner for purposes of a fishing expedition without first having initiated a valid complaint based on a reasonable suspicion. It would otherwise mean that the exercise of this power would be unrestricted because there is no prior judicial scrutiny ...

68. *Woodlands Dairy* (SCA), above n 21, para 10.
69. Id at para 35.
70. Id.
71. Id at para 36.
72. Competition Commission, 'Media Release: Commission withdraws case against Clover, Ladismith, Nestle and Parmalat', 20 April 2011. Available at http://www.compcom.co.za/2011-media-releases/.
73. *Competition Commission* v *Netstar* (CT), above n 22. Section 4(1) of the Competition Act provides:

> 4(1) An agreement between, or concerted practice by, firms, or a decision by an association of firms, is prohibited if it is between parties in a horizontal relationship and if –
> (a) it has the effect of substantially preventing, or lessening, competition in a market, unless a party to the agreement, concerted practice, or decision can prove that any technological, efficiency or other precompetitive gain resulting from it outweighs that effect; or
> (b) it involves any of the following restrictive horizontal practices:
> (i) directly or indirectly fixing a purchase or selling price or any other trading condition;
> (ii) dividing markets by allocating customers, suppliers, territories, or specific types of goods or services; or
> (iii) collusive tendering.

74. *Netstar* v *Competition Commission* (CAC), above n 22.
75. Id at paras 48, 59–63.
76. Id at paras 12, 18, 37–40, 44–45, 48–49, 57–64.
77. Id at para 27.
78. Id.
79. Id.
80. Id at para 26.
81. See note 73 above for the text of section 4(1)(b) of the Competition Act.
82. *Competition Commission* v *Yara South Africa* (CT), above n 23, para 35.
83. See note 39 above where section 49B(3) and (4) is set out.
84. *Competition Commission* v *Yara South Africa* (CT), above n 23, para 40.
85. *Glaxo Wellcome*, above n 47, para 16.
86. *Competition Commission* v *Yara South Africa* (CT), above n 23, para 43.
87. *Yara South Africa* v *Competition Commission* (CAC), above n 23.
88. *Yara South Africa* v *Competition Commission* (CAC), above n 23, para 23, citing *Glaxo Wellcome* at paras 18–19 (emphasis in the original).
89. Id at para 30.
90. See Harms JA's comment discussed above in the text to note 71.

91. *Yara South Africa* v *Competition Commission* (CAC), above n 23, para 40.
92. Id at para 38.
93. M. Bleby, 'SAB case closed but not resolved', *Business Day*, 11 April 2011.
94. *SAB Dismissal: Reasons* (CT), above n 24, para 156.
95. Id at para 108.
96. Id at paras 101–109.
97. Id at para 138.
98. Id at para 110.
99. Id at para 92.
100. Id at para 148.
101. Id at para 147.
102. Id at paras 130–131.
103. Id at para 131.
104. Competition Commission, 'Media Release: Competition Commission Invites Construction Firms to Settle,' 1 February 2011, available at www.compcom.co.za/2011-media-releases/.
105. *Competition Commission of South Africa* v *Senwes Ltd* [2012] ZACC 6; 2012 (7) BCLR 667 (CC) (12 April 2012), paras 29, 48 & 50. The ruling has been received as a boost for the Commission and the Tribunal. It appears that the competition authorities may yet enjoy a little more room to manoeuvre in South Africa.

4. The political economy of the competition regimes in Thailand and South Korea: a comparison

Deunden Nikomborirak

INTRODUCTION

Thailand was the first among the ten Association of Southeast Asian Nations (ASEAN) to pass a competition law, the Price-Control and Anti-Monopoly Act, in 1979. Two decades later, the law was replaced by the Trade Competition Act of 1999, which contains more comprehensive provisions to address restrictive practices. Despite the comparatively early adoption of the law, not a single firm has been subject to administrative or legal sanctions under either law. Thailand now lags far behind other emerging Asian countries, which have adopted and implemented their own laws, including Chinese Taipei (1992), Singapore (2004) and Indonesia (2000). Although the enforcement of competition law in these countries is not necessarily free from political interference and is still subject to certain institutional limitations, at least there have been decisions that have served to set legal precedence. The total failure of the Thai competition regime makes it an interesting case study for examining the kinds of challenges a country may face in implementing a competition law.

This chapter seeks to investigate factors that have contributed to the apparent failure of the Thai competition regime in a political-economy context, as well as those that have accounted for success in the case of South Korea. The exercise will help to point out factors underpinning the success or failure of a competition regime which may be useful for countries that are considering adopting a competition law or that are in the process of redesigning their existing competition regime.

The chapter describes the dynamics of the political economy that were at play behind the promulgation of competition law, first in Thailand and then in South Korea. It then compares the specific economic characteristics of each country, to explain the significant differences in their competition regimes. This is followed by an overview of the institutions behind the competition law in each country, as well as the extent of public support for competition law.

THE POLITICAL ECONOMY OF COMPETITION LAW

The Thai Case

According to its website, the Thai Trade Competition Office has handled 76 complaint cases (17 cases involving abuse of dominance, 17 cases for collusive practices and 42 involving unfair trade practices) since its inauguration 10 years ago, averaging only 7 cases per year. And, as mentioned earlier, not a single case has been submitted to the court and no administrative fines or remedies have ever been issued.[1] This dismal record is not surprising, given that between 1999 and 2006 the Trade Competition Commission met only nine times, four of which took place during the first year after the law came into effect under the democratic government.[2] From 2001 to 2006, the commission met only five times, an average of once a year.

Perusing the Thai Trade Competition Office's website, one finds no information about the nature of the alleged anticompetitive trade practices, the names of the companies involved, the results of the investigations and the decisions of the commission. All this points clearly to a competition regime that has failed.

We need to ask why a country would pass a law that it never intended to implement. This question is particularly pertinent in view of the fact that the promulgation of both competition laws in Thailand was a product of a unilateral decision by the domestic government, rather than a fulfilment of international obligations, in the form of a free trade agreement (Singapore), WTO accession commitments (Vietnam), or compliance with a conditionality imposed by international organisations that may be providing financial assistance to a country in the region (Indonesia).

To understand why a home-grown law with broad parliamentary support was never properly implemented, one needs to examine the economic and political context in which the two laws were passed.

Thailand's general political landscape is characterised by frequent military coups, totalling 18 between 1932 and 2006. This has resulted in fluctuations in the political regime from unstable elected civilian governments to interludes of military takeover that usually followed a situation of widespread corruption among bureaucrats and politicians. Interestingly, the promulgation of both competition laws in 1979 and 1999 were products of the military-installed governments, rather than elected civilian governments.

The Price-Control and Anti-Monopoly Act of 1979

The Price-Control and Anti-Monopoly Act of 1979 was passed during a military regime in response to the public outcry about the widespread price-fixing behaviour of businessmen and the ineffectiveness of the Excessive Profit Act of 1974 to rein in price increases that were being fuelled by the global oil-price shock. The new law would allow the state to control the prices of all products declared to be 'controlled products' and to regulate the pricing behaviour and trade practices of businesses that are declared to be 'controlled businesses'.

As the main objective of the promulgation of the law was to restrain price increases that were affecting citizens' cost of living, the price-control provision was promptly implemented for a variety of products. Interestingly, the law did not provide any basis on which a product could be declared a 'controlled product' and, hence, be subject to price-control. Instead, the implementing authority had full discretion to choose any product whose price it wished to control. Given that the Department of Internal Trade, the designated implementing authority, was also responsible for constructing and calculating the consumer price index, products that were subject to price-control were those that carried significant weight in the basket of consumption used to calculate the inflation rate. Most of the products were therefore basic necessity consumer goods such as eggs, rice and soap.

Indeed, the implementation of the price-control mechanism received wide support from the public as lower prices provided direct and immediate relief from the rising cost of living. However, there was little economic rationale behind the selection of these products for price-control, as most of those selected were provided in highly or relatively competitive markets. The established price ceilings imposed are also rarely binding on suppliers or retailers as they result from a series of negotiations between the supplier and the authority on cost data. Given the asymmetry in relation to information about costs – with producers knowing more than regulators – producers often get their way. In fact, in certain cases, the price ceilings facilitated parallel pricing, and were used as a basis for collusion.

The anti-monopoly provisions of the law were completely ineffective, however. This was because, according to the law, to be considered a controlled business, an enterprise must have carried out monopolistic or restrictive trade practices. Since the law was silent on what kind of practices were considered to be monopolistic or restrictive, except for rice trading, no business was ever declared a controlled business throughout the 20-year period that the law was in effect. Apart from this legal limitation, strong opposition from large businesses was likely to be a further factor contributing to the lack of enforcement.

The Price-Control and Anti-Monopoly Act of 1979 served mainly to stabilise prices to prevent the cost of living from rising too quickly and to keep the national inflation rate low.[3] As the price-control mechanism was able to appease the public, the enthusiasm needed to properly address the problem of collusion and other restrictive practices eventually waned. To this day, price regulation remains the most widely-employed instrument of competition policy.

The Trade Competition Act, 1999

In 1991, another military coup overthrew a civilian government that was allegedly engaged in widespread corruption practices, mainly associated with the granting of lucrative exclusive concessions to the private sector to develop several multi-billion-baht infrastructure projects. At the time, the military appointed a former-diplomat-turned-businessman, Anand Panyarachun, as the new prime minister. During the short term of his interim government, lasting from March 1991 to April 1992, he launched a series of economic reforms. The technocrat-dominated government expressed a clear vision of a free-market policy. It adopted policies of economic liberalisation, deregulation and privatisation. In addition to a freer trade policy, it instructed the Minister of Commerce to establish a committee consisting of bureaucrats and legal academics to revise the anti-monopoly law so that it could be enforced. The draft competition law was approved by Cabinet within 8 months, but Parliament was dissolved in April 1992, before the law was passed.

It took 8 more years and four more elected governments to promulgate the law. The exuberant economic growth in the early 1980s, fuelled by the bubble economy, undermined all market-reform efforts. It was not until 1999, 2 years after the Asian financial crisis that, as part of its post-financial-crisis reform, the democratic government at the time finally passed the Trade Competition Act of 1999. The new law dealt solely with restrictive practices as the price-control provisions were transferred to another new law, the Goods and Services Price Control Act of 1999. Two different commissions were established by the laws: the

Goods and Services Price Control Commission, responsible for price controls; and the Trade Competition Commission (TCC), for safeguarding fair competition in the markets. The secretariats of both commissions remain within the Department of Internal Trade, under the Ministry of Commerce.

Against the expectations of those who advocated the passing of the competition law, the law was never implemented. Although several major cases were investigated in the first year that the law came into effect, including the case of the cable-television monopoly and the beer and whisky tie-in sales cases, progress came to a halt with the change in government in 2000, when the Thai Rak Thai Party replaced the Democratic Party.

Greacen (2005)[4] describes this change in the government to the Thai Rak Thai party led by the charismatic former Prime Minister Thaksin Shinawatra as the end of the neo-liberal era. The new government that came in after a landslide victory at the polls was dominated by businessmen rather than professional politicians or technocrats. It played on nationalistic sentiment that has been fuelled by the belief that the International Monetary Fund and Western countries sold Thailand short during the aftermath of the 1997 financial crisis by withdrawing funds and imposing unreasonable structural adjustment conditions. An example of this is the government at the time advocating the building of 'national champions' in the energy market rather than opening up the sector to greater competition. National champions not only won the hearts of the nationalists and non-governmental organisations, but expanded state enterprises also translated into larger rents that could be captured. The members of the Cabinet, including the prime minister himself, were mainly from large businesses operating in various industries including the telecommunications, media and automotive sectors. Clearly, these businessmen-turned-politicians had no interest in introducing greater competition into markets in which they operated.

The change in the political environment had a significant direct effect on the enforcement of the competition law as, by design, the Thai Trade Competition Commission comes under the purview of the executive power. The commission is still chaired by the Ministry of Commerce with the permanent secretary of commerce, the top-ranking bureaucrat, as the deputy-chairperson and the director-general of the Department of Internal Trade as the secretary. Commissioners include the permanent secretary of finance and between eight and twelve 'experts' in the field of law, economics or business administration, half of whom must come from the private sector. The subordinate law governing the selection of these expert commissioners stipulates that private sector experts are to be nominated by the two most prominent trade associations, namely, the Federation of Thai Industries and the Thai Chamber of Commerce. Each association is to nominate five names from which the minister will pick two or three to be commissioners. As for the remaining expert commissioners, the Ministry of Commerce and the Ministry of Finance would each put forward two to three names designated to be commissioners. As the law does not specify the qualification criteria of these experts, the composition of the commission is determined largely by the discretion of the ministries and the trade associations. The final list of names of candidates for commissioners is proposed by the Minister of Commerce and appointed by the Cabinet.

The current selection process has many flaws. First, the two trade associations tend to be dominated by big businesses, such that small and medium businesses stand little chance of ever occupying a seat in the commission allocated to the private sector. Second, the nomination and selection process of commissioners from both the public and the private sector quota is done behind closed doors without any public announcement or solicitation for qualified candidates. The names of candidates, their qualifications, and the selection criteria for their appointment are never publicly disclosed.

Political interventions and corporate lobbying to resist the law

According to Poapongsakorn (2002),[5] political interventions and corporate lobbying – both explicitly and behind the scenes – occurred throughout the period that the Trade Competition Act was in force, in particular during investigation periods. Perhaps the most blatant and damaging lobbying by big businesses was the delay in the promulgation of the dominance threshold that would make the provision on abuse-of-dominance enforceable.[6] In June 2000, the Trade Competition Commission proposed a dominance threshold of 33.33 per cent market share and 1 billion baht sales revenue in the relevant market. With the prevalent abuse-of-dominance cases being investigated at the time, it was hoped that the passing of the threshold would ensure that the relevant provision was enforced. But opposition by the Federation of Thai Industries (FTI) did much to prevent the Cabinet from approving the proposed definition of market dominance.[7] The new government that came into office in early 2001 decided to return the proposed dominance threshold to the Trade Competition Office for review. The counter-proposal by the business sector was a 50 per cent market-share threshold. The proposed threshold would severely circumscribe the scope of application of the law, as only a handful of companies would be classified as being dominant. Even then, the dominance threshold never made it through Cabinet until 2008 when the Ministry of Commerce, led by a technocrat installed by a military government, decided to push it through Cabinet. The rule for submitting mergers and acquisitions notification has not been established to this day.

Another study, by Takasila and Chitmunchaitham (2002),[8] attributes the lack of enforcement of the competition law to conflict-of-interest problems frequently confronting competition commissioners. For example, the authors found that in 2000, one of the commissioners considering the tie-in-sale case of whisky and beer was a director of a company affiliated with the powerful whisky conglomerate. The conglomerate is known to be one of the largest contributors to all political parties, charities and sports events and it is staffed with high-ranking retired bureaucrats who have strong ties with the relevant regulatory authorities. Another commissioner – in fact, the secretary to the fair trade commission, the director-general of the Department of Internal Trade himself – was also found to be a director of a company affiliated with the cable-television monopoly alleged to be bundling cable services and charging the excessive monthly fee mentioned earlier. There is no evidence that these commissioners ever declared their conflict of interest and recused themselves from meetings during which these cases were discussed.

But large businesses are not the only opponents of the law. Many ministries have also been resistant to the law. Some have been genuinely concerned about whether conventional competition rules can apply to state enterprises that operate on a non-commercial basis, claiming, for example, that subsidised services may be seen as predatory pricing. Others, however, feared competition rules would erode the lucrative rents that state enterprises under their purview enjoyed. As a result, the Trade Competition Act of 1999 contained a carve-out for state enterprises. This was to appease various ministries that would like to retain full control over enterprises under their supervision. This blanket exemption for state enterprises no doubt undermines the effective implementation of the law, as state enterprises are dominant in a broad range of sectors – in particular energy, transport and utility. According to Nikomborirak and Lertamphainond (2009),[9] state-owned enterprises and their respective affiliated companies contribute to 52 per cent of the Stock Exchange of Thailand (SET) market capitalisation. And the PTT, the country's energy flagship company, and its affiliated companies alone contribute to 45.6 per cent of market capitalisation. Indeed, these large state-owned enterprises operating in the infrastructure and utility businesses all carry certain monopoly rights which can be easily manipulated to restrict competition from private competitors. Worse, to maximise their monopoly rents, many of these enterprises auctioned off their statutory monopoly rights to private concessionaires in exchange for a handsome royalty fee, thus legitimising the monopoly arrangements and extending them to private enterprises.

A good illustration of this is the very first competition case investigated by the Trade Competition Commission (TCC) in 1998. A privately-owned cable-television monopoly was alleged to have raised the monthly subscription price excessively and restricted customers' choice of lower-priced packages. However, as the company operated under a concession granted by the state-owned broadcasting company, the Mass Communication Organisation of Thailand (MCOT), and was subject to the latter's rules and regulations, its practices did not fall within the jurisdiction of the competition authority.

Carve-outs

Although it is commonplace that trade practices undertaken in compliance with state regulations are exempted from competition law, this case warrants deeper investigation. Like many developing countries, Thailand did not have a fully-fledged sectoral regulatory body, bar the financial sector, until 2001, when the Telecommunications Business Act of 2001 established a truly independent regulatory body, the National Telecommunications Commission (NTC).[10] As a result, the state enterprise that provided the broadcasting service assumed the regulatory role. In this case, the MCOT owned the cable-television concession in question and enjoyed an annual concession royalty fee equivalent to 6.5 per cent of the company's revenue. It is no surprise, therefore, that when the case was handed over to the MCOT, nothing was done to further investigate the alleged excessive pricing practices of the private cable company. There was a similar occurrence in the telecommunications market, where private concessionaires were alleged to have fixed the monthly fee for cellular phone services during 1998–1999, the period before competition in the market intensified. The same defence that the fees were regulated by the state enterprise that handed out the concession was invoked. This shows that the state enterprise carve-out practice leaves a gaping hole in the enforcement coverage of the competition law.[11]

Indeed, carve-outs are not uncommon among competition laws, even in countries with well-developed competition institutions, as they serve to ensure that the application of the law does not undermine the effective implementation of other state policies, in particular industrial policy.

While the case of South Korea is discussed in more detail in the next section, it is pertinent to mention a few points about it here. It has also had its share of sectoral carve-outs such as in the fishery, agriculture, forestry and mining sectors. It has also allowed the fixing of fees by professionals when these fees were approved by the relevant regulator. But these exemptions were repealed before the end of the twentieth century so that the Monopoly Regulation and Fair Trade Act (MRFTA) applies almost universally, except for business conduct authorised by other regulations. The Korea Fair Trade Commission (KFTC) maintains jurisdiction over unregulated aspects of business practices undertaken by state enterprises as well as private companies. For example, in 1999 it fined KEPCO, the majority state-owned electricity generation company, for unfairly awarding tenders to its own subsidiaries. More recently, in 2008, the KFTC slapped a surcharge of US$15.4 million on the Korean Development Bank (KDB) for the undue subsidisation of its subsidiary. To prevent KDB Capital (one of its affiliates experiencing financial difficulties) from facing a suspension order from the Financial Supervisory Commission, the KDB undertook large amounts of privately-placed corporate bonds issued by ADB capital at interest rates of 4.79 to 5.86 per cent, while the corresponding figures announced by the private bond rating agencies were between 7.32 and 11.6 per cent.[12]

The likelihood that the Thai competition authority would ever take up a similar competition case against a state enterprise – should the law allow it to do so – is almost nil. This is because the TCC is merely a commission at the departmental level and therefore cannot be expected to challenge a state enterprise under direct supervision of another ministry. This 'turf' problem is particularly taxing in a minority or coalition government where ministers come from different parties with different agenda of their own. There is no doubt that elevating the status of the fair trade commission to the ministerial level, as in the case of South Korea, underscores the commission's success in enforcing the competition law against state enterprises.

The South Korean Case

The birth of competition law in South Korea is in many ways similar to Thailand. South Korea passed the Price Stabilisation Act in 1973 in response to the surging prices resulting from the first oil shock. The law was enacted to establish a fair trade order by banning the practice of refusal to sell as well as placing price ceilings on goods and services. The law was replaced by the Monopoly Regulation and Price Stability Act in 1975, which contained more substantive provisions on unfair trade practices.

For a while, South Korea seemed to be following the same path as Thailand, with little enforcement of the newly-founded fair trade law, due to staunch lobbying from the private sector. But the continued expansion of the formidable *chaebols* (the large, conglomerate family-controlled firms of South Korea with strong ties to government agencies) in the 1980s, which threatened the survival of many small and medium enterprises, into all areas of business, called for the active implementation of the competition law. In addition, the *chaebols*' questionable standards of corporate governance also engendered much distrust among the public.

And, like Thailand, the implementation of the competition law at the time focused mainly on price-control rather than monopoly regulation (Lee 1998).[13] The difference, however, is that the South Korean government quickly recognised that controlling the end-effects of market concentration via price-control may easily distort the market, leading to unintended consequences such as production cancellation, the creation of double prices, market cornering and the hoarding of products.[14] As a result, within 5 years, a comprehensive competition law that was designed to deal with market concentration, the Monopoly Regulation and Fair Trade Act 1980 (MRFTA), was passed under that military government of General Chun Doo Whan, which came into power after staging a coup in December 1979.

Although the promulgation of South Korea's MRFTA in 1980 took place after the military coup that put General Chun Doo Whan in power, it received support from a much wider constituency than the Thai law did. According to Seung Wha Chang and Yoonjin Jung (2005),[15] by that time, the public's opinion of the *chaebols* was 'souring noticeably'. Intellectuals, consumer groups, the media and workers all shared the view that the large business conglomerates created by the state industrial policy and politicians were designed to exploit the South Korean people. Clearly, due to the specific economic environment, the competition law in South Korea has always had a much broader constituency of support than the Thai law.

It would not be wrong to say that the existence of *chaebols* and the problems they created and the opposition to them helped the KFTC become the prominent and effective institution that it is today. As the following chart shows, the KFTC's level of activity has been more or less constant since 1996, except between 1999 and 2003, the years after the Asian economic crisis in 1997, during which the number of judgements fell by almost a half. Since 2007, the number of corrections issued has increased dramatically, mainly from cases involving abuse of dominance, cartels and unfair business practices.

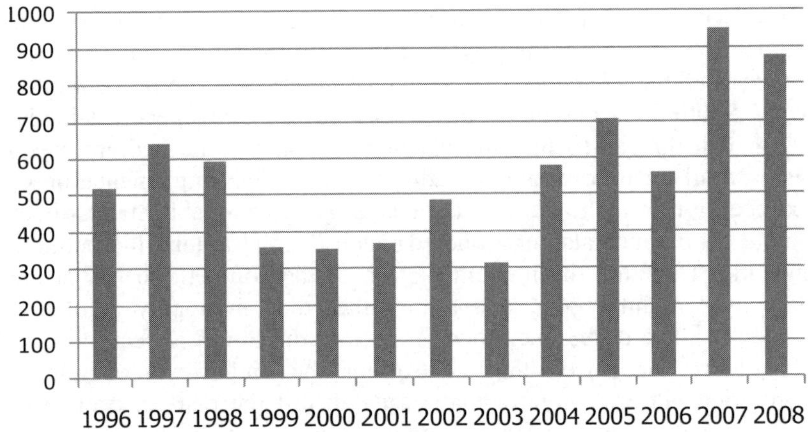

Sources: KFTC (2005), 'Annual report on Competition Policy Development in Korea'. Available at ftc.go.kr/data/hwp/20061214_101629.do for data from 1996–2004 and KFTC's 'Annual report 2008' for data from 2005–2008.

Figure 4.1 The number of corrections issued by the KFTC related to the violation of restrictive and unfair trade practices from 1996 to 2008

The composition of the Commission's staff has also been constant. Although commissioners are appointed by the country's president on the recommendation of the chairman of the Commission,[16] which could be seen as a form of political intervention, the law clearly specifies that they need to be qualified. Article 37(2) of the law stipulates that commissioners are required to have prior experience as a public official in monopoly and fair trade issues, or 15 years' experience as a judge, lawyer or prosecutor, or 15 years of academic experience in law, economics, or business administration, or 15 years of business or consumer-protection experience. However, broad criteria for qualification are not a sufficient guarantee against political meddling with the appointment process, as there is not a transparent nomination and selection procedure. As in the Thai case, the absence of such a procedure leaves the composition and qualification of commissioners entirely to the whim of the minister.

The influence of vested business interests on politics has been waning. According to Lee Sung R. (2003),[17] successive governments in South Korea have targeted the middle class rather than the business elite as their main political support. Seung Wha Chang and Youngjin Jung (2005) explain that the growth-oriented policy during the 1960s and 1970s did much to alleviate poverty and increase the wealth of average South Koreans. More economically-secure South Korean voters are more inclined to take interest in the issue of equity and wealth distribution. The fact that the regulation of large businesses has always been one of the key issues in any South Korean political party's campaign is evidence of this.

The KFTC's regulation of *chaebols* initially helped to de-concentrate the market. According to Sung-hui Chwa (2002),[18] market concentration decreased in the 1990s compared to the 1980s, but returned to an increasing trend in the mid-2000s. The phenomenon was attributed to the expansion of exports by major *chaebols*, which helped to drive the South Korean economy. The study also shows that economic resources have been gravitating towards the top five *chaebols*. This view is confirmed by the KFTC, which found that out of the 400 industries it investigated between 2004 and 2008, 46 industries were dominated by oligopolies, with a single company dominating more than half of the market, or the top three companies occupying more than three quarters of the market.[19] There is no doubt that there is little that the KFTC regulations and competition rules can do to prevent the concentration of economic power in the hands of a few large *chaebols*.

THE ECONOMICS BEHIND COMPETITION LAW: THE DIFFERENT CASES OF THAILAND AND SOUTH KOREA

This section examines the economic and political conditions in the two countries, and attempts to explain why South Korea embraced competition law principles more readily than Thailand.

Although the political economy behind the enforcement of its competition law contributes largely to the failure of the Thai competition regime, the economic environment has also played an important role in this.

According to a study by Stephan (2005),[20] there are three main rationales for adopting a competition law, based on the survey of competition regimes in over 160 countries. The first is the need to establish competition rules to ensure free and fair competition in markets following the privatisation of state enterprises, the deregulation of major sectors and the liberalisation of formerly protected and concentrated markets. The second is the need for an effective legal tool to address collusive practices and mergers and acquisitions of foreign businesses that restrict competition in the domestic market. The third is the belief that free and fair competition will lead to greater efficiency, which will help to promote the competitiveness of the local industry.

The promulgation of the competition law in South Korea in 1980 was perceived by policy-makers at the time as an integral part of the country's industrial reform that sought to replace state-led industrial growth with the market. There was universal recognition in the government that while state support and protection may have helped the industry to achieve the scale of production desired, the overwhelming market power of the large business conglomerates or the *chaebols* proved to be damaging to the domestic industry and thus, had to be circumscribed.[21]

It is common for rapidly industrialising economies to be faced with an intensifying problem of market concentration, which needs to be properly addressed. The history of the development of antitrust law in the United States reveals a similar story. Back in 1890, when the Sherman Act was passed, several large business conglomerates controlled the steel, oil and railroad markets. The law was designed to deal with these 'trusts'; a term commonly referred to big manufacturing business conglomerates much like the *chaebols* in South Korea.

Unlike South Korea or the United States, however, Thailand did not have an immediate problem with trusts or *chaebols*, or other problems that called for the promulgation and implementation of a competition law. As mentioned earlier, although high market concentration can be found in certain sectors, such as cement, steel and energy, the prices of these products are closely monitored by the Goods and Services Price Control Commission, so that consumers feel that they are not 'overly' excessive.[22] But the sense of being protected may be false as price ceilings established by the Commission also accommodate parallel pricing among suppliers.

Privatisation, another rationale for having a competition law, was on the government agenda at the time, but little connection was made between privatisation and competition law. Rather, academics and civil society demanded an independent regulatory body that could ensure not only fair competition, but also a proper licensing and access regime and fair regulated prices. Local cartels were prevalent in certain industries, but since many had the blessing of the government agency, cartels become more or less accepted practices. Trade associations in Thailand will not think twice about announcing the 'recommended price or fee' for their products or services. Finally, bid-rigging in government procurement was rife, but the practice falls within the jurisdiction of the National Counter Corruption Commission. So, in short, there was not a clear constituency for the competition law.

Also, unlike in South Korea, the Asian financial crisis that hit in 1997 did not help the competition law cause. At the time that the law was promulgated, in 1999, the Thai economy was struggling to recover from the Asian financial crisis of 1997, of which Thailand itself was the source. Many laws were passed that year to assist in the financial recovery process, such as the bankruptcy law and the foreclosure law. The corporatisation law was also passed to allow the government to privatise state enterprises to consolidate its dire fiscal position as well as improve efficiency in the state-dominated sectors. In addition, the new Foreign Business Act was promulgated to relax restrictions on foreign equity share in Thai businesses, to mobilise foreign direct investment.

It was not at all clear where competition law and principles fitted into the scheme of things at the time. The crisis in Thailand was perceived to be a result of monopolisation or lack of competition in the market, and bad corporate governance in banks and other financial institutions that led to reckless lending. Hence, post-crisis reform concentrated mainly on tightening the prudential regulation of financial institutions and building good corporate governance in the private sector. Liberalisation or market reform, which would foster greater competition, were clearly not on the reform agenda.

The 'statement of rationale' written at the very end of the Trade Competition Act of 1999 was too general and vague to reveal any sound underlying rationale for having the law. It simply states that a competition law is essential to establish a systematic competition regime to ensure free competition and prevent unfair trade practices.

Perhaps the law was perceived merely as a part of the general economic reform agenda of the country at the time. It was possibly seen as something a country should have, as competition is universally believed to be associated with greater efficiency and more equitable distribution of wealth. Besides, most economically advanced countries all have a competition law to safeguard free and fair competition. Alternatively, the law might have been passed simply to fulfil the mandate established by the new Constitution to advocate for free and fair competition. Article 50 of the Constitution assures citizens of their right to engage in free and fair competition, while Article 87 stipulates that the state shall pursue a free economic system through market forces, ensure and supervise fair competition, prevent direct and indirect monopolies and refrain from engaging in businesses in competition with the private sector. While lofty principles enshrined in the Constitution has resulted in the drafting of legislation, the apparent lack of conviction and will on the part of policy-makers has resulted in poor implementation and enforcement.

This begs a deeper question: Why did Thai policy-makers, unlike their counterparts in South Korea, never view competition as an integral part of its economic reform? Economic plans in South Korea, such as those that seek to steer the economy towards a knowledge-based one, explicitly recognise the need to foster competition in the market in order to attain economic goals.

Perhaps the answer lies in the structure of the economy. Although both Thailand and South Korea are export-oriented economies, with exports contributing to 73 and 46 per cent of GDP respectively in 2008,[23] the underlying market structure of the two countries is fundamentally different. Most large South Korean firms or *chaebols* – such as Hyundai, Samsung and LG – operate in the manufacturing sector, which is a traded sector. As tariffs continued to fall persistently as a result of WTO and FTA commitments, these conglomerates needed to boost their efficiency to sustain competitiveness in the global market. The South Korean government reckoned that competitive pressure can be effective for sharpening the much-needed competitive instinct of these large conglomerates.[24]

On the contrary, large Thai conglomerates, such as the PTT group (formerly the Petroleum Authority of Thailand) or the Siam Cement Group, operate mostly in the non-traded sector, namely energy and cement. Except for the agricultural-based Chareon Phokaphand (CP group), Thailand cannot boast any local manufacturing conglomerate that competes in the global export market. Nikomborirak (2009) found that among the 50 largest listed companies in the stock exchange of Thailand ranked by the size of the turnover in 2008, 32 operated in the non-traded sector.[25] Large exporters, such as automobile assemblers and electronic and electric parts and supplies producers are mainly foreign multinationals rather than local companies. Most large Thai companies are comfortably shielded from competition as foreign companies are barred from engaging in any service business in Thailand.[26] Moreover, a large number of these large companies are state-owned and still carry statutory monopolistic privileges. As market liberalisation and the introduction of competition into these markets are likely to have severe implications for the economically (and likely politically) powerful incumbents, it has been difficult for any government to embrace a 'competition culture'.

At the same time, market protection explains why many large Thai businesses, both public and private, are willing to put so much effort into undermining not only the competition law, but also other government policies such as trade liberalisation and deregulation, that may dislodge their entrenched market power. In the past, they have often drummed up nationalistic sentiment to undermine planned liberalisation in trade or investment as this tactic has usually resulted in ready support from NGOs. To ward off any government privatisation and deregulation plan that would take away their lucrative monopoly rights, state-owned enterprises often demonise private companies as profit-maximising suppliers providing inferior quality goods or services at excessively high prices.

Given the private sector's strong resistance to competition, it is therefore not surprising that Thailand has not made any meaningful commitment to any of the many trade agreements that are in effect. These include bilateral agreements like the Japan Thailand Economic Partnership Agreement (JTEPA), the Thailand Australia Free Trade Agreement (TAFTA) and the New Zealand Thailand Closer Economic Partnership (NZTCEP); regional agreements like the ASEAN Free Trade Agreement on Services (AFAS), the ASEAN–China Free Trade Agreement, the ASEAN-India Free Trade Agreement; or multilateral agreements like the GATT, to open up its highly protected non-traded sector.[27]

South Korea, on the other hand, decided to join the OECD in 1996, voluntarily removing much of its protection for non-traded service sectors. This opened up its legal service[28] and financial sectors[29] and removed restrictions on capital flows and foreign direct investment. The fact that South Korea chose to join the 'rich men's club' showed that it was ready to commit itself to market principles and to undertake major economic reforms to bring its domestic laws and regulations into line with international standards.

THE INSTITUTIONS BEHIND COMPETITION LAW

The success or failure of any policy or regulation depends largely on the capability of the institutions involved, in particular for policies or rules that are conceptually and technically complex, such as competition law. Without political commitment, it is unlikely that a non-independent competition authority can hope to have access to the resources required to build up capacity and to properly enforce the law.

Indeed, in Thailand, the lack of political commitment explains the trade competition office's relatively modest status within the hierarchy of the Ministry of Commerce. The office is only a small unit within the Department of Internal Trade under the Ministry of Commerce. Its annual budget in 2010 was less than US$100 000 and it only had 28 non-administrative staff. The Office of Trade Competition Commission has always been seen as the 'orphan child' of the Department of Internal Trade under which it resides, as competition law enforcement often ranks in terms of priority well below other more apparently pressing and more publicly-visible policies such as agricultural price support, price control and export promotion. It is likely therefore that the minister would neglect his or her role as the chairperson of the Commission, which explains why so few meetings of the Commission have been called.

This stands in stark contrast to the Korea Fair Trade Commission (KFTC), which was first established within the powerful Economic Planning Board. In 1990, the decision-making powers over competition-law-related matters had already been transferred from the Minister of Economic Planning Board to the KFTC, and in 1995 the office acquired its independence when the Economic Planning Board was merged with the Ministry of Finance to become the Ministry of Finance and Economy. The head of the Competition Commission holds a ministerial position and thus attends Cabinet meetings. The Commission also holds the statutory power to review government rules and regulations that may inhibit competition in the market. There is no doubt that competition law and policy are perceived to be an integral part of South Korea's economic development.

Resource constraints naturally lead to capacity constraints. But the problem of institutional capacity in Thailand is not unique to the trade competition office or the Ministry of Commerce. The problem runs much deeper. Enforcement of competition law often involves 'winners and losers' between sellers and buyers and upstream and downstream businesses, as it takes away rents from one party, thus lowering the cost burden shouldered by the other party. And Thai bureaucrats and politicians are loath to get involved in this inevitable redistribution of income between different industries. Doner (2009)[30] attributes the lack of industrial policy in Thailand to the unwillingness of politicians and bureaucrats to 'pick and choose' industrial sectors to promote, as such a policy would involve winners (promoted industries that would receive subsidies or other state assistance) and losers (supporting industries and upstream and downstream industries that would be exposed to greater competition to boost efficiency). According to the author, the country has been very successful in diversifying its manufacturing base from rice, rubber and sugar to include cars, garments, prawns, chicken and disk drives, without any state guidance or support. But the country's long-standing diversification strategy into natural resource and labour-intensive industries is pushing its limits as Thailand now faces stiff competition from emerging economies with cheaper labour and better natural resources, in particular those of Vietnam and China.

The luxury of there always being 'a new pasture' has allowed policy-makers to avoid making the hard decisions that would be involved in correcting the inherent structural deficiencies that hamper the country's competitiveness. This would include monopolisation or the lack of competition in many of its upstream industries such as steel or agricultural industries as well as in many supporting service industries such as education, energy, banking and telecommunications. As a result, Thailand has not been able to upgrade its industries into ones that exploit technology and skills more intensively as is the case in Taiwan and South Korea, since industrial upgrading requires more efficient (lower cost) upstream and supporting industries, many of which remain heavily protected in Thailand.

The situation in South Korea couldn't be more different. Although – according to existing literature on the subject – whether the state-led growth in South Korea was considered to be successful is debatable, one cannot deny the exceptional ability of the South Korean government to coordinate the complex implementation of its industrial policies. Chang (1993)[31] attributes South Korea's success in industrial policy to political and institutional factors, including elite bureaucracy. Lee (2007)[32] agrees. In his view, South Korean administrative elites played an important role in the policy-making process as well as the implementation and appraisal of such policies. Like Doner, he asserts that economic planning and engineering involve highly specialised knowledge, while implementation requires deep administrative insights and a keen evaluative perspective. Because the South Korean government has always assumed the key responsibility in the development of the economy, the bureaucracy has been consistently deeply involved with vital decision-making processes that require special skills in assessment and evaluation.

PUBLIC SUPPORT FOR THE LAW

As mentioned earlier, the KFTC enjoyed much wider support from various groups than did the Thai competition law when it was promulgated in 1999. Perhaps one of the reasons was that the KFTC deals not only with competition issues, but also consumer protection issues such as unfair advertisement and labelling, as well as unfair contract and franchising that involved numerous small and medium-sized enterprises. The KFTC has built up, over time, a strong support from consumers and SMEs. This has not happened in the case of Thailand, where consumer law and unfair contract laws are handled by the Office of Consumer Protection Commission, in the Office of the Prime Minister. Price-control, the most visible regulation to the average consumer, is handled by the Price Control Commission.

Most non-governmental organisations in Thailand do not perceive the competition authority as their ally, as they do not see how competition law affects the welfare of the average consumer. Most believe that the law deals solely with settling 'disputes between businesses' that have nothing to do with consumers. In the absence of broad public support, the law could not withstand the strong resistance from large, politically influential businesses.

CONCLUSION

This comparative study of the political economy behind the competition regime in Thailand and South Korea shows that the legislation for the competition authority in both countries was passed after military coups. This is because civilian governments were often associated with big businesses and the incoming military regime wanted to break the cosy relationship that may be concentrating power in the hands of a few wealthy families. But from this point, the paths of the two countries diverge completely. The Korea Fair Trade Commission has gained prominence and become a very powerful organisation whose chairman holds ministerial status. The Thai Trade Competition Commission, on the other hand, has remained a very small office under the Department of Internal Trade, within the commerce ministry.

Thailand's experience shows that simply having a competition law does not guarantee effective enforcement. After 10 years of existence, the Thai Trade Competition Commission has not been able to bring any legal case against companies alleged to have pursued restrictive practices. Yet, in 2008 alone, the KFTC handed out over 800 corrections related to violations of restrictive and unfair trade practices.

What are the factors responsible for such contrasting performances?

A possible explanation is the marked difference in the corporate structures of the Thai and South Korean economies. Although both countries are relatively open economies that rely on export as the engine of growth, in Thailand it is mostly foreign companies that operate in the traded sector, while in South Korea it is mostly local companies. Because most large businesses in South Korea, such as Samsung, LG and Hyundai, must compete in the global market to be able to survive, they are more receptive to competition than are the Thai conglomerates that operate mainly in the non-traded sector.

Large Thai conglomerates, such as Siam Cement Group, the state owned PTT Group, or even the Chareon Phokapand Group that grew from the highly competitive food export business, all have operations in the non-traded sector, such as cement, energy or telecommunications. And these are comfortably shielded from foreign competition. This highly influential group of businesses is therefore not accustomed to open competition and perceives protection, rather than competition, to be the best way to survive.

In addition, the culture of competition among businesses and policy-makers is not enough to promote competition in the face of the strong lobbying of large powerful businesses, and where there is no public support for the law. This study finds that the South Korean competition law received broad public support since its promulgation, as the law was specifically designed to deal with the politically and economically powerful *chaebols* that were perceived as the bad guys by the South Korean people. Also, the Korea Fair Trade Commission Office handles not only competition rules, but also consumer protection rules such as those governing unfair contracts, false advertisements and labelling, product liability, and so on. This brings the office into direct contact with a large number of consumers, which has helped to build its reputation over time.

The Thai competition law, on the other hand, has had little public support from the very beginning. The public never demanded the law. In fact, very few people know about the law. Most people probably never came across the Thai Trade Competition Office, as it deals solely with business competition issues such as abuse of dominance, mergers and unfair trade practices. Nor has enforcement of the law been on the agenda of any political party's campaign platform in any election.

To conclude, a prerequisite for a successful competition regime is broad public support for the competition law. Thus, the most important and challenging task facing competition law advocates is how to convince ordinary citizens that the law can help to improve their wellbeing or the health of the economy as a whole. Making the link between competition law and welfare is not an easy task. Only with strong public backing can one hope to save this controversial law from being held hostage by its politically and economically powerful opponents who are loath to see their monopoly rents eroded by its effective implementation.

NOTES

1. The only time that the Trade Competition Office decided to lodge a lawsuit against private firms for breaching the law was a case involving exclusive dealing in the motorcycle business. However, the public prosecutor refused to submit the case to court on the grounds that the investigative process was not in-keeping with the law.

The Trade Competition Office is authorised to bypass the public prosecutor and submit the case directly to the court, however.

2. www.dit.go.th (only available in Thai) as of January 2006. The department now no longer discloses records of the commission's meetings. However, news of trade competition commission meetings is extremely rare.
3. The Department of Internal Trade, the keeper of the competition law, is also responsible for calculating and annoucing the consumer price index.
4. Greacen, Chris (2005), 'Privatisation of profits, socialisation of costs and risks: Privatisation in Thailand's Power Sector', powerpoint presentation, Windsor Hotel, Bangkok, 16–17 July 2005. Downloadable at http://www.slideserve.com/chelsey/privatization-of-profits-socialization-of-costs-risk-privatization-in-thailand-s-power-sector.
5. Poapongsakorn, Nipon (2002), 'The new Competition Law in Thailand: Lessons for institution building', *Review of Industrial Organisation*, 2, 185–204.
6. Ibid.
7. As in n 30.
8. Takasila, Suriyasai and Chitmunchaitham, Rajitkanok (2002), 'Monopolies and politics', in *Building Constituency for Competition Policy and Competition Law*, eds Thailand Development Research Institute (TDRI), funded by the World Bank. The paper is available online at www. info.tdri.or.th/unpublished/.
9. Nikomborirak, Deunden and Lertamphainond, Sirikarn (2009), 'Monopolies and economic inequality', paper presented at the Thailand Development Research Institute Annual Academic Conference, Bangkok, 29–30 November 2009.
10. Thereafter, similar bodies were formed in the insurance and energy sectors, though with less autonomy than the NTC.
11. The Ministry of Commerce has proposed to lift the exemption for state enterprises that are public companies as they operate on a purely commercial basis, seeking maximum shareholders returns. There are currently over 120 state enterprises in Thailand, only a dozen of which are public companies. Hence, the proposed amendment will have only a marginal impact on state enterprises. The draft amendment, first proposed in 2007 during the military-installed government and revised by the Council of the State, is currently under review by the ministry of commerce in the current civilian government.
12. KFTC's annual report 2008, pp. 74–75.
13. Lee, Kyu Uck (1998), *Competition Policy, Deregulation and Economic Development: The Korean Experience*, Korea Institute of Industrial Economics and Trade.
14. KFTC (2009), 'Evolution of Korea's competition law', OECD website: www.globalcompetitionforum.org/asia.htm#korea.
15. Chang, Seung Wha and Joong, Yoonjin (2005), *Competition Policy and Development in Asia*, eds Douglas Brooks and Simon Evenett, UK: Palgrave Macmillan, pp. 161–195.
16. Except for the Chairman and the Vice-Chairman, which are considered to be political appointmments, commissioners are recommended by the Prime Minister and appointed by the President.
17. Lee, Sung R. (2003), 'Political change and regulatory policy change: An exploring study in the regulation of economic concentration by big corporations'. Paper downloadable from www.kapa21.or.kr/data.
18. Chwa, Sung-hui and Sung-Hee Jwa (2002), *The Evolution of Large Corporations in Korea: A New Institutional Economics Perspectives of the Chaebol*, Cheltenham: Edward Elgar Publications.
19. *The China Post*, 23 December 2010. Downloadable from www.chinapost.com.tw/business/asia/korea/2010.

20. Stephan, Johannes (2005), 'Adopting competition laws', in *Competition Policy Foundations for Trade Reform, Regulatory Reform and Sustainable Development*, coordinated by Simon J. Evenett. A Research Project Funded under the Sixth Framework Programme, DG Research, European Commission. The paper can be downloaded from http://cordis.europa.eu/documents/documentlibrary/124856901EN6.pdf.
21. Jacobs, Scott H. (2000), *Regulatory Reform in Korea*, Paris: OECD Publications.
22. These products are subject to soft price control mechanisms whereby there are no price ceilings imposed but suppliers have to consult the Office of Goods and Services Price Control Commission before making any price increase.
23. Central Intelligence Agency, *The World Factbook 2010*. Downloadable at www.cia.gov/library/publications/the-world-factbook/.
24. KFTC (2009), ibid.
25. See note 9.
26. The Foreign Business Act 1999 stipulates that the direct foreign equity share of all businesses operating in the service sector must not exceed 49 per cent.
27. Thailand Development Research Institute (2009), 'Service sector master plan', paper submitted to the National Economic and Social Development Board (in Thai with English executive summary).
28. Woong Shik Shun (2000), 'Liberalization of legal services market in Korea', paper downloadable at www2.law.columbia.edu.
29. Sang In Hwang, Inseok Shin and Jungho Yoo (2000), 'Korea's liberalisation of financial services trade', in *NBER East Asia Seminar on Economics*, Vol. 11, eds Takatoshi Ito and Anne O. Krueger, Chicago: University of Chicago Press.
30. Doner, Rick (2009), 'Politics and Thailand's uneven economic development', paper presented at the Thailand Development Research Institute Annual Academic Seminar, Bangkok, 29–30 November 2009.
31. Chang (1993), 'The political economy of industrial policy in South Korea', *Cambridge Journal of Economics*, 17(2), 131–157.
32. Lee, Hyung-U. (2007), 'Characteristics of Korean bureaucracy', downloadable from http://riss.dongguk.ac.kr/riss/2007140108.pdf.

5. The role of SMMEs in the formal and informal economy in Zambia: the challenges involved in promoting them and including them in competition regulation

Thula Kaira

INTRODUCTION

The development of an economy in any country is closely linked with the development of the small business sector. Formal and informal small businesses are often the nurseries of bigger companies, even multinationals, which have become a symbol of industrialisation. As the foundation of the industrial base of a country, small businesses therefore need policies and legal frameworks to facilitate their development. The role of government is indispensable in ensuring that the course of industrial growth and development is not obstructed by anticompetitive or abusive market practices that may frustrate the entry and growth of small businesses.

The small business environment thrives in countries like the United States, India and China. And there are signs of this in Zambia too. A walk in the high-density residential areas, known as 'compounds', shows thriving businesses along the streets, both in and outside homes, and on every corner. Even in the leafy suburbs, the 'home shop' has become a common feature. The people running these businesses are the millions of self-employed that the formal sector has not been able to absorb. The businesses offer a way for people with relatively low levels of education or training, finance and social sophistication to enter into economically gainful activities and thus establish their own social safety net.

However, the challenges for small formal and informal businesses are many. They range from lack of finance to high capital finance costs. For example, for some, packaging, location and logistics hamper expansion into upmarket segments as well as expansion of existing capacities. This paper recognises and explores the importance of small, micro and medium-size enterprises (SMMEs) in the formal and informal economy in Zambia. It goes further to consider the myriad challenges involved in promoting and protecting the development of SMMEs and how this may be applied in relation to competition regulation. The paper discusses the genesis of competition law in Zambia before analysing some of the core issues.

BACKGROUND TO THE DEVELOPMENT OF THE SMME SECTOR IN ZAMBIA

Zambia's big business sector has historically been dominated by private foreign firms or state monopolies. Small businesses, on the other hand, have traditionally been middlemen or suppliers of components and services to the private or state-owned dominant firms. In 1968, 4 years after independence, the Zambian government announced a major policy shift towards a centrally-planned economy, through the Mulungushi reforms. These were implemented vigorously, particularly from 1972 onwards, when the government nationalised key industrial sectors such as sugar, cement, clear beer, national retail, public transportation, insurance, soaps and detergents, edible oils, and bread and milk, into state-owned monopolies. The desire to have one company supplying a product such as cement or a service such as public transport was based on socialist economic principles. The final phase of nationalisation involved the turning of the previously privately-owned copper mines in 1982 into the state-owned Zambia Consolidated Copper Mines (ZCCM). One of the spinoffs of this was the creation of a small business industrial base that mainly supplied input goods and services to the giant mining conglomerate.[1]

Between 1972 and 1991, private business expansion was limited to the SMME category, as growth in larger businesses would either mean nationalisation or a mandatory 51 per cent government stake in the enterprise. Other than state-owned enterprises (SOEs), most enterprises were SMMEs and competition turned on gaining access to and meeting the supply requirements of the SOEs.

Within the domestic economy, there was no substantive competition to the SOEs. While protection from foreign competition may be good in some cases, when the protection is absolute it tends to induce complacency in the protected industry or entity. The economist Adam Smith recognised this when he explained that while it is possible that the monopoly of the home market frequently gives great encouragement to the particular type of industry which enjoys it, and perhaps helps to create and protect jobs, there is doubt about whether it leads to sustained industrial growth in the long term.[2] This is definitely what started to happen in Zambia. The SMMEs had been dependent on the efficiency of the SOEs, which was unfortunately not sustained. In 1992, there was thus a return to market economy principles, and the ensuing privatisation process saw the collapse of the SOEs, as well as the SMMEs that had relied on their existence.

THE STATE OF COMPETITION IN ZAMBIA

Like most sub-Saharan countries, Zambia's market has traditionally been protected from competition. Policies in the telecommunications sector, for instance, still show explicit protectionist tendencies, including high licence fees as well as reserved areas.[3] SMMEs are frequently wary of any foreign business within their vicinity because of their obvious size and lack of financial and technical capacity to compete with more resourceful, larger opponents. Strong lobbying activity and calls for government to reserve certain geographical and product areas for SMMEs are common. Ironically, even bigger and more resourced firms in Zambia also make similar calls. For instance, in the sugar industry, a successful lobby has maintained a closure to importation of domestic sugar for almost 10 years, with prohibitive procedures in place for obtaining a licence for importation of industrial sugar. A market study by the Commission revealed that as a result of this, sugar prices in Zambia were about three times higher than those obtaining in neighbouring countries.[4] With such entrenched conduct in the economy, competition needs protection and promotion. It needs clearly-identified supporters and defenders. The need for a systematic legal basis on which to address undesirable market behaviour that is likely to adversely affect fairness and equity in and access to business opportunities cannot be overemphasised. Recognising the need to address this, the Zambian government spearheaded through Parliament the enactment of the Competition and Fair Trading Act, Act number 18 of 1994.

The Competition and Consumer Protection Commission (formerly the Zambia Competition Commission) has continued to be a lead enforcement agency for competition and fair-trading matters in the economy. Playing the dual roles of competition regulator and consumer enforcement agency, the Commission has grown from a position of relative obscurity, when it started, to being an enforcer to be reckoned with in commerce and industry. Between 2009 and 2011, the Commission was engaged in court actions against multinationals such as Zambian Breweries (licensees for Coca-Cola and subsidiary of South African Breweries), British American Tobacco and Mercury Express. During the same period, the Commission managed to successfully prosecute Zambian Breweries/South African Breweries, with one case involving abuse of dominance. With these kinds of cases, competition enforcement in Zambia has created unprecedented levels of interest among businesses on how to comply with the Act. Companies such as Zambia Sugar PLC (associated with the Illovo Sugar and Associated British Foods companies) and Lafarge Cement have invited Commission staff to conduct in-house training programmes on compliance with competition law.

With increased enforcement activity, there was increased public concern about the weak powers of the Commission and the low fines, the maximum of which was K18 million (US$3600). Further, the Commission did not have powers to subpoena persons or demand the submission of documents or information. In a State-of-the-Nation address to Parliament, the President of the Republic of Zambia acknowledged the inadequacies of the Competition and Fair Trading Act and announced in September 2009 as follows:

> Competition and consumer protection are paramount in a developing economy such as ours. Unfortunately, the current legal framework governing this is weak and requires an overhaul. To this effect, government will be introducing a consumer and competition protection bill to this august house to strengthen the legal framework.

As per the presidential promise, in March 2010 the Zambian government adopted the comprehensive National Competition and Consumer Protection Policy. Following the adoption of the policy, the previous Competition and Fair Trading Act was repealed and replaced in August 2010 with the Competition and Consumer Protection Act of 2010. In terms of the new legislation, the Commission has been granted powers to subpoena witnesses and by a binding notice demand the production of documents or the supply of information relevant to the investigation. In terms of powers, the Commission can now fine up to a maximum of 10 per cent of an enterprise's turnover. However, with increased powers, fines and vigorous enforcement, the big business sector is not going to comply without some resistance. In a socio-political environment where big business is consecrated and can virtually 'do no wrong', it will require competition enforcers and adjudicators who are tenacious. Competition enforcement implicitly threatens entrenched business strongholds.

The National Competition and Consumer Protection Policy implicitly notes Zambia's long-term vision to become a middle-income country by 2030. In order to achieve this vision, the country is expected to improve the productivity and competitiveness of firms, and private and public institutions. The policy further recognises that the small size of the Zambian market makes it susceptible to anticompetitive practices, those facilitated by corruption of public officers or through certain policies that create ad hoc investment concessions, which in turn create an uneven playing field in the market place. This tends to frustrate other prospective and thriving entrepreneurial activities in the economy.[5]

Zambia's key industries are characterised by SMMEs playing roles of intermediaries or supply-chain players. The sugar industry is dominated by Zambia Sugar (a subsidiary of Illovo Sugar/ABF) with over 90 per cent market share; clear beer by Zambian Breweries/SAB-Miller with over 90 per cent market share; carbonated soft drinks (over 70 per cent of the market); cement by Lafarge with over 80 per cent market share; railway by Railway Systems of Zambia (a 100 per cent monopoly); electricity generation and transmission (ZESCO with over 75 per cent market share); and oil refinery (INDENI with 100 per cent market share). There has also been increasing concern over the monopolisation of key government infrastructural development projects by the Chinese.

Given these structures, and the small size of the market, a large SMME sector has developed to largely supply input and facilitate the sale downstream of the products of the dominant/monopoly firms. High sunk and entry costs into most of the sectors have dwarfed SMMEs and made it difficult for them to sustain their existence.

CHALLENGES IN PROMOTING FAIR COMPETITION AMONG SMMEs IN BOTH THE FORMAL AND INFORMAL ECONOMIES

There is a lot we can say about theories of competition and the benefits to consumer welfare in view of a low-cost and efficient producer vis-à-vis our traders, our farmers and other business people that have been subjected to what they feel is 'unfair' competition. What kind of conduct amounts to 'unfair' competition? The Zambian economy, like all others, is more open to international competition than before – and it is not only happening in the auto or clothing sectors but also in relation to the selling of chickens.

A survey done for this paper shows that the majority of the informal sector as well as formal SMME players consider that big firms are a threat to their existence. Measures to ease access to working capital have also been significant. Unfortunately, the interest rates for lending in Zambia are as high as 25 per cent. Generally, banks have been averse to lending to informal sector players as well as start-up SMMEs. The alternative has been family and friends as sources of both start-up capital and for recapitalisation purposes.

The Competition and Consumer Protection Commission has continued to receive complaints from informal traders about the unfair trading practices of their wholesale suppliers, which either supply them with defective products, or engage in anticompetitive practices such as discriminatory pricing. In the context of high unemployment and the HIV/AIDS epidemic that has created orphans and widows, a more social approach, as opposed to a purely economic approach to the enforcement of competition law, has been adopted. This means that the Commission does not always apply the economic rigours of competition analysis. For example, it may not first analyse the 'relevant market' by dealing with the matters on a case-by-case basis – regardless of whether the culprit trader is a dominant firm or not.

From the other side, in the manufacturing process, there have been accusations by large firms of unfair competition from informal businesses in the form of infringement of intellectual property rights, largely through trademarks and repackaging, and unfair trading practices in the supply of products that could cause injury and harm, due to the lack of attention to health and safety regulations, as well as many cases of false representation. It is therefore no surprise that certain segments of society may regard this sub-economy with contempt. But it needs to be remembered that the market players in this sub-economy are key to the survival of millions of men and women, who would otherwise be where?

THE SMME SECTOR

The Role of Formal and Informal SMMEs in the Economy

There are no reliable estimates as to the numbers of SMMEs in the Zambian economy. Figures from the Registrar of Business Names and the Registrar of Companies are useful only as an indication of registered businesses and companies, but not so much for whether such businesses are actually operating. However, in terms of employment, conservative estimates suggest at least 1.5 million people are employed in the sector. The Zambian government has been working towards creating dynamic SMMEs that are expected to contribute 30 per cent of jobs by 2013. The government hopes that this would be achieved through its national SMME policy, which it adopted in 2009.[6]

The term small, micro and medium-sized enterprises (SMMEs) includes small formal and informal enterprises. And it is necessary at the outset to recognise the crucial role they play in the Zambian economy. They provide a safety net, in terms of the scale of jobs that are created through them, and a self-managed 'social-welfare' system that the state is not able to adequately provide. Both the formal and informal SMMEs are a hub of entrepreneurial activity that is perhaps unparalleled in terms of the time and effort that goes into surviving and growing the businesses on a daily basis compared to larger and more formalised businesses. These market participants also play a critical role in re-positioning products according to the needs of their target customers that they have acquired through personal or established business links.

SMMEs in the Formal Economy

Business-related legal reform has been promoted through the World Bank-sponsored Private Sector Development Programme. Under this, a one-stop-shop concept was promoted that saw the amalgamation, through the creation of the Zambia Development Agency Act (11 of 2006), of four standalone institutions: the Zambia Investment Centre, the Export Board of Zambia, Zambia Export Processing Zones Authority, and the Small Enterprises Development Board. Following this process, the laws governing the dissolved institutions were repealed, including the Small Enterprises Development Board Act. The Act included detailed definitions of the terms 'small', 'micro' and 'medium'-size business. Among other things, the Zambia Development Agency (ZDA) was expected to promote SMMEs, whose classification is to be recommended through regulations under the ZDA Act. In defining SMMEs, the Act takes into account the four business variables used by the policy:

> 'Micro business enterprise' means any business enterprise whose total investment, excluding land and buildings, and annual turnover and the number of persons employed by the enterprise does not exceed the numerical value or number prescribed.
>
> 'Small business enterprise' means any business enterprise whose total investment, excluding land and buildings, and annual turnover and the number of

persons employed by the enterprise does not exceed the numerical value or number prescribed.

The Small Enterprises Development Board Act's definition for micro-enterprises was an entity with less than ten employees, investments in plants and machinery of less than 10 million Kwacha (US$2000) and an annual turnover of less than 20 million Kwacha (US$4000). Most micro-enterprises, however, have a much lower initial investment and turnover, and a workforce often not exceeding one employee. Enterprises between 10 and 30 employees, investments of less than K50 million (US$10 000) and an annual turnover of up to K80million (US$16 000) were defined as small and medium-sized enterprises (SMEs).

However, the Micro, Small and Medium Enterprise Development Policy of April 2009[7] defines SMMEs based on the following business variables:

- total fixed investments;
- sales turnover;
- number of employees;
- legal status.

Definitions of SMMEs as provided for in the policy:

(a) Micro Enterprises

A micro enterprise shall be any business enterprise registered with the Registrar of Companies;

(i) Whose total investment excluding land and buildings shall be up to Eighty Million Kwacha (US$16,000)
(ii) Whose annual turnover shall be up to One Hundred and Fifty Million Kwacha (US$30,000)
(iii) Employing up to ten (10) persons.

(b) Small Enterprises

A small enterprise shall be any business enterprise registered with the Registrar of Companies;

(i) Whose total investment, excluding land and building, in the case of manufacturing and processing enterprises, shall be between Eighty Million and Two Hundred Million Kwacha (US$16,000–$40,000) in plant and machinery;
(ii) In the case of trading and service providing enterprises shall be up to One Hundred and Million Kwacha (US$30,000)

(iii) Whose annual turnover shall be between One Hundred and Fifty Million and Two Hundred and Fifty Million (K151,000–K300, 000,000) Kwacha (i.e. after US$30,000 to US$60,000)
(iv) Employing between eleven and forty nine (11–49) persons.

(c) Medium Enterprises

A medium enterprise shall be any business enterprise larger than a small enterprise registered with the Registrar of companies;

(i) Whose total investment, excluding land and building, in the case of manufacturing and processing enterprises, shall be between Two Hundred Million and Five Hundred Million (K201,000,000–K500, 000,000) Kwacha (i.e. above US$40,000 to US$100,000) in plant and machinery.
(ii) In the case of trading and service providing shall be between One Hundred and Fifty One Million and Three Hundred Million (K151,000,000–K300,000,000) Kwacha (i.e. above US$30,000 to $60,000).
(iii) Whose annual turnover shall be between Three Hundred Million and Eight Hundred Million (K300,000,000–K800,000,000) Kwacha (i.e. between US$60,000 and US$160,000)
(iv) Employing between fifty one and one hundred (51–100) persons.

Survey findings and reports on SMMEs

Several reports have been published on the SMME sector in Zambia. The latest is the Zambian Business Survey (ZBS) of 2010.[8] The survey shows that Zambian businesses are sharply divided into two worlds – one comprising large business and the other a wide range of SMMEs. Most SMMEs are informal, owner-operated businesses. The survey showed that most SMMEs have no paid employees and are more like home-based, income-generating activities than clearly structured businesses. Most are in rural areas (81 per cent) and are involved in agricultural production (70 per cent) or wholesale/retail trade (21 per cent). Very few SMMEs are registered with any government agencies.

Further, most SMMEs are reckoned as not having access to basic infrastructure such as energy, transport and water, whereas most large enterprises do. Similarly, few SMMEs have access to formal financial services, whereas almost all large enterprises use some form of financial services.

Close to 60 per cent of SMME owners said that lack of access to finance services, including bank credit, was a serious constraint to their operations. Concern was particularly high among the smallest micro-enterprises and among farm owners. About 40 per cent of SMMEs do not have physical access to bank branches that can provide these services.

The effect of not having access to these facilities is highlighted by the finding that SMMEs which do have energy, transport, water and information communication technology (ICT) are far more productive than those that do not. SMMEs using financial services are also observed to be more productive than those that do not. However, the effective use of these in the entrepreneurial activity was also observed to be linked to education. Low levels of education, with a few exceptions, have affected outcomes. The ZBF report rightly noted that education was equally important. For instance, non-agricultural SMME owners who had completed secondary school were 25 per cent more productive than their counterparts who lacked a secondary school education. This was the same for players in the informal sector operating in high-density urban neighbourhoods, as they are not targeted in public awareness information programmes.

Government's attempts to facilitate SMMEs as an important sector

There is a general perception that certain business sectors should be left to the informal or SMME players. These sectors include the supply of goods and services such as stationery, cleaning services, minor road maintenance works, landscaping, and car hire to the government and its agents. As government is viewed as having the key to creating employment, its role would facilitate sustainable sources of wealth for the SMMEs. Government has come up with policies and laws that ensure that its role as the largest consumer of goods and services in the economy does assist in spreading wealth throughout the economy. Besides the competition and consumer protection legislation, the government created a revolving fund system to assist SMMEs to establish themselves more formally and also to enhance their growth cycles. This process was more pronounced in the Citizens Economic Empowerment Act in 2006.

The Citizens Economic Empowerment Commission Until 2006, anti-competitive practices in public procurement were quite common, where SMMEs could be crowded out by their not being able to comply with the unrealistically stringent conditions during pre- and post-tendering processes. In addition, abusive monopolies could be created through executive orders for the supply of certain services that SMMEs are made to buy at exorbitant prices or in unfavourable conditions. In Zambia, part of an answer to this has been the Citizens Economic Empowerment Commission, which was set up in terms of the Citizens Economic Empowerment Act in 2006.

The aim of the Act was to facilitate 'broad-based' economic participation of 'targeted' citizens, which, in the Zambian socio-economic stratum, largely includes women, the disabled and any other people who would demonstrate some form of vulnerability that has unfairly impeded their economic welfare. Prior to the enactment of this Act, there was fierce debate about the scope of beneficiaries under the Act, with South Africa's renowned Black Economic Empowerment (BEE) policies providing inspiration. While Zambia has not had a racial history as volatile or pervasive as South Africa's or Zimbabwe's, there has been general concern over the perceived growing immigrant community from within and outside the Southern Africa Community doing business that should be 'reserved' for 'Zambians'. Over the years, with the growing urban and metropolitan lifestyles, there has also been a debate about who exactly should be strictly classified as a Zambian for the purposes of benefiting any prescribed needs under the Citizens Economic Empowerment Act. SMMEs in both the formal and the informal economy were ardently in favour of specific restriction of foreign entry into sectors that should be prescribed for 'locals' only.

To facilitate economic fairness, the Citizens Economic Empowerment Commission (CEEC) came up with measures to assist SMMEs involved in the supply to government or related institutions with bridging finance if they are unable to secure funding. In addition, where the citizen-owned or -influenced SMME fails to secure bid security in a tender, the CEEC may come in and secure the bid security on behalf of the SMME. While this appears to have provided some form of fair competition for the formal SMMEs, businesses in the informal sector are actually not recognised *per se* and cannot benefit from the CEEC facilities until they formalise their businesses.

The loan facilities provided for under the Citizens Economic Empowerment Act have been a shot in the arm for small businesses. However, while the CEEC has been set up and has done remarkably well, its focus has been more on the formal sector, although efforts have been devised to facilitate support through cooperative arrangements in markets, more targeted at women.

Zambia's SMME policy of 2009: contribution of SMMEs to the economy

The contribution of SMMEs to employment, growth and sustainable development is a widely accepted fact.[9] The development of the SMME sector is inevitably critical to the achievement of broader national development goals, which include:[10]

- reduction of unemployment levels;
- increased participation of citizens in economic development;

- creation of avenues for equitable wealth distribution;
- increased utilisation and value addition of local raw materials.

Formal SMMEs appear to have been well catered for under the SMME policy. While the SMME policy focuses on key developmental pillars of capacity, access to market opportunities and an enabling environment, the practical realities of the SMMEs hinge to a large extent on big business contracts. These had begun to reduce during the period 1988 to 2000, owing to the privatisation process that had started, the low copper production and the lack of sufficient inflows of foreign direct investment. However, things began to change from 2001, when the mines that were nationalised in 1982 started to attract private investment and began to record modest but promising growth.

Most of these developments, however, ignore SMMEs in the informal economy.

SMMEs in the Informal Economy

Zambia's economy is historically tied to the mining and allied industries. A shock in commodity prices of copper and cobalt has a telling effect on both the socio-economics of the country as well on the political landscape. It is common knowledge in Zambia that the loss of formal jobs on a significant scale began with the process of the transformation of the economy from a state-controlled one in 1991 to a market economy. At this time, most of the major parastatals were privatised, including the giant conglomerate Zambia Consolidated Copper Mines (ZCCM). New owners could not retain the large labour force that had been engaged during the period of state ownership. Retrenchments, redundancies, forced retirements and the outright abandonment of workers in some cases cast the jobless into the streets. The result was an unprecedented wave of 'street vending'. Many people struggled to find market stalls as well as embark on any entrepreneurial activity that came to mind or that they saw their neighbour take up.

The result of this structural adjustment was a rise in poverty levels, to 80 per cent of the population living below US$1 a day. Unemployment rose to about 50 per cent. However, by 2006, the situation looked much more positive, with poverty levels dropping to about 60 per cent and the unemployment rate to 30 per cent on the national average.[11] It is clear that the informal sector was filling the sizeable vacuum, largely due to the absence of entry barriers and the consequent ease of entry. In some cases, people would just set themselves up on the street, ready for any opportunity that came their way.

Zambia's informal sector is, even from casual observation, a very large and significant part of the socio-economic dynamics of Zambia and has for a long time been a source of self-employment for millions of people. Due to the overall weak economic performance, there has been a general inability on the part of government to stimulate formal sector entry and expansion. The problem has been aggravated by the failure of government to provide adequate employment promotion policies or social security since the oil crisis of the mid-1970s, which got even worse between 1982 and 1992. Moreover, apart from retrenchees and retirees, the trade unions have seen the need to promote self-employment and to organise the informal economy as a whole, as it is increasingly becoming the main source of livelihood for the majority of Zambians.[12]

Definition of the informal sector

While there is no single definition of what constitutes the informal sector, it is generally considered that sole traders or business arrangements that are not registered with the Registrar of Business Names or the Registrar of Companies are informal.

Descriptive terms of the sector have included the second economy, underground economy, the black market, the hidden economy, illegal economy, unobserved economy, unrecorded economy, and unreported economy.[13]

The SMMEs in the formal and informal economies are spread across the vast landmass that is Zambia. While the survey done for this paper was based on Lusaka respondents, the nature of the players and their operations is similar elsewhere. The most recognisable informal trader in Zambia is the street vendor and the market trader. While we may limit ourselves to the word 'trader', some operators are engaged in some form of manufacturing of goods and services. Traded goods include second-hand clothes and tyres, plumbing materials and agricultural produce. The manufactured goods include fast foods, confectionery, finger-snacks, herbal medicines ('muti') etc., sold in the streets. The services range from welders, tyre-mending, barber shops, women's hairdressers, pirate taxis, traditional African counsellors and fortune-tellers, handy-men who can do anything from plumbing to construction of houses, including the 'real estate agents' and the infamous 'ng'wang'wazi'– the noisy mini-bus callers who call out for passengers to board designated mini-buses. In fact, issues of competition have arisen in this latter segment as a cartel has been created which prevents some mini-buses from loading passengers if they do not agree to pay certain unofficial levies or to charge certain fixed bus-fares. The Lusaka survey confirms the trend of 'charging the same prices as the competitors' in the taxi industry.

The informal sector, which is predominantly active in markets in the sprawling metropoles of Zambian towns, provides more employment to a larger segment of the population than the formal sector. Despite this, not much has been done to help improve the working conditions of participants in this sector. The structures that have been put in place over the years are not sufficient to allow businesses to thrive in most markets. Market traders cannot be expected to continue selling their merchandise in their designated trading areas where there is poor drainage and infrastructural problems, putting their health and that of their customers at risk. This is clearly one of the reasons why most traders engage in kerbside hawking (street vending) and are forced to sell on the streets.[14]

The informal sector is perhaps the most dynamic and innovative part of the economy and its managers astute hands-on market analysts who survive largely on a day-to-day basis. Competition is fierce and brutal with intense bargaining the order of the day and every price open to negotiation.

SMMEs: THEIR ROLE IN EMPLOYMENT, OUTPUT AND CONSUMPTION

A casual walk in any town or city in Zambia shows the large numbers of people who are striving to beat poverty and empower themselves by creating their own jobs and wealth and take charge of their destiny. Men and women undertake a range of activities that includes carpentry, brick-making, stone-crushing, selling food, and other service-industry businesses such as hairdressing and real estate. All these have created job opportunities that are not readily available in the bigger economy. According to a survey by the Central Statistics Office (CSO),[15] the size of the overall labour force grew from 2.4 million persons in 1986 to 4.9 million persons in 2005. By 2006, employment levels remained above 80 per cent for both the 1986 and 2005 Labour Force Surveys (LFS). The 2005 LFS results showed that 16 per cent of persons in the Labour Force were unemployed, 14 per cent of the males in the labour force and 17 per cent of the females. Higher rates of unemployment were observed in more urbanised parts of the country than less urbanised ones. Comparing the two LFS, the proportion of unemployed persons registered a marginal increase from 13 per cent in 1986 to 16 per cent in 2005. At the national level, the labour force in the age group 15–19 showed the highest unemployment rate at 25 per cent. Of all persons aged 15 years and above, 80 per cent were economically active while 20 per cent were economically inactive. Eighty-six per cent of the males and 74 per cent of the female population were economically active.

Of the total number of employed persons in Zambia, 43 per cent were self-employed, 17 per cent were paid employees, 38 per cent were unpaid family workers and 1 per cent were employers. Most of the literate persons (44 per cent) were self-employed, whereas the majority of illiterate persons (54 per cent) were unpaid family workers.

Zambia has an unemployment rate that would threaten the stability of a developed democracy. Out of a population of 11 million 10 years ago, only 500 000 were in formal employment by the year 2000 and were the backbone of all remuneration-based taxation. However, the formally employed have been steadily increasing with the opening-up of old and new copper mines, including those dealing with iron ore, uranium and gold.

The Zambia Congress of Trade Unions and the Mine-workers Union of Zambia have observed that since the change from a state-controlled to a free market economy was started in 1991, Zambia has experienced a number of negative impacts, especially on the labour market. Mismanaged privatisation, lack of economic growth and the inevitable rationalisation in a competitive and globalised economy left scores of former employees in the formal economy jobless, forcing them to look for one of the few other formal employment opportunities, facing unemployment or starting a business in the informal economy. The informal economy in Zambia, however, does not only have to absorb the former government and parastatal employees, but it is also the source of survival for those ninety percent of Zambians who never even had a chance to enter the formal labour market.[16]

A major obstacle for an improved economic performance by informal sector operators is their lack of qualification for an increasingly competitive market. 'From the characteristics of the informal sector it is evident that the level of education among participants is low and they generally lack skills'.[17] This is also a problem for many former miners, who form the majority of retrenchees. They are either unskilled or semi-skilled, and their often one-sided qualifications from the mines do not help them to set up a business in another field.[18]

It is still debatable if the informal economy has the potential to lead to strong and sustainable growth and transform itself eventually into the broader formal economy, or if it is a mere means of survival and a reservoir for cheap labour and services, subsidising the shrinking formal economy. Nevertheless, efforts have to be made to develop its entrepreneurial capacity systematically in order to enhance their progression and ultimate graduation into the formal sector. Despite its economic and social importance, labour in the informal economy is still being insufficiently supported (if not hampered) by government, but also underrepresented within the labour movement. Typical for the informal economy is its complexity of labour relationships and diversity of trades, which have also made it difficult for the trade unions to engage themselves in organising the sector. Generally, labour in the informal economy is:

- unrecognised: not registered by the appropriate state agencies;
- unprotected: labour laws are not being implemented or are not even applicable;
- excluded: from services like infrastructure provision or banking facilities;
- underrepresented: by trade unions or other civil society organisations.

Results from a survey conducted in Lusaka by United Kingdom-based consultancy Natural Resources International showed that the informal food-vending sector in Lusaka alone was worth approximately US$10 million per year and employed about 16 000 people in seven major markets. About 5300 vendors were trading in seven markets, and these collectively employed the 16 000 workers who were serving more than 81 million meals per year. The study, which was undertaken in three African capital cities in Zambia, Ghana and Zimbabwe and the city of Kolkata in India, revealed that the sector contributed significantly to the respective national economies. In Accra, Ghana, the sector was reckoned to employ around 60 000 people, making about US$24 million annually, while India's Kolkata city had 134 000 vendors on the streets and around the markets who were generating a turnover of US$100 million. The report concluded that about 40 per cent of the low-income households generally depended on informally-vended foods.

According to the report, the vendors were still not recognised in most cases by their governments and there were a number of health and environmental risks associated with unhygienic trading activities by the vendors.[19] The nature of informal trade is generally that they are neither established by nor operated under written law. It therefore goes without saying that compliance is not prioritised.

Government Response to the Informal Sector

Zambia's Central Statistics Office (CSO) has acknowledged that the informal sector has been growing faster than the formal sector in Zambia, in terms of business, since 1992. As a result of this, the Zambia Revenue

Authority (ZRA) attempted to target the informal sector in the late 1990s because it realised how fast this sector was growing. As recognised by the CSO, accurate statistics played an important role in the development and planning of the national economy.

Generally, however, government has not supported the street vendors because of the nuisance factor. Street vendors or hawkers have been seen to operate right outside authorised and formal retail outlets, selling the same merchandise as the shop right behind or in front of them. Shop owners have complained of the unfair positioning of the street vendors in front of their shops, and, to address this 'unfair competition', the shop owners have subcontracted a handful of unemployed youths to sell their merchandise on commission basis outside the shop or wherever they may hawk or peddle. Another dimension is that what appears to be a scattered lot of informal traders may in fact be agents of formal businesses trying to ensure that they cash in at the front-line marketplace.

Government has recognised the importance of its role in facilitating and creating formal employment. However, even in relation to the informal sector, there have been numerous government efforts to create larger and new market structures from where market traders can operate. The uncontrollable rural–urban drift has led to crowded urban settlements as rural-dwellers trek into towns and cities for greener pastures. A significant number end up in informal street or market trading. There has been an increasing scramble for market space, which has compelled government to make both planned and ad hoc arrangements to curtail unrest in markets.

The local authorities have also added grief to the informal sector by carrying out 'dawn raids' on their makeshift and often illegal physical business infrastructures. The informal player's cry has either been that there are not enough business premises or infrastructure to accommodate everyone or that the levies are too high for them to break even and compete effectively with the formal businesses.

The local authorities, mainly in the cities and larger towns, have set up fast-track courts to deal with street vendors and fine them accordingly. The majority of these street vendors have changed their tactics by getting small lots of merchandise which they hawk or peddle around, making them more mobile and able to run away quickly and fuse into crowded areas with their merchandise the moment they detect the presence of the police or local council officials.

Formalising the informal sector

The government in Zambia has embarked on major private sector development reforms aimed at streamlining businesses and attracting the informal sector to formalise their existence. The Minister of Local Government in Zambia was reported to have proposed the abolition of 38 trading licences, including stone sales licences (for informal stone crushers), to be replaced by a direct levy aimed at reducing the cost of doing businesses and supporting the growth of small businesses. According to a report in the *Business Times of Zambia* of September 2010, stone crushers along the roads had been tormented as a result of their operating illegally without trading licences. One of the stone crushers reported that it was difficult to register a business at offices where they only speak English as the traders felt intimidated and out of place.[20] However, it is yet to be clarified whether the direct levying following the removal of the stone sales licence would inevitably legalise the existence of illegal quarrying and sales of crushed stones along the streets of Lusaka. This business niche serves the crushed-stone needs of people buying this product in smaller quantities in their small-scale construction activities – unlike the industrial or larger-scale constructors who go to formalised and larger quarry mines and stone-crushing companies for bulk purchases.

COMPETITION ISSUES AFFECTING INFORMAL AND FORMAL SMMEs

As the informal sector and formalised SMMEs substantially cover critical employment and social-welfare gaps in less developed economies, it is critical for a competition authority to be concerned with anticompetitive trade practices that affect these vulnerable sectors. Consumer welfare may be further advanced by including the informal and formal market beneficiaries and victims in the broader competition scenario. An important question has thus been: Should competition agencies care about the informal sector? And the answer is: 'Actually, yes', as informal firms can operate in the same product or geographic markets as formal firms and therefore affect the level of competition. The next question is therefore: So what can competition agencies do to address the informal sector? However, in relation to this, an interesting issue was raised at the 2008 OECD Global Forum on Competition's dedicated session on the informal sector, which shed light on the other side of the coin: it was recognised that unregistered firms may be unfair competitors to the formally registered companies because informal firms can gain price advantage by not paying taxes and not complying with regulations. But here, the competition agencies have very limited power, as the enforcement of these regulations is often outside their jurisdiction. This then led to the question: 'Are informal firms also guilty of uncompetitive practices?'

At the forum there was general consensus that the correct approach to the informal sector is not to suppress it because it has some unfair advantages over the formal sector, but rather to reduce regulatory barriers to entry in the formal sector so that the informal sector can become formalised more easily.

Because of their small size, as well as the lack of a sustained and organised unified voice, SMMEs in the formal and informal sector have borne the brunt of abuse of market power by dominant firms which may, for instance, engage in predatory pricing or the creation of barriers to entry, putting these small firms at a significant disadvantage. This contributes to the high failure-rate of small firms, or to them constantly reviewing and changing their products and services to try and stay afloat. Another feature of this is the reliance on personal relationships and other acquaintances for sustaining their operations. On the other hand, the nature of intervention that a competition authority should make to benefit the SMMEs, and, if at all, the informal sector as well, has been misunderstood. There has been a general perception and expectation that the competition law should 'protect' SMMEs from all competition from dominant or foreign firms. There have also been calls to have certain sectors of the economy (for example, market trading) to be reserved only for local SMMEs. Should the competition authority allow the so-called 'competitive process' to run its course or should it protect the smaller guys down the road? SMMEs in the formal and informal sectors in Zambia have generally viewed the competition authority as the protector of the weak, in terms of businesses and consumers. There have also been calls to have a policy, and in some cases a law, to prevent foreigners from engaging in certain economic activities that should be reserved for local SMMEs and the informal traders.

The Informal Sector and the 'Chinese Problem'

Since the late 1990s, there has been an influx of small and medium-sized Chinese-owned firms entering the Zambian market. Most of the Chinese businesses operate in the same locations and serve the same markets as the Zambian businesses. During a question-and-answer session when the Commission appeared before a parliamentary committee in April 2010, a member of the committee asked what the Commission was doing about 'the Chinese who were selling their chickens at K5000 (about US$1) and thus bringing about unfair competition as the Zambians were not able to raise chickens within one week and sell at such a low price like the

Chinese'. The chair of the committee intervened and said: 'But do you want Zambians to continue to be backward and have production processes that take long to produce something and also that Zambians should continue to be subjected to high prices when there was a cheaper alternative?'

A lot has been said about the influx of Chinese businesses trading alongside the struggling Zambian traders even in the marketplaces. Evidently, the Chinese brought in levels of competition that the Zambian traders have never been subjected to before. It is the kind of competition they cannot ordinarily understand or master because they had for long been used to communicating prices among themselves and the profit margins were relatively reasonable for every trader. The Chinese came, and they came with huge differences in prices that destroyed the price-fixing arrangements that existed at the market.

This parliamentary discourse was reminiscent of an incident during the festive break at the end of 2009 and beginning of 2010. I heard from a group of angry traders from Lusaka's famous Soweto Market who had previously come to the Commission offices and wanted to see me over 'unfair competition brought in by the Chinese'. During our meeting, they angrily asked for intervention (and protection) as their source of livelihood was being robbed by foreigners. I sat quietly and listened as one trader after the other explained just how unfair the Chinese have been. It was evident that what was happening to them was posing a real threat, not only to their businesses, but to their lives. As I listened, my mind went through the Competition and Fair Trading Act, CAP 417 of the Laws of Zambia to try and find a provision to deal with the issue. Then I raced through the theories and other concepts on competition and consumer welfare to try and ensure that when I opened my mouth to speak, I was going to say something that was going to make sense to the traders – and that this was not going to be just another lecture on liberalisation, privatisation, commercialisation, free market enterprise … and eventually competition.

The issue, the traders recounted, was that the Chinese were running farms and selling their farm produce to the traders who then resold it at the Soweto Market. The produce included various vegetables and poultry products such as chickens and eggs. This arrangement apparently worked very well until the Chinese discovered that they could make more money by removing their middleman and going straight to the market themselves. This process either eliminated the traders or made them compete with the Chinese at the Soweto market. The traders claimed that the Chinese were selling their cabbages as low as K500 (ca. US$0.10) at retail level and that their chickens were about K12 000 (ca. US$2.40), while the Zambian traders sold the cabbage at K1500 (ca. US$0.30) and chickens at least at K20 000 (US$4). With the Chinese operating downstream, it was not possible for the traders to compete 'fairly'. To add insult to injury, the Chinese arrived at the market at about 03:00 am to sell their produce. By the time the Zambian traders had arrived to do the same at closer to 05:00, they found that the Chinese had already flooded the market with cheap produce. The traders also contended that at about 03:00 am, there were no market officials to ensure that the Chinese, who even traded in the open streets around the market as street vendors, were paying the prescribed levies.

The traders made the following plea to the Commission:

1. that the Chinese should only operate at wholesale and not retail level;
2. that market trading should be reserved for Zambians only;
3. that the Chinese should be stopped from selling their merchandise at 03:00 in the morning;
4. that the Lusaka City Council should be advised to patrol the market at about 03:00 am and ensure that the Chinese pay the levies that the Zambian traders are subjected to.

The complaint by the traders is not unique to the Soweto market. Similar experiences have been reported in the restaurant business and the textile business too. While traders have complained, other farmers have also complained about the 'fast rate' at which the Chinese grow their vegetables and chickens, and then the very low prices at which they are sold.

With sympathy, I acknowledged the evident damage that was caused to their businesses and evidently, the source of their livelihood. I asked whether there was a market committee and what they and the Lusaka City Council had done about the 03:00 issue as well as the levies. From their account, nothing had been done. I promised them that the Commission would write to the council as well as the relevant market committee to find out how to deal with issues of the trading at around 03:00 am, the street vending at that hour as well as the lack of payment of levies at that hour. On the issue of the Chinese being involved in retailing, I advised that if the Chinese were given any incentive to trade at the market that was not made available to other traders, then this would be an issue the Commission could deal with. Otherwise, the Commission could not stop any wholesaler from engaging in retail business.

In answer to the parliamentary query, I said that there is a lot we can learn from the Chinese. They have become an economic superpower and are projected to be a leading world player over the next 20 years. The world has been developed by people learning from and even spying on others' more effective ways of doing things. We need to learn about the new methods of farming, trading and running businesses because they are here to stay, and if we lag behind, it is at our own peril.

How Competition Law can be Formulated and/or Implemented to Promote Entrepreneurship

There is evidently the need for more targeted advocacy efforts directed at the SMMEs in order for them to derive greater benefits from the existence of a competition authority. The repealed Competition and Fair Trading Act, 1994, CAP 417 of the Laws of Zambia, had as one of its objectives 'to promote the base of entrepreneurship', but it did not specify whether such entrepreneurship should be formal or informal, micro, small or medium. Under Section 2 of this Act, a person was defined to include '... an individual, a company, a partnership, an association and any group of persons acting in concert, whether incorporated or not incorporated'. While the word 'enterprises' was used in parts dealing with restrictive business practices, cartels and mergers, the word 'person' was used in the section dealing with unfair trading. For instance, a person 'shall not supply a defective product'. The word 'enterprise' was not defined in the Act and thus common law was used. Going by the literal translation, there would appear to be no provision in the current Act to limit the involvement and/or enforcement action of the Commission based on whether the culprit or victim is an informal player or not, an SMME or a multinational entity. Driven more by practice than by legality, the Commission has historically concentrated more on formalised enterprises while the local authorities have dealt with the informal sector.

While the informal sector is evidently not legally recognised and is the subject of criticism for anything ranging from littering to tax evasion, its role in a less developed country in terms of providing a source of income and livelihood for the vast majority of the population who have no alternative/s is clearly very important. Thus, a generous approach to dealing with informal sector needs and problems becomes paramount. While competition law may provide some solutions, this is just one of the many interventions that should be carefully analysed. Whether competition laws should only deal with formal businesses continues to be a subject of debate and often ignoring the informal sector is used as a weapon to compel them to formalise their businesses.[21]

It is interesting to see what other countries are doing in relation to small businesses and competition regulation.

Other Countries' Treatment of Competition Law and SMMEs

While Zambia's competition law does not expressly address the SMMEs' needs, similar legislation in other jurisdictions have addressed this. Reference to SMMEs is made in merger assessments under Section 31(e) of the Competition and Consumer Protection Act, which states as follows:

> The Commission may, in considering a proposed merger, take into account any factor which bears upon the public interest in the proposed merger, including –
>
> (e) the extent to which the proposed merger may enhance the competitiveness, or advance or protect the interests, of micro and small business enterprises in Zambia; …

This is an important provision, which unfortunately may only be used in times when the Commission is considering a merger application. Some countries have also enshrined provisions to deal with SMMEs, as shown below.

Korea

Some competition laws have interesting references to the SMME sector, such as the Korean Fair Trade Commission (KFTC), in which competition regulation aims at: 'creating a foundation on which parties to transactions who have different economic power can compete freely and fairly on a level playing field'.

Canada

Section 1.1 of the Canada Competition Act provides that: '… the purpose of this Act is to maintain and encourage competition in Canada … in order to ensure that small and medium sized enterprise have an equitable opportunity to participate in the Canadian economy …'

Australia

The Australian Competition and Consumer Commission (ACCC) has long recognised that small businesses do not have the same sort of resources as big businesses to address education and compliance. There is a dedicated small business unit within the ACCC to focus on the sector. However, the ACCC has continued to assert that it is not the role of competition policy to favour one sector over another – competition policy is not about preserving competitors, it is about promoting competition – as ably noted by an economic adviser to the Competition Commission of India.[22]

India

The case of India provides interesting lessons. There, the Federation of Indian Micro and Small & Medium Enterprises (FISME) commissioned a study on competition commission framework in India and SMMEs. The study was expected to give SMMEs an idea of how to leverage the new Competition Commission of India (CCI) dispensation to their advantage. According to the promoters, SMMEs were viewed as largely ignorant of their rights and responsibilities in the new competition policy regime. While the CCI had taken some initiatives to create awareness through seminars, the FISME believed that the absence of documentation of instances and typology of restrictive practices is diluting its efforts. The study had two aims. The first was to compile a list of anticompetitive practices in order to help SMMEs identify practices of this kind that affect their own enterprises, and let them know the remedial measures that are available under the law to mitigate their hardships, as well as the processes to be followed for initiating action. Second, the study was envisaged to suggest to SMMEs, the CCI and other stakeholders an actionable agenda for effective advocacy, to instil competition principles in public policies in India.[23]

Four tasks were planned to be undertaken in the exercise. The first was to be a study of competition policy frameworks in India and abroad from the perspective of SMMEs, and the capturing of best practices and any special dispensations for SMMEs that may be in use in other countries. The second was to be a classification of various types of anti-competitive practices (with a view to developing a typology) that SMMEs encounter at the hands of dominant corporates and other entities, relating to public procurement, raw material supplies and public policies. The third was to be a study of the rights and privileges of SMMEs under the CCI dispensation, and measures that SMMEs could take to mitigate their grievances against anti-competitive practices.

The fourth was aimed at identifying existing mechanisms in place – agencies, experts, law firms and service providers in the field – and deficiencies, if any, from the perspective of SMMEs. Rising protectionist tendencies in the wake of the global financial crisis and the resulting slowdown in India, which had restricted Indian SMMEs' access to competitively-priced inputs and access to public procurement, have lent the issue a sense of urgency.

Useful lessons for Zambia

The foregoing examples from these commonwealth countries provide useful lessons for Zambia, whose competition law has been largely influenced by developments in key commonwealth countries. India's development path provides a useful model for Zambia as the two countries both have high unemployment rates and a high level of SMME businesses. And Korea provides a good example of a country that has developed rapidly over the last 30 years, with previously small companies like Samsung and LG now being global brands.

CONCLUSION

Since 2001, Zambia has continued to register an average of 5 per cent GDP growth after the government began to review its then decade-long 'Government-has-no-business-in-business' policies and reposition its strategies, particularly those dealing with influencing the growth and sustenance of SMMEs. The establishment of the Zambia Development Agency, the Citizens Economic Empowerment Commission, the adoption of the national competition and consumer protection policy, and the enabling legislation and reformation of the Zambia Competition Commission to the Competition and Consumer Protection Commission all contributed to this. While competition law and policy play a big role in fostering a culture of competition in an economy and allow for transparent and open markets where SMMEs thrive, there are a number of problems that affect the entry and growth of SMMEs in an economy such as Zambia's. These include the barriers to entry created by the dominant firms as well as the lack of finance for the SMMEs to access, and the lack of formal and technical education and/or knowhow that would allow the SMME entrepreneurs to easily tap into the wealth of available business and financial management intelligence.

The growth and development of SMMEs in Zambia does not hinge on any one piece of legislation. Rather, it depends on a suite of legislation that needs to be harmonised so that SMMEs are optimally included in the economy. Competition policy or its enforcement is an important part of the industrial development mix but not the only answer to all the structural and behavioural obstacles that SMMEs encounter. It would, however, be important in future, as in the Trade Practices Act of Australia, to have some specific provisions in Zambia's competition law that address and promote SMMEs explicitly, which would go beyond the current arrangement that the competition law does not protect any market players but just the so-called 'competitive process'. SMMEs therefore need some explicit protection from competition laws and related policies.

As long as countries such as Zambia do not create sufficient jobs and also facilitate sustainable self-employment opportunities, the problem of the informal traders will continue to plague the country for a long time. While efforts have been made to facilitate the entry and growth of the formal SMME through such initiatives as the Citizens Economic Empowerment loan facilities, anticompetitive trade practices that affect market entry need to be addressed at policy level as well as at implementation level.

Both the informal and the SMME sectors remain critical sources of employment, and therefore vital crime-prevention mechanisms on which the formal economy actually thrives. While competition among the informal as well as the formal SMME sectors may appear to be uncoordinated in the form of meetings in boardrooms and golf courses, the reality on the ground is that the mode of coordination is by word of mouth and observation. Price-fixing in mini-bus and taxi fares is common. While this may be a subject of control by the competition authority, the undisciplined nature of such markets makes it difficult to effectively enforce most laws.

Uncontrolled and/or crowded streams of informal traders will remain a nuisance and perhaps a menace to fair and formal competition. However, these traders do play a key role in disciplining the potential abuse of 'market power' of some well-established traders and manufacturers in terms of offering a substitute distribution system for the niche trader or manufacturing SMME and negotiated price alternative to the consumer.

NOTES

1. Kaira (2009).
2. Smith (1776), Book IV: Of Systems of Political Economy, ch. II.
3. See Kaira (2011).
4. Zambia Competition Commission (2006).
5. National Competition and Consumer Protection Policy (2010), paragraph 2.1.
6. Dr Buleti Nsemukila, Permanent Secretary, Ministry of Commerce, Trade and Industry, 'State, SMEs to create 30 per cent jobs', *Times of Zambia*, 21 February 2011, available at: http://allafrica.com/stories/201102210841.html.
7. Micro, Small and Medium Enterprise Development Policy of the Government of Zambia (2009).
8. The report/s are available from the Zambia Business Forum (www.zbf.org.zm, secretariat@zbf.org.zm); Private Sector Development Reform Programme (www.psdrp.org.zm); FinMark Trust (www.finmark.org.za, julietmunro@iconnect.zm); and World Bank Zambia Country Office (www.worldbank.org/Zambia, Pyramid Plaza, Plot No 746 Church Road, Lusaka. Tel: 260-1 252 811).

9. Micro, Small and Medium Enterprise Development Policy of the Government of Zambia, April 2009, p. 1.
10. Ibid, p. 3.
11. Central Statistical Office of Zambia (2006).
12. Muchimba et al. (2004).
13. Feige (1990).
14. Ikwueme (2010).
15. Central Statistical Office of Zambia (2005).
16. Ibid.
17. Muneku (2001), p. 93.
18. Mwanalushi (2001), p. 6.
19. *Times of Zambia* (2010).
20. Maimbolwa (2010).
21. Ramalho (2009).
22. Augustine (2008).
23. *Business Standard Reporter* (2010).

REFERENCES

Augustine, Peter (2008), 'Treatment of micro, small and medium enterprises (MSMEs) under Competition Act 2002'. Presentation to: Associations of MSMEs, Economic Adviser Competition Commission of India, India International Centre, 27 November.

Business Standard Reporter (2010), 'Competition framework for MSMEs to be drawn up', New Delhi, 15 June 2010, downloaded on 7 September 2010: http://www.business-standard.com/india/news/competition-framework-for-msmes-to-be-drawn-up/398181/.

Central Statistical Office of Zambia (2005), *Labour Force Survey (LFS) 2005.*

Central Statistical Office of Zambia (2006), *Zambia Living Conditions Survey 2006.*

Feige, E.L. (1990), 'Defining and estimating underground and informal economies: The new institutional economics approach', *World Development*, 18(7), 989–1002.

Ikwueme, Kabukabu Kawanambulu (2010), 'Zambia's informal sector facing major challenges', *Lusaka Times*, 12 February. Available at: http://www.lusakatimes.com/?p=23967&wpmp_switcher=mobile?p=23967&wpmp_switcher=mobile (downloaded 7 September 2010).

Kaira, Thula (2009), 'The role of competition law in national economic development', paper presented to the Honourable Members of the Parliament of Zambia at the National Assembly Buildings, 26 October.

Kaira, Thula (2011), 'State of competition in the telecommunications industry in Zambia', *Africa Journal for Information and Communication* (AJIC), issue 11, 22–38.

Micro, Small and Medium Enterprise Development Policy of the Government of Zambia (2009), April.

Muchimba, Charles, Adrian Shikwe and Georg Heidenreich (2004), *Employment Promotion by Trade Unions in Zambia, A Strategic Approach,* produced with the support of Friedrich-Ebert-Stiftung (FES), Lusaka, Zambia.

Mulikelela, Maimbolwa (2010), reporting on the Hon. Eustarckio Kazonga MP (then Zambia's Minister of Local Government), *Business Times of Zambia*, 8 September.

Muneku, Austin (2001), *An Exploratory Study on Impact of SAP on Informal Sector in Zambia,* Lusaka, Zambia: International Labour Organisation (ILO).

Mwanalushi, Muyunda (2001), *A Study of Retrenchees on the Copperbelt,* Lusaka, Zambia: Frederick Ebert Stiftung.

National Competition and Consumer Protection Policy of the Republic of Zambia (2010), March.

Ramalho, Rita (2009), 'Should competition agencies care about the informal sector?', downloadable from http://blogs.worldbank.org/psd/should-competition-agencies-care-about-the-informal-sector (accessed on 17 December 2012).

Small Enterprises Development Board Act, CAP 425 of the Laws of Zambia of 1996.

Smith, Adam (1776), *The Wealth of Nations*.

Times of Zambia (2010), http://www.times.co.zm/news/viewnews.cgi?category=12&id=1132002949 (downloaded on 7 September 2010).

Zambia Competition Commission (2006), 'Report on the excessive pricing of sugar in Zambia', June.

Zambia Development Act No. 11 of 2006.

PART II

Multinational issues and initiatives

6. The past and future of international antitrust: gaps, overlaps and the institutional challenge

Eleanor Fox, John Fingleton and Sophie Mitchell

INTRODUCTION

International antitrust has expanded rapidly since the third quarter of the twentieth century. The need to fit national laws to the reality of global markets has led not only to nations looking beyond their borders but also to the contemplation of international modalities and instruments. We do not have world competition law and are unlikely to get it in the foreseeable future. We ask in this chapter: what level of protection do we have against global restraints; what trans-border problems remain unattended; and, in the absence of world competition law, what initiatives (if any) might the existing institutions take to fill the gaps in the web? In the first part of this chapter we describe the evolution of international antitrust. In answering the policy questions in the second half of this chapter, we focus in particular on the International Competition Network. Finally, we make some suggestions for modalities to address the problems that currently have no 'home'.

A KALEIDOSCOPE OF CHANGE

The story of antitrust begins in the late nineteenth century. Antitrust was national.[1] Intimations of world antitrust came during World War II. Cartels organised from Germany threatened US defence. US Assistant Attorney General Thurman Arnold began the first campaign against international cartels, linking them to their totalitarian sponsors.

In this era of war, the United States law expanded to reach offshore actors. It did so in the notorious *Alcoa* case (148 F.2d 416, 2d Cir. 1945), in which the court held that US law reaches an offshore cartel when the actors intend to affect and do affect the US market.

In the years that immediately followed, and in view of the lessons of the war, nations proposed the first multilateral antitrust agreement. This was the Havana Charter, which was negotiated in 1947 and 1948 as the blueprint for the first world trade agreement. The Havana Charter would have required nations to take measures against transnational restrictive business practices including price-fixing, market division, and restraints limiting market access and fostering monopolistic control. The United States, however, withdrew its support from the enterprise, fearing loss of sovereignty, and the Charter was never adopted. The Charter did, however, pave the way for the General Agreement on Tariffs and Trade (the GATT, 1947), which marked the start of the long and continuing process of bargaining among nations for ever-lower barriers to world trade.

Still, until the 1970s, antitrust was domestically-focused and mostly American. Trade barriers, though constantly lowered, remained high. In the United States, major industries were protected from foreign competition. The largest US corporations were politically and economically powerful, and they became flabby and unresponsive, as was the case with the makers of automobiles and steel.

Meanwhile, conditions were changing. The European Economic Community had been formed in 1957. The European Commission got enforcement powers in 1962. European competition law began its rise to world visibility in the early 1970s. As world trade barriers shrank, German and Japanese producers successfully contested the US steel market and the US automobile market. American producers, in turn, set sights on foreign markets. The first wave of the modern era of globalisation had begun. The United States, the European Community, Canada and others negotiated bi-lateral agreements as platforms for cooperation with one another; at least to advise one another when one party was planning to bring antitrust proceedings that would affect the interests of the other party, and to consider sympathetically the important interests of the other with a view to according 'comity' – implying respect and accommodation.

The late 1960s and early 1970s also saw the growth of multinational firms. Foresightful firms saw the world as their playing field. They would locate factories abroad, wherever they could get cheaper labour; thus, a first wave of outsourcing took place. To the host country (in spite of jobs and technology transfers) the multinational enterprises (MNEs) appeared to be exploiting their workers and displacing local businesses. The expanding corporations were accused of predatory business practices including blocking the exports of the host subsidiary and influencing politics towards right-wing capitalism, bolstering dictators such as Chile's Pinochet. When the MNEs found better economic opportunities elsewhere, they would close their plants, abandon the workers, and leave the host. Such, at least, was the story told by Jean-Jacques Servan-Schreiber in THE AMERICAN CHALLENGE (1967) and Anthony Sampson in THE SOVEREIGN STATE OF ITT (1973).

Most of the restrictive practices complained of were then illegal *per se* under US law if they were done by Americans to Americans. Developing countries, hurt by the practices, were powerless to protect themselves. They triggered talks under the aegis of the United States Conference on Trade and Development (UNCTAD) to obtain universal rules to constrain the MNEs. Americans seized the opportunity as an occasion to educate the developing countries in economics and efficiency and as a chance to bring the proliferating state-owned enterprises into the purview of antitrust. Negotiations began. The negotiating groups were the industrialised countries, the developing countries, and the Communist bloc. The nations reached consensus at the end of the 1970s, and, in 1980, the United Nations promulgated the agreement – the Set of Multilaterally Agreed Principles and Rules for the Control of Restrictive Business Practices (RBPs) (also known as the Set or the UNCTAD code). The United States signed onto the Set – but not before bargaining for everything it strongly wanted: state-owned enterprises were not excluded from coverage, transfer pricing within one firm was excluded, all RBPs could be justified as reasonable, and the code was voluntary, not mandatory; there were no sanctions for its breach. There was a deep irony. The year the code was signed, 1980, was also a turning point year in US antitrust law as Ronald Reagan was elected President of the United States. The concern that had animated US antitrust for most of a century and that had such resonance for developing countries – law to contain the power of the largest firms and clearing the path for the underdog – transmogrified into the concern that antitrust law should not interfere with efficiency. As the United States turned its sights on competitiveness in the world, US antitrust law became a blueprint for the freedom and efficiency of even the dominant firm.

The 1980s was a busy decade for international antitrust. We mention four markers. First, the Foreign Trade Antitrust Improvements Act of 1982 (the FTAIA). US business was complaining about being handicapped by too much antitrust. It complained in particular that US antitrust law was following American business into foreign markets, handicapping them worldwide. Congress responded. It enacted the FTAIA. The Act cut back US antitrust jurisdiction over conduct that had effects only in foreign markets (or clarified that US law did not reach so far). Thus, it decreed no jurisdiction over export cartels. Moreover it was eventually construed, in the famous worldwide vitamins cartel case, not to allow foreign victims to invoke the Sherman Act even against harm from world cartels that hurt Americans unless the foreign victims were harmed by the effect of the cartel in the United States.[2]

Second, many nations began to enforce their antitrust laws not only against domestic actors but also against actors abroad. In Europe, the Court of Justice was asked to opine on its jurisdiction over an offshore cartel. In *Wood Pulp* ([1988] ECR 5139), the court adopted an iteration of the effects doctrine, without using those words. Europe realised that effects jurisdiction is necessary to protect citizens from offshore acts.

Third, more dramatic events were to come at the end of the decade. With trade barriers reduced, Japanese firms were making great inroads into US markets, out-competing the Americans in their home country. Americans, however, were making slow progress in contesting Japanese markets. Best-selling books, THE RISING SUN (Michael Crichton) and HEAD TO HEAD (Lester Thurow), mirrored Americans' anxiety.

Japan was under trade obligations to reduce structural barriers that protected its market from outsiders, but barriers persisted. In 1989 the United States under the first President Bush and Japan under Prime Minister Uno launched the Structural Impediments Initiative. The Japanese undertook to reduce non-tariff barriers in regulated markets such as insurance and financial markets. They insisted that they had in fact eliminated unnecessary state restraints in the non-regulated areas. The United States Trade Representative replied in effect: If you have removed your state restraints and still our firms cannot successfully compete in Japanese markets, then you must be tolerating private restraints in violation of your antitrust laws. If your firms are closing Japanese markets by anticompetitive acts and Japan's FTC does nothing, we will sue your firms (for example, photographic film, paper, glass) under our antitrust laws.[3]

Thus, an epiphany. Antitrust was a world matter. In a world integrated by freedom of trade and establishment, antitrust cannot stop at a nation's shores. The closing of markets to protect one's own is a violation of norms and perhaps law; if by state restraint, it is a violation of the GATT; if by business restraint, it could be a violation of antitrust if a court has jurisdiction and the authority has the incentive to enforce the law. But there was a problem. It might be the case that no nation has both jurisdiction and the incentive to sue. These are world problems. It began to seem that an antitrust dimension of the GATT/WTO could not be far away.

Fourth, the major transforming event of the late 1980s was yet to come. Communism had lost its grip. The Soviet peoples rebelled. Not only did they want political freedom; they wanted economic freedom. Communism's command-and-control economic system that had promised a decent standard of living had failed. Markets promised benefits: freedom to participate in the economic enterprise; access to goods and services, and at affordable prices. Not incidental was the technology and information revolution. The quality of life in market-based economies was now well known even behind the iron curtain; radio, television and ultimately the Internet had pierced the iron veil.

In late 1989 the Berlin Wall fell, literally and figuratively. The fall of the Berlin Wall marked a major turning point in the story of antitrust. One by one, the post-communist countries adopted democracy and market systems. When they adopted market systems, they adopted the usual set of economic laws to control private firm excesses and abuses and help the market work. On the list was antitrust.

Later events, including the successful conclusion of the Uruguay trade round in 1994, combined to trigger adoption of antitrust law by scores more countries, resulting today in more than 100 countries in the world antitrust family.

Beginning approximately with the end of the Uruguay round, which launched the World Trade Organisation (WTO) as the umbrella over the GATT, policy-makers and civil society began to observe a dilemma: The principle of free trade was strong and becoming stronger. Yet freer trade had impacts. It affected the environment, labour and competition. Policy-makers began to consider an array of subjects of 'trade and …' and to ask whether tensions between freer trade and other values and disciplines should be explored and accounted for in the context of the WTO.

The European Union launched a project on trade and competition. The project originated in the early 1990s within the Competition Directorate under the leadership of Competition Commissioner Leon Brittan and later Competition Commissioner Karel van Miert. The Europeans, steeped in the harmonising impulses of community, were the first to develop intellectual underpinnings for a cosmopolitan world competition policy.

Animating their project was the reality that competition law is national but transactions had become significantly international. The proliferation of international effects required a conception of the whole; law that would internalise externalities, minimise or bridge disparities, and provide coherence. The Europeans proposed to begin with building blocks of information-sharing and cooperation, international norms of due process, transparency and non-discrimination, and undertakings by developed jurisdictions to provide technical assistance and capacity-building to less-well-off nations. A second stage would see the adoption of consensus substantive principles such as anti-cartel and abuse-of-dominance principles. Eventually, world norms could include the full panoply of substantive principles and dispute resolution, within a procedural framework of largely national enforcement.

American officials and the US antitrust bar reacted with hostility. They largely opposed an international antitrust regime or framework of any sort, and they especially opposed the WTO as a forum. Detractors called the European proposal a 'code' and characterised it as requiring and supporting a world antitrust authority and world antitrust enforcement. They argued that the proposal would necessarily entail adopting substantive rules of the lowest common denominator because that is what would evolve from multi-nation bargaining, with nations around the bargaining table seeking to protect 'their' competitors rather than to unleash efficiency. They particularly worried about an expansive conception of abuse of dominance that would handicap the efficiency of large firms. Moreover, they argued that a world system would create a faceless, untrustworthy and unaccountable bureaucracy at the top, run by politician/bureaucrats who did not understand antitrust. They argued that the WTO was an inappropriate forum because it was run by trade officials, and trade officials bargain; trade law *is* a bargain; on the other hand antitrust law is principled; it entails application of rules of law, insulated from political trade-offs.

Responding, the European Commission trimmed the sails of its proposal on successive occasions, resulting finally in the proposal that made its way onto the agenda for the Doha round of trade talks in 2001. But Doha gets ahead of the story.

The WTO was not, of course, the only relevant international institution with competition interests. UNCTAD, discussed above, was another forum. So too was the Organisation for Economic Co-operation and Development (OECD). The OECD was designed to advance cooperation among the developed countries of the world. It, like UNCTAD, has no enforcement powers; only the power to make recommendations to its member states. In the OECD Competition Law Committee, the member states share their experiences; they discuss and debate procedural and substantive practices and issues; and the secretariat publishes research reports on various subjects of interest.

Not happy with the WTO as a forum and equally unhappy with abuse of dominance as a centrepiece of antitrust, US antitrust officials introduced a recommendation against cartels at the OECD. The proposal was simple and its adoption feasible. It was infinitely less complicated than inaugurating a world competition regime. It attracted interest and, although somewhat watered down, became the Recommendation of the [OECD] Council concerning effective action against Hard Core Cartels, adopted in 1998. The recommendation states that: 'Member countries should ensure that their competition laws effectively halt and deter hard core cartels'; that their laws should provide for effective sanctions and should include adequate provisions for document discovery and detection; and that the member countries should cooperate in detection and enforcement while safeguarding confidential information. 'Hard core cartel' was defined to exclude anything the member country's law exempts. The recommendation advises that member countries continually examine their laws for undue exemptions and seek to eliminate them, and that they should make their exemptions transparent.

Meanwhile, several clashes of jurisdiction occurred, adding urgency to the quest for international norms. Famously, the Boeing/McDonnell Douglas merger was cleared by the United States and nearly prohibited but ultimately cleared with conditions by the European Commission,[4] and the GE–Honeywell merger was cleared by the United States and enjoined by the EU.[5]

Talk of a WTO antitrust competence continued. Then, at the turn of the century, the United States convened an international antitrust review committee (International Competition Policy Advisory Committee, or ICPAC) to study problems and solutions for international competition issues. Among other things, the ICPAC recommended a new, 'virtual' global forum for antitrust. This global forum was not to have a secretariat or bureaucracy, and its recommendations were to be entirely voluntary. It would be devoted only to antitrust issues; not trade and antitrust, as some had proposed for the WTO. Its membership would be the antitrust agencies of all nations (not just industrialised nations, as per the OECD). ICPAC presented its report to US Attorney General Janet Reno and Assistant Attorney General Joel Klein. At an international antitrust forum in the fall of 2000, Klein made a proposal taken from the pages of the ICPAC Report: that the antitrust agencies of the world form a virtual network and devote their work to solving practical problems capable of solution. Although at first greeted with suspicion, the idea got increasing traction. A meeting convened at Ditchley Park near London, focusing principally on the wasteful, multiplicitous merger systems of the world, consolidated support from the business community. Within a few months, leading antitrust authorities warmed to the idea of a grassroots-up world antitrust forum, and, at Fordham Law School in October 2001, the International Competition Network (ICN) was launched.

One month later, the WTO held its ministerial meeting at Doha, Qatar, and the ministers adopted an agenda for the trade round – the Doha Declaration of 14 November 2001. The document recognised that the developing countries had not equally shared the gains from the prior trade rounds, and declared that this round was to be the Doha Development Round. The Doha agenda contained three paragraphs on the interaction between trade and competition. The declaration 'recognise[d] the case for a multilateral framework to enhance the contribution of competition policy to international trade and development' and the need of developing countries for enhanced technical assistance and capacity building, and it proposed work of the WTO Working Group on the Interaction between Trade and Competition Policy (which had been launched in December 1996 in Singapore) to clarify 'core principles, including transparency, non-discrimination and procedural fairness, and provisions on hardcore cartels; modalities for voluntary cooperation; and support for progressive reinforcement of competition institutions in developing countries through capacity building'.

The Doha antitrust agenda, however, was not to see light. The negotiations, begun in Cancun, quickly faltered. The United States and the European Union failed to offer sufficiently serious cuts in their agricultural subsidies – which notoriously harm the developing world and which was the main item on the agenda. To help revive the negotiations, the nations agreed to remove several agenda items, including competition law. At this writing, despite attempts to restart the stalled Doha round negotiations even without the competition item, it appears that the entire round has failed.

The fate of the ICN was quite to the contrary. The ICN blossomed. The competition agency heads and officials, with non-governmental advisers present, held their first annual meeting in Naples in the fall of 2002. Much preparatory work was done in advance, with meetings of working groups held largely by telephone and Internet. At the first annual meeting, the problem of disparate requirements for pre-merger filings was addressed, and recommended practices – such as when the merging parties can file, so as to allow coordination of the scores of pre-merger filing systems – were adopted. Successive annual meetings were held in Merida, Seoul, Bonn, Cape Town, Moscow, Kyoto, Zurich, Istanbul, The Hague, Rio de Janeiro and Warsaw. Projects are underway on cartels, merger standards, unilateral conduct, advocacy, agency effectiveness, and a video-training curriculum. Workshops are held throughout the year. Through recommended practices, guidelines, and multitudinous opportunities for personal interactions, convergence of antitrust law and procedure has occurred and is further occurring, and mutual understanding and cooperation have increased.

The world centre of the international competition conversation has shifted from the WTO to the ICN, and from a formal hierarchical structure to informal horizontal networking. Until such time as policy-makers around the world are willing to embark on an over-arching global competition initiative,[6] convergence, appreciation and cooperation provide the best prospects for addressing the challenges arising from a system of predominantly national competition regimes in a globalised economy. This system can result in a failure to address certain private anti-competitive behaviour, unwarranted public restrictions on competition, potential chilling effects from differing substantive standards and policies, and burdens caused by duplicative and inconsistent procedures. The ICN has emerged as the best hope for convergence, by establishing recommended practices and guidelines, improving understanding of divergence, and constant learning from cross-fertilisation. The ICN has lived up to and surpassed the modest expectations of its founders. We now ask: What remains to be done?

THE PROMISE OF NETWORKING: OPPORTUNITY FOR THE ICN

The antitrust community was debating the merits of a virtual forum in the fall and winter of 2000 and the spring of 2001. Skeptics queried whether antitrust needed yet another body, and speculated that this new creature, if indeed created, would be a headless horseman[7] or, to use a different metaphor, an empty vessel. What would it do? What could it do? What could it do that was not already being done or for which existing institutions were not well placed?[8]

Already, network literature was emerging. It focused primarily on international and human rights law and was not immediately noticed as relevant to the policy world of competition. The most prominent scholar and thinker of networking as an alternative to the fearsome dream of world governance was Anne-Marie Slaughter, who, in 1997, published a seminal article, The Real New World Order, in *Foreign Affairs*.[9] Slaughter articulated 'the globalisation paradox': 'needing more government and fearing it'. Networking was an answer.[10] Slaughter's work describes the emerging phenomenon of government networks as an alternative to world law. Located in an atmosphere of informality, flexibility, and freedom from bureaucracy and coercion, stakes of agreement are low. Network participants more easily find common ground. Networks were becoming the instrument of choice to galvanise common positions and solve the multiplying problems of coordination.

On its separate track (for only later, when David Lewis of South Africa and Bill Kovacic of the US became vice chairs of the ICN Steering Group, did the ICN leadership begin to draw from the insights of the networking literature), the ICN became, figuratively, Exhibit A to The New World Order.

By all accounts, the ICN is a success as a modus operandi for cross-fertilisation, better understanding, and the resulting convergence and informed divergence on principles and process of competition law. Perhaps the ICN's greatest advantage lies in its inclusiveness, both as regards its membership – any competition agency around the world is eligible to participate – and the involvement of 'non-governmental advisers': representatives from business, consumer groups, academics, and the legal and economic professions. This broad participation ensures that the ICN's work product is balanced, lends it legitimacy, and facilitates its use and implementation by a broad range of jurisdictions.

Another major key to this success has been the ICN's 'virtuality': its lack of either rule-making or enforcement powers. The very structure of the ICN has produced candour, trust, receptivity and sympathetic regard. These traits have had payoffs for networks in general, not least for the ICN. When the financial crisis of 2008 hit the world, networks brought together central bankers and other experts to share wisdom and devise solutions, and facilitated helpful common policies. For example, at the annual economic symposium in Jackson Hole in 2008, central bankers, finance ministers, academics and financial market experts from around the world met to discuss the financial crisis and its implications for the broader economy. This was followed 6 weeks later by an unprecedented coordinated interest-rate cut by the US Federal Reserve, European Central Bank, Bank of England, Bank of Canada, Sweden's Riksbank and Swiss National Bank.[11] Subsequent meetings of the Basel Committee on Banking Supervision have brought together banking supervisors and central bankers from 27 countries to discuss ways to strengthen the regulation, supervision and risk management of the banking sector.

In the wake of the financial crisis, the ICN, too, profited from mutual trust and respect. Many nations' first responses to the crisis were protectionist: bailing out their own firms, by cash or merger. Having built a reservoir of understanding, competition officials conferred seamlessly across borders. Conversations of top competition officials flowed from South Africa to Australia to the UK to the European Union to the United States. Advocacy strategies for 'competition policy in troubled times' crafted in the UK[12] were disseminated and used internationally. Mario Monti, a former Commissioner for Competition in the European Union, gave a keynote speech at the American Antitrust Institute in June 2009 articulating a common competition policy against protectionism[13] – a speech that he refined in several fora and which inspired the ICN Steering Group to prepare a set of key messages on the case for competition policy in difficult economic times which were sent to all ICN member agencies in October 2009 for use as they chose in their own internal policy and advocacy.

With a modest profile, the ICN is the facilitator of its members' reform initiatives. With the anchor of the ICN's recommended practices, many of its member authorities have proposed legislative reforms to their own legislatures. The ICN's voice appears to have added legitimacy to the efforts and fuelled their success. In 2009, in response to a request from the Brazilian authority CADE, the chair of the ICN Steering Group wrote a letter to CADE stating: 'I would like to … express my support for the changes to the Brazilian merger notification and review system proposed … The … provisions that conform to the ICN's Recommended Practices for Merger Notification and Review Procedures should contribute to more effective and efficient merger review'. Its effort for legislative reform was successful. The ICN has given similar support to the Pakistan Competition Commission.

SHOULD THE ICN MOVE TO ANOTHER STAGE OF ENGAGEMENT?

Introduction

We believe and accept that the ICN is a useful forum, intermediary and facilitator. It does what it does well, and is working at refinement and improvement. But should it do more?

We have noted the four principal international institutions that play a role in world competition policy; namely, the WTO, UNCTAD, OECD and ICN. Given the work of the four institutions, can we now conclude that all the problems emanating from world competition, world markets, and world-affecting restrictive practices have been or are being addressed? If not, which institution is best placed to fill the need in which interstice? Might there be a role for the ICN?

To explore answers to these questions, we ask: What are the problems that remain to be solved? Then we consider: What organisation is best placed and most likely to solve these problems, and how might solutions evolve?

A Thought Experiment

A paper written by John Fingleton as incoming chair of the ICN Steering Group[14] was based on a thought experiment. First, let us consider the European Union. Consider what the European Commission's Directorate General for Competition achieves, sometimes in collaboration with neighbouring directorates, by the deep integration of trade, competition and all other internal market policies. Now suppose that there is no European Union. All European States apply only their national laws. What are the gaps? How close could these multifarious national regimes come to tackling the world's competition problems and filling the gaps? Would there be the ability and the will to catch and put an end to the Quinine cartel? To rein in Électricité de France, Deutsche Post, Deutsche Telekom, Microsoft?

Next, superimpose a network. Can the network close the gaps? How far do convergence and cooperation projects go to close the gaps? Given the unlikelihood of a competition regime in the WTO in the short term, should there be an ambition of the ICN to help make the world competition system more seamless?

Addressing the Challenges of Private Anticompetitive Behaviour, Unwarranted Public Restrictions, Differing Substantive Standards, and Duplicative and Inconsistent Procedures

The ICN has had some notable successes in fostering procedural and substantive convergence through the development and promulgation of recommended practices and practical guidance. For example, the ICN Recommended Practices for Merger Notification and Review Procedures have been cited by nearly two-thirds of ICN members which have made or planned changes to their merger regimes as having played a role in initiating or shaping their merger reforms; and the ICN's work on cartel leniency has proved influential in the introduction and reshaping of many leniency programmes.

But much remains to be done. In its early years, the ICN focused its energies on the 'low-hanging fruit': projects chosen in part for their non-controversial and practical nature. The ICN broke new ground in 2006 with its work on unilateral conduct, but other 'controversial' areas such as non-horizontal mergers and agreements remain thus far largely unexplored.

The ICN's role in facilitating networking and relationship-building across the international competition community – cited by ICN members as a key benefit of participation – has also helped foster the trust and mutual understanding necessary for cooperation on cases with cross-border effects, such as that seen with the Marine Hose cartel in 2007–2008. There is demand among ICN members for more work aimed at facilitating international cooperation.

The ICN also supports its members' efforts to tackle public restrictions on competition through its work on competition advocacy, which focuses on providing a forum for members to share their domestic experience of competition advocacy, and on developing practical guidance on conducting market studies as well as competition advocacy more generally.

Gaps, Overlaps, Myopic Vision and the Problem of Bounded Concern[15]

Gaps

The ICN has devoted much time to soft convergence. Soft convergence tends to alleviate conflicts and facilitate the flow of trade and investment. But it does not cure the essential discontinuities that naturally stem from 100 national laws and world markets. Gaps can be seen from both a horizontal and a spiral (or world) perspective. The most obvious gap involves export cartels and world cartels that differentially harm outsiders, for national laws are inward-looking; they do not take account of external harms. An example of this gap was spotlighted by Frédéric Jenny in a letter to the editor of the *Financial Times* in August 2010,[16] regarding the potash export cartel in Canada. Potash is a necessary ingredient of fertiliser. Fertiliser is indispensible to farming, and farming is the life-blood occupation in developing countries. Higher-priced potash means less fertiliser, which means less food in the poorest nations of the world. It is easy to say that the victim nations can sue, but practically, they cannot. They do not have the resources. Moreover, as with pollution, the efficient cure is at the source.

The second palpable gap is anticompetitive state action, including state encouragement and facilitation of cartels, building of national champions, and launching – through state-owned enterprise or privileged cronies – monopolistic abuses that predominantly or significantly hurt foreigners.

A less gaping discontinuity is the divergence of substantive law in its application to cross-border transactions. Do we need bridging protocols that would tend to increase certainty, diffuse conflicts, and thereby help to complete a more seamless common world market?

These are not the 'low-hanging fruit' that the ICN at first set out to address. They do not necessarily lie within the spirit of the early epithet 'antitrust all of the time'. They may be seen as adjacent territory. But they are problems that may have a larger significance to the world economy and the welfare of people than convergence of national laws.

Overlaps

A number of nations' antitrust laws may apply to the very same conduct or transactions, and nations' treatments, including remedies, may be inconsistent, conflicting or overregulatory.

The ICN addresses the overlap problem by working towards greater convergence of substantive and process principles. This is the meat of the ICN's work, and much has been accomplished.

There is also much work left to do. There is considerable demand among ICN members for work aimed more squarely at cooperation: subjects that might be addressed include further coordination on cartel leniency programs, merger process (consideration of a common clearing house?), abuses by world-dominant firms, and coordination of damages and fines so as to guard against duplicate penalties. Some of these subjects are precisely within the ICN's 'traditional' work. Trans-border discontinuities and world coordination are not.

Myopic vision and bounded concern

Nations normally have myopic vision and bounded concern. Understandably, they care about themselves. This phenomenon feeds back into gaps we described above; in general, condoning conduct that differentially hurts outsiders. A vision from the top – such as achieved in the European Union – underscores the reality that the gap problem is not just horizontal, nation-to-nation. It is a problem of lack of community-wide vision, wherein the authority sees and takes account of a total transaction and its total impacts.

Along with export cartels and undue state restraints, anti-dumping laws and subsidies with significant external impacts cut a big hole in the project of relatively seamless world competition.[17]

Summary

All of the above are problems that should be addressed if a cure is feasible and worth its costs. Solutions need exploration. We therefore ask, for each problem, is one or another of the four international institutions best placed to address it? The OECD is an organisation of developed countries; it is essentially a research forum and a facilitator of dialogue among its members. It could helpfully interact with the other institutions if a project were to proceed. UNCTAD is devoted to the problems of developing countries. It, too, could helpfully interact on a project. We focus our thinking hereafter on how the ICN might seek to address these problems, and whether there is still a role for the WTO in doing so.

CURING THE PROBLEMS

Towards Convergence, Cooperation, and More Effective Domestic Advocacy and Enforcement

A comprehensive survey of ICN members and NGAs seeking their views on the priorities for the ICN in its second decade, carried out in 2010,[18] revealed that competition agencies and non-governmental actors alike would like to see international convergence in more areas as a result of the ICN's work. In addition to developing recommended practices, the ICN carries out comparative work which can be very useful in fostering 'informed divergence' in areas where convergence is not possible over the short to medium term. This means identifying the nature and sources of divergence and understanding and respecting the divergent underlying rationales. Such an understanding can offer clarity and transparency to business and consumers and can lay the groundwork for possible convergence over the longer term. However, it is imperative that the ICN continue to seek areas ripe for further recommended practices aimed at achieving convergence in the short to medium term where possible.

There is little point in the ICN developing work products if they are not then implemented or used. The ICN is increasingly focusing on promoting implementation and use of its work product, through efforts to measure implementation and use of existing work product and to identify and address barriers to implementation in future. The ICN should allow sufficient space in its forward agenda for such efforts, without compromising its virtual nature.

The ICN's work on advocacy will be particularly beneficial in helping its members address public restrictions on competition. The ICN has an important role to play in promoting recognition among national policymakers of the importance of international welfare, even where domestic interests may not necessarily be affected by or aligned with international interests.

Fundamental to the ability of competition agencies to address these challenges is the effectiveness of the agencies themselves. To that end, the ICN has a working group focusing on agency-effectiveness issues which has held workshops for competition agency heads to discuss, in an informal and confidential setting, best practices in various aspects of running an agency. Additionally, in response to demand from members, the ICN is developing a comprehensive curriculum of training materials to serve as a virtual university on competition law and practice for competition agency officials and their staffs.

It is also crucial to ensure that the ICN's governance structure ensures that inclusiveness and continuity are maximised. Maintaining inclusiveness and diversity of engagement in all of the ICN's work is a particular challenge in a network with over 100 members and at least as many non-governmental advisers. Continuity and institutional memory also pose a challenge in a network without a 'bricks and mortar' organisation. Efforts are under way to optimise the ICN's governance structure to ensure that the network is well placed in future to meet the needs of all of its members, and to serve the interests of consumers in each of its members' jurisdictions.

Overlaps of Substantive Law that Create Conflicts Despite Soft Convergence

Soft convergence does not solve all problems of systems-clash. In many respects divergences remain, whether because jurisdictions have different standards, apply the same standards differently, reach different conclusions because their markets are different, or have a different appreciation of appropriate remedies. From a world welfare or community perspective, it may make sense to develop bridging protocols, such as conflict and priority rules in the event of a clash. Bridging protocols could serve one of two purposes: (1) making the world and its law more seamless, and thus producing efficiencies and enhancing world welfare; and, even if this cannot be accomplished, (2) conferring legitimacy on different approaches – which itself could tend to allay protective or retaliatory responses such as were threatened in *Boeing/McDonnell Douglas*.

What institution is best situated to develop this infrastructure? The ICN seems very well placed. It could launch conversations with a view towards developing best practices. It could be aided in this task by discussions within the OECD.

Gaps and Positive Obstructions

Anti-dumping laws and subsidies

Anti-dumping laws and subsidising regimes distort the market. These, however, are typical WTO problems at the core of WTO work. Advocacy against the distorting regimes is a fair and important subject for advocacy by competition agencies; but the work belongs, as it is, in the WTO.

Non-coverage of export cartels

Export cartels are different. Anti-cartel law is the centre of antitrust policy of most nations. The same nations that unequivocally condemn cartels as the worst possible antitrust restraint have blinkered vision when the victims are abroad. They may say: let the victims sue in the victim country; it is their problem. But the victims often cannot sue; they lack the resources and detection and enforcement power. As said above, the efficient cure is at its source. This gap in national concern is exactly the profile for problems that need an international solution.

There is also another tack, and networks can help. The Basel Convention on disposition of hazardous wastes is a model. Under this Basel agreement, nations that wish not to be a home for shipments of hazardous wastes can so notify their fellow members who are party to the convention. If they do so, it becomes an agreed offence to ship hazardous wastes into that territory. A competition agreement could go one step further. Hazardous wastes need to be deposited somewhere; cartels do not. World welfare is better without them. Nations might consider an agreement not to export their (consensus) antitrust harms. They could do so out of self-interest. (It is more efficient for all.) They could do so out of a communal regard for others. But these motivations have failed. They could do so because otherwise they will invite world law to make them do so. These issues and aspects could usefully be discussed in the ICN and/or the OECD. This work could also help pave the way for a possible world framework.

State action and actions of state-owned enterprises

State action defences shield some of the most harmful anticompetitive conduct, and much of the conduct imposes harms on outsiders. Many scholars and some agency heads have identified state action defences as overbroad to protect the interests of the state. The WTO has waded into the area, but only modestly. Article 11 of the Safeguards Agreement prohibits nation states from encouraging or supporting the adoption or maintenance by private enterprises of measures equivalent to voluntary export restraint exercised by the government, which may include export cartels.[19]

There is room for considering the appropriate scope of a state action defence, particularly where it shields voluntary private conduct that differentially harms foreigners.

States may also cause anticompetitive harms in the form of privileged state-owned enterprises. Sometimes SOEs are subject to the national competition laws; sometimes they are not. Often states confer anti-competitive privileges on recently-privatised successors. The European

Union is one model for limiting state privilege that harms the market. This, too, may be a sympathetic subject for the ICN, at least to define the contours of the problem and investigate possible solutions. Helpfully, in 2013 the Advocacy Working Group launched a project to prepare guidance on the competitive effects of proposed and existing government regulation. This could be a first step towards a more concrete identification of the problem.

Specific Regulatory Coordination Problems

Coordination may hold palpable benefits. While progress has been made in reducing the time and cost of multijurisdictional merger filings due in large part to the work of the ICN, the need for multiple merger filings continues to present one such problem. A common clearing-house for first-stage merger filings would save enormous costs. It could be voluntary. The US Antitrust Modernisation Commission has proposed the exploration of such a body,[20] as have scholars.[21] There are obstacles to reaching agreement, including confidentiality problems. The ICN would be an ideal forum to consider the virtues and structure of such a coordinating centre.

Other cross-border coordination is for the common good. The ICN put a toe in this water at the time of the 2008 financial crisis. Other such issues, including appropriate boundaries of industrial policy versus market policies, might arise; and perhaps again on an emergency basis. The ICN is well placed to explore foundations and modes of thinking, coordinating and proceeding in the future.

CONCLUSION

International antitrust has evolved dramatically from one nation's taking action against offshore actors to protect its market, to world-scale institutions and fora to address the global problems of competition law.

We have told the story of the growth of competition laws, the institutions and interactions in response, the flirting with global frameworks, and the critical role of the ICN as a grass-roots provocateur in crafting network solutions to global problems.

While problems of national law and standards have been and are being well attended, we have directed the spotlight to issues of cross-border impact and we find them relatively unattended. We have tried to define what these issues are, and which of the competition-involved world institutions are best placed to offer the best solutions. Some of the unresolved problems fit naturally within the WTO. But others might helpfully devolve to a grass-roots level, at least for preliminary consideration. We find the ICN particularly well placed to consider these linking issues; to use its network, in effect, to mimic the barrier-levelling function of the EU but without any ambition of centralisation.

NOTES

1. Note that Canada adopted its law in 1889, the year before the US (in 1890).
2. *See F. Hoffmann-La Roche Ltd.* v *Empagran S.A.*, 542 U.S. 155 (2004).
3. *See* Department of Justice press release, 'Justice Department Will Challenge Foreign Restraints on U.S. Exports Under Antitrust Laws', 3 April 1992.
4. U.S. Federal Trade Commission, Statement, 5 CCH Trade Reg. Rep. (CCH) [Transfer Binder 1997–2001], ¶ 24,295 (July 1, 1997); European Commission Case IV/M877, O.J. L 336/16 (Dec. 8, 1997).
5. *See* Eleanor Fox, *GE/Honeywell: The U.S. Merger that Europe Stopped – A Story of the Politics of Convergence*, Chapter 12 in ANTITRUST STORIES, eds E. Fox and D. Crane (2007).
6. A well-argued and evidence-based case for such an initiative was made by David Gerber in *Global Competition: Law, Markets and Globalization* (2010).
7. *See* Lawson Hunter & Susan Hutton, 'Global Competition Initiative: A "Headless Horseman"?', in *International Antitrust Law & Policy: Fordham Corporate Law Institute 2000* 25, ed. B. Hawk (2001).
8. Eleanor Fox, 'Linked-in: Antitrust and the Virtues of a Virtual Network', 43 *International Lawyer* 151 (2009).
9. Anne-Marie Slaughter, 'The Real New World Order', 76 *Foreign Affairs* 183 (1997).
10. *See* Anne-Marie Slaughter, *A New World Order*, Princeton University Press (2004).
11. Fed, ECB, 'Central Banks Cut Rates in Coordinated Move', Bloomberg, 8 October 2008.
12. John Fingleton speech, 'Competition Policy in Troubled Times', 20 January 2009, available at: www.oft.gov.uk/shared_oft/speeches/2009/spe0109.pdf.
13. Mario Monti speech, 'Competition Authorities of the World, Unite!', 18 June 2009, available at: www.antitrustinstitute.org/content/former-european-commissioner-competition-mario-montis-keynote-address-aai-national-conferenc.
14. John Fingleton, 'Competition Agencies and Global Markets: The Challenges Ahead', 5 June 2009, available at: www.oft.gov.uk/shared_oft/speeches/2009/spe0909paper.pdf.
15. This section draws from Fingleton, supra, and Fox, 'Antitrust Without Borders: From Roots to Codes to Networks', in *Cooperation, Comity and Competition*, ed. A. Guzman, Oxford (2010).
16. Frédéric Jenny letter, 'Potash Cartel and Double Standards', *Financial Times*, 31 August 2010. *Also see* 'Professor's Critique of Hostile Bid Triggers Discussion of Export Cartels', 99 *BNA Antitrust & Trade Report* 339, 17 September 2010.
17. A reasonably seamless world system would contemplate more state sovereignty than does the EU. We do not imply a 'united world' but merely mean to tease out problems that are going unattended.
18. *See* www.internationalcompetitionnetwork.org/second-decade.aspx.

19. The article is under-enforced and might be thought relevant only when connected with emergency action taken by a state where its domestic industry is seriously injured or threatened with serious injury caused by a surge in imports of particular products.
20. Report, April 2007, Recommendation 38, p. 217.
21. *See, for example,* Fox, Separate Statement in Report of International Competition Policy Advisory Committee to the Attorney General and Assistant Attorney General for Antitrust (ICPAC), at Annex A-1 (2000).

7. Regional agreements

Alberto Heimler and Frédéric Jenny

INTRODUCTION

Fighting anticompetitive practices or transactions, whether domestic or international, is crucial for developing countries that are more prone than developed countries to being victimised by them. The awareness of the cost inflicted on developing countries by anticompetitive practices has increased significantly during the 2000s, and a large number of jurisdictions have adopted a competition law and set up a competition authority to fight them. This movement has been accelerated by the proliferation in the 1990s and the early 2000s of trade liberalisation agreements which have led domestic economies to be opened to competition and, as a result, accelerated the setting up of market-oriented institutions.

Yet, as trade liberalisation has progressed, the gap between the rapid internationalisation of markets and the fragmentation of the systems of domestic antitrust laws has meant that competition authorities in developing countries have experienced considerable difficulties in fighting the transnational anticompetitive practices which originate abroad but have a negative effect on their domestic markets or to adequately intervene against transnational transactions initiated in other countries but affecting their home markets. To try to address this problem, the international competition community has experimented with a number of possible solutions ranging from a failed attempt to promote a multilateral cooperation system in the area of competition to voluntary bilateral cooperation agreements between developed and developing countries. So far, those solutions have been mostly unsuccessful and frustrating for developing countries. Regional agreements on cooperation in competition seem to be more promising largely because the cooperating countries may have more of an incentive to cooperate than pairs of developed and developing countries unequal in size and with different stakes and unbalanced trade flows.

Background to Increased Awareness of Competition in Developing Countries

Up to the beginning of the 1990s there was little research on domestic anticompetitive practices in developing countries and little awareness of their existence or their importance.[1] This has changed progressively since then. A number of factors seem to have contributed to this shift.

First, the economic structure of the world has changed. We have moved from a bipolar world, a situation characterised by the pre-eminence of two large economic blocs competing with one other, based on opposite conceptions of economic and social mechanisms, each having in its sphere of influence a number of affiliated developing countries, to a multipolar world characterised by the disappearance of the socialist bloc, the slowing down of the economic growth of the western bloc and the emergence of new sources of economic power. The economic rise of the BRICS countries (Brazil, Russia, India, China and South Africa) has revealed the enormous potential of developing countries to promote economic growth in the world and has created a renewed interest for the issue of economic development.

Second, as is well known, the 1990s was a period during which economists put a great deal of confidence (some would argue too much faith) in the ability of competitive markets to promote static and dynamic efficiencies. Market-based solutions such as deregulation, privatisation, trade liberalisation, the abolition of price controls, and so on, became the fashionable tools of economic development, whether in transition economies or in developing economies. Hence research on market conditions in developing countries became a more important focus of attention of researchers.

Third, at the initiative of the European Union, the agenda of the negotiations of the WTO Doha Round included the question of whether multilateral trade discipline should be extended to include a competition dimension. For reasons outside the scope of this chapter there was fierce resistance on the part of a number of developing countries to enlarging the scope of traditional multilateral trade negotiations. In the WTO Working Group on Trade and Competition, set up in Geneva in 1997, a number of developing countries argued that they had no experience with competition law, that since they were for the most part small open economies they did not need to have a domestic competition law and that their main competition problems came from abuses of dominant positions by multinational firms based in developed countries or export cartels also originating in developed countries. The debates within the WTO Working Group on Trade and Competition and the assertion of developing countries that competition law was not relevant to them increased interest in gathering data on market conditions in developing countries.

Fourth, the Internet revolution of the 1990s made it easier for researchers to access material produced by local news organisations in developing countries. This gave economic researchers interested in assessing market conditions in developing countries a first set of evidence that competition issues were an important source of concern in those countries and that, at the local level, there were widespread allegations of market abuses or cartelisation by domestic firms in developing countries in markets for consumer goods or services or in markets for intermediate products or raw materials. These press reports also showed that in many developing countries governments were the object of intense lobbying on the part of domestic and international firms seeking shelter from competition.

Fifth and last, a large number of developing countries adopted their own competition laws in the 1990s and the beginning of the 2000s. For example, in the 1998–2008 period, more than 60 countries adopted a competition law and the vast majority of these countries were developing countries or countries in transition.[2] It is interesting to note that in a number of developing countries the adoption of a competition law was the consequence of negotiating a bilateral or multilateral trade agreement with other countries. More and more of these trade agreements were negotiated as it became clear that WTO negotiations for a new multilateral agreement were encountering serious difficulties. In a number of cases, such trade agreements provided for the fact that the parties to the agreement would cease to use the antidumping instrument against one other. But if the negotiating parties were willing to give up one of the protectionist instruments on which they had relied in the past to shelter their domestic firms from international competition, they also wanted to be assured that their firms would have access to the markets of the other party (or parties) to the trade agreement and that they would have a means of recourse if their firms encountered difficulties accessing these foreign markets because of domestic anticompetitive practices such as abuses of dominant positions by local firms or import cartels. Thus a negotiating party was willing to abandon trade protectionist measures only if the other party to the free trade agreement had (or adopted) a domestic competition law. For example, Singapore, which between 1997 and 2003 had been a leading opponent to the European initiative on competition in the WTO Working Group on Trade and Competition, passed its competition law in early 2005 to fulfil its obligations under the US–-Singapore bilateral free trade agreement. Similarly, a number of other developing countries, such as Vietnam and China, adopted their competition laws to meet WTO accession commitments.[3]

Although more than 100 countries in the world have adopted a competition law, the enforcement of these laws has not always been very effective. First, identifying a restriction of competition is not an easy task. The existence of a cartel must be proved and the proof is often only available through some sort of cooperation with one or a number of cartelists. Such cooperation, which is unlikely to be motivated by the mere existence of a leniency programme, requires a well-established competition culture, seldom found in developing countries. As for abuse of dominance, the widespread adoption of an effect-based approach must be accompanied by complex analysis, aimed at proving the existence of exclusionary effects, and which requires a highly competent antitrust authority and an equally competent judiciary. Furthermore, anti-competitive practices, especially when originating from a merger, increasingly produce effects in a number of jurisdictions, suggesting that national authorities, unauthorised to look at market effects beyond national borders, are not well placed for disciplining them.

Different Types of Cooperation Agreements

Voluntary bilateral cooperation agreements are common among major OECD countries and are widely used to coordinate authorities action, especially in areas such as merger control where the identification of appropriate remedies may be challenging in the case of multi-jurisdictional mergers. Although these agreements do not often allow competition authorities to exchange confidential information, in order to favour speedier and more effective decisions, merger parties may waive the confidentiality exception.

These agreements are not very common in the developing world.

First of all, not every developing country has a system of merger control in place, so the benefits originating from bilateral agreements among countries with different legal provisions are very small.

Second, bilateral cooperation agreements between competition authorities in developing and developed countries have proved to be disappointing tools for developing countries when they try to fight transnational anticompetitive practices and transactions. The source of this disappointment is the fact that competition authorities in developed countries are reluctant to commit themselves to enter into cooperation agreements with competition authorities in developing countries (especially when the developing country is small) and the fact that such cooperation agreements usually provide that the contracting parties *may* cooperate but do not have an obligation to cooperate. This feature of voluntary bilateral cooperation seriously limits the effectiveness of the instrument.

However, it should be noted that bilateral agreements represent a very important information source on actions undertaken in the cooperating jurisdictions. They may lead to greater substantive and procedural convergence, may represent an effective learning experience on how to solve technical, political or institutional issues and may be the first step in a regional integration process. Unfortunately, bilateral agreements among neighbouring countries are very rare in the developing world.

Moving from the bilateral level to the multilateral level, attempts to promote a multilateral agreement on competition in the context of the WTO between 1997 and 2004 were unsuccessful and it is highly unlikely that the issue will be reopened until the Doha Development Round negotiations are successfully completed, which may take a number of years.

The last possibility, and the key focus of this chapter, is regional competition agreements.

This chapter will look at specific regional agreements in the developing world and analyse their effectiveness in combating anticompetitive practices. It will then give an overview of the institutional arrangements in the EU and how these facilitate effective competition enforcement, and how developing countries could start to apply some of these successful models.

A CLOSER LOOK AT REGIONAL COMPETITION AGREEMENTS IN THE DEVELOPING WORLD

Such agreements are entered into by neighbouring countries, often in the context of a free trade regional agreement, rather than by pairs of developed and developing countries. A number of such agreements exist in the developing world, such as the Mercado Commun do Sul (Mercosur), the Andean Community, the Common Market for Eastern and Southern Africa (COMESA), the Caribbean Community (CARICOM), the West African Economic and Monetary Union (WAEMU), the Economic Community of West African States (ECOWAS) and the South African Development Community (SADC), to name a few. Such agreements also exist, although there are fewer of them, in the developed world. The best known is the European Union.

What is striking about such regional agreements is the diversity of their institutional features, the fact that their competition provisions have very different scope, and the fact that they have had variable success.

On the basis of past experience, the institutional arrangements of regional cooperation agreements in the area of competition matter a great deal. A number of characteristics influence their effectiveness.

Some agreements create a supranational antitrust authority with enough powers and resources to be able to start an action. A weaker alternative is to create extensive cooperation among the different national competition authorities of the region. But the cost of enforcement is likely to be lower if there is a supranational authority than if the enforcement of competition law is done through multiple domestic agencies (this of course is only true when enforcing the law to cross-border practices).

Institutional arrangements favouring the participation of national authorities in the decision-making process at the central or 'federal' level are useful because they make regional antitrust action politically acceptable to the affected jurisdiction. When the regional agreement is negotiated between jurisdictions that have already introduced a competition law, great care should be exercised. Indeed, it is very difficult for any country to abandon its national sovereignty and close cooperation between the centre and the periphery contributes to the political acceptability of any agreement establishing a supranational enforcement mechanism. Regional agreements which exclude the jurisdiction of national competition authorities on competition cases affecting only their territory are unlikely to be as effective as agreements which contain a flexible system of case allocation and encourage cooperation in the enforcement of competition law by all institutions concerned. In Europe the application of the principle of subsidiarity is not only very effective for a more thorough enforcement of competition law, it also reduces rivalry between institutions and encourages cooperation.

Finally, regional agreements should make it clear to all concerned which law they are subject to and which authority is in charge. Uncertainty about procedural issues is likely to create problems, increase the amount of litigation and block the functioning of the agreement.

Free Trade Area Agreements

The creation of a free trade area may be the first step for establishing regional cooperation in antitrust enforcement. Two examples of cooperation agreements in the context of the creation of a free trade area will be analysed: the Mercado Común del Cono Sur (Mercosur) and the Southern Africa Customs Union. Both of these agreements contain provisions promoting increased cooperation among the competition authorities of member States. However, without the introduction of a regional authority, this enhanced cooperation is insufficient. With respect to mergers, the cost associated with multiple filings may be substantial. First of all, parties would have to gather information on whether and when they would have to notify a merger. And then there would be costs associated with the different timing and requirements of the decision-making process. While soft convergence (as achieved, for example, by Mercosur) may be more than sufficient to solve these informational problems, a 'federal' merger-control system may be important in order to make sure that the accepted remedies solve all the identified competition problems at the regional level. Especially when the integration among the different national markets is strong, a regional authority would make sure that cross-border mergers are analysed within a unified framework. A regional turnover threshold would trigger notification at the regional level, while domestic authorities within the region would be responsible for mergers below the regional turnover threshold.

As for cartels, while (as we have seen) a few operate at the international level across countries and across continents, most operate nationally or regionally. Without some sort of regional agreement, it may be very difficult to ensure that domestic authorities cooperate in the investigation of cross-border violations. Domestic laws that protect the exchange of confidential information may make it very difficult for authorities operating in different jurisdictions to cooperate in a substantive way. The same would happen with the administration of leniency programs and the setting of fines. A 'federal' system can help in overcoming these difficulties.

Finally, regarding unilateral conduct, while a number of violations are domestic in nature, there are instances where the same behaviour affects more than one jurisdiction. In these instances, a regional authority may be much more effective in identifying a common remedy than a succession of domestic proceedings.

Mercado Común del Cono Sur (Mercosur)

Competition policy was introduced in Mercosur (which is an agreement between Argentina, Brazil, Paraguay and Uruguay, of which Venezuela became an additional member in July 2012) by Decision No 21/94 and strengthened by Decision No 18/96, the Protocol for the defence of competition ('Fortaleza Protocol') which has addressed issues related to institutional design, substantive standards and increased cooperation among national competition authorities. The Fortaleza Protocol prohibits anticompetitive agreements and abuse of dominance. However, instead of setting up a Mercosur-wide enforcement body, according to the protocol, proceedings against the violation of these provisions are initiated before the competition authority of each member State and only if the practice affects trade within Mercosur can the authority submit the case to the Mercosur Committee for the defence of competition for a second draft decision that needs to be confirmed by the Mercosur Trade Commission, a body specialised in trade disputes.

Without going into a discussion of whether a trade dispute body is the best suited for deciding on antitrust cases among Mercosur countries, it is worth noting that only Argentina and Brazil have adopted a competition law, while Paraguay and Uruguay still have not. Therefore only Argentina and Brazil could enforce the Fortaleza protocol, but with few incentives to do so, since there would not be much that the Mercosur bodies could add. As a result, the competition provisions of Mercosur have remained unimplemented. Paradoxically, given the institutional design of Mercosur, a bilateral agreement between Brazil and Argentina would have been much more effective.

However, it is likely that introducing a Mercosur Authority independent of member country agencies would have contributed to improving the effectiveness of the agreement. It would have made decisions that would have also protected jurisdictions that had not introduced a domestic law. Furthermore, it would have influenced all member States to adopt convergent laws and follow similar substantive standards. The cooperation envisaged by the Fortaleza protocol was far too complicated.

The Southern African Custom Union

The same institutional weakness characterises the Southern African Custom Union, an international agreement between Botswana, Lesotho, Namibia, South Africa and Swaziland. Currently South Africa and Namibia are the only member states with a competition law. Like Mercosur, the SACU agreement also contains antitrust provisions. Article 40 requires all member states to have a competition law so as to be able to cooperate. Article 41 requires the SACU to develop in an annex to the agreement 'policy and instruments to address unfair trade practices between member States'. Six years after the establishment of the SACU, article 40 is not enforced and the annex mentioned in article 41 was not developed. As a result, regional competition issues have been completely ignored. The lack of an SACU-wide institutional structure has probably been the main reason for this lack of interest in antitrust.

Other Regional Initiatives

Other regional initiatives among developing countries are much more structured and their aim is not simply the creation of a free trade area, but the building of an integrated common market. In terms of the effects on antitrust enforcement of these initiatives, however, experience shows that it is not sufficient that a federal authority be created. A number of other elements must also be present. For example, sometimes the federal law does not cover merger control, the area most likely to benefit from a regional approach (CARICOM and Andean Community). In other circumstances the jurisdictional uncertainty over which law to apply and the lack of funding at the federal level has reduced the incentives for applying the federal law (COMESA). Finally, the lack of a subsidiarity principle has eliminated the possibility of applying domestic laws, probably weakening overall antitrust enforcement (WAEMU).

The Andean Community

In 1969, Bolivia, Chile, Colombia, Ecuador and Peru joined together in the Cartagena Agreement in order to 'jointly improve their peoples' standard of living through integration and economic and social cooperation'. On 30 October 1976, Chile withdrew, while Venezuela was a member from 13 February 1976 until 22 April 2006. The Andean countries created a free trade area in 1993, and in 1997 decided to expand it into a common market.

In 1991, competition rules were introduced into the free trade Andean agreement by Decision 285, which established common rules to address distortions of competition. At the time the decision was adopted, only Colombia had a competition law.

Competition rules were strengthened at the time of the creation of the Andean Community. In 2005, Decision 608 by the Andean Community Commission reformed the system of competition enforcement in the Andean Community, by making a Community violation all anti-competitive trans-border practices originating in a country of the region or in third countries. According to Decision 608, the Andean Community has jurisdiction over a matter when there are cross-border effects. Decision 608 is based on the principle of non-discrimination, transparency, and due process and the Andean Community General Secretary is free to decide when and how to start an investigation. It can open an investigation as a result of a complaint by a private party, a member State government or ex-officio. Decisions can end with corrective measures, including sanctions, that have to be executed by the governments of member states.

According to Decision 608, a number of anticompetitive practices remain outside the reach of the Andean Community jurisdiction. First of all, merger control is fully left to national authorities. Should a merger produce its effects on a geographic relevant market beyond that of a single member State, the difficulty of coordinating an appropriate remedy, for example a divestment action in a different member State, may lead to a very ineffective decision-making. Another area in which there may be a problem is antitrust exemptions that are decided at the national level rather than at Community level (contrary to what happens in the EU). All this creates a system where the primacy of Community law is put into question and where it may be difficult to create a level playing field characterised by common rules and convergent practices in all member States.

Indeed, the Andean Community has never made an antitrust decision, probably because only Peru and Colombia have domestic competition laws and also because the Andean Commission has difficulty in claiming jurisdiction over antitrust matters.

The Common Market for Eastern and Southern Africa (COMESA)

The Common Market for Eastern and Southern Africa was conceived in the mid-1960s, but it was only in 1978, at a meeting of Ministers of Trade, Finance and Planning in Lusaka, that the creation of a regional economic community was recommended, beginning with a preferential trade area, which over a 10-year period would evolve into a common market.

Four years later, on 30 September 1982, the Treaty establishing the preferential trade area entered into force. Finally, the Treaty establishing the Common Market for Eastern and Southern Africa, COMESA, was signed on 5 November 1993 in Kampala, Uganda, and was ratified in Lilongwe, Malawi, on 8 December 1994. Nineteen countries are members of COMESA: Burundi, Comoros, Congo, Djibouti, Egypt, Eritrea, Ethiopia, Kenya, Libya, Madagascar, Malawi, Mauritius, Rwanda, Seychelles, Sudan, Swaziland, Uganda, Zambia and Zimbabwe, covering a very wide area and a total population of over 400 million people.

So far, COMESA strategy has been to emphasise the integration of the economic space through the removal of trade and investment barriers, more than the creation of an integrated area governed by common rules.

COMESA defines itself as a custom union more than a common market. Indeed the provisions of the Treaty are primarily devoted to the elimination of trade barriers, to the enforcement of antidumping rules and to the creation of a free trade area. Only recently have some new developments occurred which may effectively lead to the creation of a common market, at least with respect to antitrust enforcement.

In 2006, a full Competition Commission composed of nine Commissioners from COMESA member States was created. The Commission has been fully in place and operational since December 2009. The COMESA Competition Commission is responsible for enforcing the rules against abuse of dominance and cartel behaviour and it also has some power with respect to merger control.

The experience of the COMESA Competition Commission is still too recent to permit an evaluation of its performance. However, the institutional structure of COMESA and in particular the existence of a COMESA court of justice could rapidly lead to an efficient system of antitrust enforcement. Nevertheless, jurisdictional issues are enormous. Recently, a number of regional groupings in Africa have been created with overlapping boundaries. In particular, the East and Southern Africa (ESA) association of 16 members, created for the purpose of negotiating an economic partnership agreement with the European Union, has member states which belong to both COMESA and the Southern African Customs Union (SACU). As a result, the COMESA Competition Commission will have the preliminary task of going through the SACU, ESA and COMESA configurations when deciding on any case. The burden in terms of litigation could be enormous.

The European experience suggests that the adoption of the principle of '*effet utile*' may be a way to alleviate the jurisdictional issue faced by regional groupings such as COMESA. According to the principle of *effet utile*, what matters, even in order to determine jurisdiction, is the substance of the decision. Judges or domestic antitrust authorities could apply either community or domestic antitrust laws, but the decisions they reach should in any case conform to community case law and jurisprudence. As a result of the principle of *effet utile*, domestic competition laws became fully integrated with community law, not simply complementary to it, as it might have been presumed.

Furthermore, the COMESA treaty did not guarantee the adequate funding of the Commission. As a result, although the Competition Commission has been in place for almost a year, it has been unable to make any decisions because it lacks funding, both for the operation of the board and for recruiting staff. Adequate funds are an essential feature of any organisation. Without funds, even the best-designed institution cannot survive.

The Caribbean Community (CARICOM)

The Caribbean Community (CARICOM) was established in 1973, transforming a pre-existing free trade agreement (CARIFTA) into a common market where labour and capital would be free to circulate, and the agricultural, industrial and foreign policies of member States would be coordinated.

Contrary to the European Union, which started as a political project, CARICOM evolved from a free trade agreement. CARICOM has been characterised by widespread implementation problems, and issues of sovereignty have always impeded the achievement of a much-desired increase in the degree of economic liberalisation of the region.

The original Treaty of Chaguaramas was revised in 2001 and its new Chapter Eight created a Competition Commission responsible for enforcing the Treaty antitrust provisions on cross-border business practices. Although the Treaty requires each member State to 'establish and maintain a national competition authority', since CARICOM member countries are in some cases very small economies, they may not have the resources to establish their own domestic antitrust agency. And indeed, almost 10 years after the implementation of the revised treaty, only Jamaica, Guyana, Saint Vincent, Trinidad and Barbados have adopted domestic competition legislation. This means that in the other jurisdictions (Antigua, Bahamas, Belize, Dominica, Grenada, Haiti, Montserrat, Saint Kitts, Santa Lucia, Suriname) only the CARICOM treaty provisions are in place.

Contrary to the European Union, where the interface between the Commission and national authorities has been developed with the case law, the CARICOM treaty rules explicitly on the relationship between the CARICOM Commission and domestic authorities, creating ex-lege a working network among them. The operation of this network is rigidly defined, thereby limiting the enforcement possibilities of the CARICOM Commission. Indeed, according to Article 176 of the Treaty that rules on the possibility of ex-officio investigation by the Commission, if there are reasons to believe that a firm is behaving anticompetitively, the Commission 'shall request the national competition authority to undertake a preliminary investigation'. Only if dissatisfied with the outcome of its request, the Commission 'may initiate its own preliminary investigation'. Furthermore, should domestic authorities differ from the Commission as to whether a particular conduct is anticompetitive, the Commission must stop the investigation and refer the issue to the CARICOM Council for Trade and Economic Development. Because the Council is a political body, not a court of law, this may create opportunities for politically-based decision-making that might prevent prosecution of politically sensitive cases. Furthermore, since this protection of member State interests is introduced only in the case of ex-officio investigations, the independence of the Commission is reduced, in the sense that the adopted procedure makes it difficult for the Commission to investigate the more sensitive cases.

The treaty introduces a system of dispute settlements that is apparently only available for controversies among States. It is not clear if and where a firm can appeal a decision by the CARICOM Competition Commission. Certainly, if a company fails to adopt a remedy that the Commission has adopted, the Commission can take the firm to the Caribbean Court of Justice where the firm can defend itself.[4] In other circumstances the rules are not clear.

A final observation is that the CARICOM Commission was not given any power with respect to merger control. Especially in the case of the Caribbean Community, characterised by small island states, a regional merger control system would be particularly effective since remedies are much more easily identified in a regional setting than with a piecemeal approach State by State.

The West African Economic and Monetary Union (WAEMU)

With a treaty signed in Dakar on 10 January 1994, seven West African countries (Benin, Burkina Faso, Ivory Coast, Mali, Niger, Senegal and Togo) established the West African Economic and Monetary Union (WAEMU). Guinea-Bissau joined on 2 May 1997. All the countries involved shared a common currency, the CFA franc. The 1994 Dakar treaty shows the clear intention of these countries to evolve from a monetary union to full economic integration where the four liberties (free movement of persons, goods, services and capital) are fully guaranteed. The treaty established a set of institutions very similar to those of the European Union: Conference of Head of States, Council of Ministers, Commission, Court of Justice, Parliament, Central Bank. Furthermore, the treaty established the principle of direct applicability of community legislation and the primacy of community law over domestic laws. Finally, the WAEMU Commission was made financially independent and Articles 54 and 55 of the Treaty ensure that the Commission is properly funded. All these features are very important for ensuring the effectiveness of the WAEMU competition policy.

However, one distinctive feature of the European approach missing in WAEMU is the coexistence of domestic and community jurisdictions. In the European Union, as previously explained, the notion of '*effet utile*' has allowed national authorities to apply domestic law, under the constraint that their decisions (in situations where community law could also have been applied) be in line with the law and the case law of the EU. More recently, the principle of subsidiarity has been strengthened in the EU, with the Commission, domestic authorities and judges all applying the same European rules. As a result, in the EU system the same law is applied by different bodies across the whole common market, with very flexible rules for case allocation and no possibility of litigation over jurisdictional issues. By contrast, the Court of Justice of WAEMU has ruled that only the Commission is in charge of applying community law, without exactly defining what 'competition in the Union' means and without identifying a role for domestic competition authorities.

The territory of WAEMU is extremely large and leaving all antitrust enforcement to the WAEMU Commission may contribute to weakening enforcement, by not providing incentives for consumers, competitors or customers to report their complaints on strictly national cases to a distant authority.

According to the WAEMU Court of Justice, the only role for a national authority is to cooperate with the WAEMU Commission. However, an institution has an incentive to act when it receives recognition for its actions. Very rarely will an institution act efficiently when it is only feeding into the decision-making process of another one. Indeed, domestic authorities have almost no role in the WAEMU Commission enforcement record. Adopting a principle of subsidiarity, similar to the one adopted in the EU, may help domestic competition authorities find an identifiable role in the procedure, leading to a much more effective system of antitrust enforcement.

This does not mean that WAEMU has been ineffective. On the contrary, the WAEMU Commission has taken up a number of important antitrust and state aid cases in a variety of sectors, such as cement, kraft paper bags for cement, broadcasting, flour, pipelines, oil distribution, postal services, mobile telephony, audiovisual, and maritime transport. WAEMU has been by far the most successful of all the regional competition agreements in terms of enforcement. The point is that a better treatment of subsidiarity would enhance the role of domestic authorities with a multiplying effect on the number and the relevance of cases.

A LOOK AT THE EU

The Institutional Arrangements that Facilitate Overall Enforcement

Many of these regional agreements between developing countries have in common with the EU the objective of creating a common integrated market across neighbouring countries. However, they have been created much more recently than the EU, and therefore have not had the time to set up all the necessary infrastructure to be successful.

The most important feature of the EU Treaty is that it introduces a 'federal antitrust law', with European Commission decisions subject to the judicial control of the European Courts. This feature is common to a number of regional agreements such as COMESA, WAEMU and CARICOM. However, with the exception of WAEMU, in these other agreements the role of the Courts is marginal and much less influential than in the EU, where the Courts became key players for enhancing European integration. In particular, the European Court of Justice did not limit itself to a narrow view of competition policy. Following the Commission, the Court promoted a very broad interpretation of the rules of the Treaty, setting the foundations for the important developments that competition policy, both with respect to liberalisation measures and antitrust enforcement, would have in the Community.[5]

One of the cornerstones of the EU system, and of its success, is the principle of supremacy of community law, combined with a procedural relationship between centre and periphery, which assigns a specific role for every institution. This was facilitated in the EU because the EU Treaty was adopted long before domestic antitrust laws were adopted at the national level, with the exception of Germany, whose antitrust law was implemented the same year as the EU Treaty. In some of the other regional agreements the process is the opposite. As a result, while establishing supremacy of community law occurred easily in the EU, it is much more difficult when it requires reducing the sovereignty of established domestic authorities.

The fact that EU Community law was established first also had positive spillovers on the evolution of member States' institutional settings. While only Germany had adopted a competition law at the time of the signing of the Treaty, almost 55 years later all member States have a competition law and an institutional structure very similar in substance (and procedurally) to the European one. The imitation of a very successful model was the major driving force of such positive developments, with the necessity of better cooperation within the network of European competition authorities playing an additional reinforcing role. In the antitrust field, consensus on substantive provisions and institutional design mainly originated in the deliberate choice of an efficient model. Furthermore, member States, equipped with a competition regime aligned with the European one, were able to play a more influential role in European decision-making on competition matters, thereby reinforcing their incentive to conform to the European model. This model could be used by developing countries as well, since in most existing regional agreements only a few member States have already adopted a domestic law.

All regional agreements, including the EU Treaty, are applicable only on matters that affect trade between member States. Since the effect on trade is not a very precise measure to determine jurisdictions, there is always the risk that litigation may be based not on substance but on jurisdictional issues – that is, not on whether a practice would actually be restrictive of competition, but whether the law to be applied is domestic or European and would thereby block the functioning of any agreement.

Because the European Court of Justice understood the risk of being blocked by endless jurisdictional litigations, it rapidly developed the concept of '*effet utile*', leading to a fully coordinated body of law, with no substantive distinction between domestic and community provisions.

Instead of forcing institutions to cooperate on investigations, the EU system left each institution in charge of its own cases, maintaining for each the right incentive for action. Indeed, the fact that each member State adopted a domestic law and created an independent domestic institution, responsible for enforcement, made competition better known at the member State level and enhanced the overall level of enforcement. Domestic competition authorities apply both domestic and community laws and are fully integrated with the European Commission. In other words, Treaty provisions can be enforced by the Commission, national authorities and judges. This flexibility in the application of common legal provisions has added effectiveness to the system and legal certainty to firms that they are subject to the same antitrust provisions across the Union.

In an integrated system, an effort had to be made in order to avoid conflicts over case allocations and clarify the principles to be used. Indeed the 2004 European Commission notice on case allocation[6] suggests that

> an authority can be considered to be well placed to deal with a case if the following three cumulative conditions are met: 1. the agreement or practice has substantial direct actual or foreseeable effects on competition within its territory, is implemented within or originates from its territory; 2. the authority is able to effectively bring to an end the entire infringement, i.e. it can adopt a cease-and-desist order the effect of which will be sufficient to bring an end to the infringement and it can, where appropriate, sanction the infringement adequately; 3. it can gather, possibly with the assistance of other authorities, the evidence required to prove the infringement.

In practice, the Notice suggests that national authorities would deal with national cases while the Commission would deal with cross-border cases. This is, however, a general statement and in exceptional circumstances the Commission may deal with national cases as well. For example, this may occur when the case addresses a new competition issue or when the Commission may ensure more effective enforcement. As a result of this flexibility, litigation on case allocation would be almost impossible.

The system requires strong cooperation between national authorities and the Commission in order to ensure that case allocation does not lead to inefficiencies and to the lengthening of proceedings. In particular, the Notice requires that 'all authorities ... be informed at an early stage of the cases pending before the various competition authorities'. As a result of this early information exchange, the process of case allocation in the 6 years since the notice has been issued has always run very smoothly.

Since the effect on trade is not a precise measure for establishing jurisdiction, the approach taken in the EU has also been to give domestic authorities the power to apply community law, while case allocation is governed on the basis of the principle of opportunity – that is, according to which institution is better placed with respect to the investigation. In this way, not only does litigation over jurisdiction become irrelevant, but more importantly the incentives to enforce antitrust law by domestic authorities are maintained, if not significantly strengthened.

Finally, a very important part of the success of the EU is that the Treaty addresses directly the issue of funding and the EU institutions are to be funded according to their needs as established by the Council of ministers through the tax revenues of member States.

Competition Rules, the New Member States and Convergence

In the case of the EU, joining a well-functioning regional agreement has had a positive effect on domestic rules. A similar virtuous circle could be triggered among developing countries as well.

Right after the fall of communism in 1989, the European Commission started a process of bilateral short-term technical assistance with the former Eastern European countries. The programme was quite ineffective because the Commission relied on outside consultants, mostly university professors with limited experience in the workings of a State administration. Furthermore, since the projects were short term, consultants had only a very general understanding of the specific circumstances of the recipients of their assistance at best, and, as a result, their advice was not very useful. In 1998, the Commission launched the 'twinning projects'. These projects (approximately 1000 of them) covered all areas of

Community interest and have addressed sectors such as agriculture, customs, police cooperation, competition and State aid. Fifteen of these projects have been concerned with competition policy and have benefited Bulgaria, Croatia, Estonia, Lithuania, Macedonia, Malta, Morocco, Romania, Poland and the Czech Republic. New ones are starting in Albania, Algeria, Moldavia and Ukraine.

The idea behind these projects is to train the administration of a beneficiary country with the help of an administration of a member State by means of a long-term relationship, whose aim is to bring the beneficiary administration in question to the 'European standard'. In practice, this has not only meant convergence on 'hard' law, which was the easier part, but also on 'soft' law, on organisational matters, and on the application of the law. While the bilateral short-term advice used before 1998 was a one-shot exercise, this long-term relationship between sister administrations was very successful because the assistance was fine-tuned to the needs of the beneficiary and policy suggestions were followed up, either by the member State administration or by the Commission itself.

The success of these projects is related to the fact that there is a real demand for modernisation on the part of the beneficiary. The process would start from a demand for technical assistance. Member States would then compete to supply the services that the beneficiary requires. A contract would then be written with all the details of the project, including a precise indication of the results to be achieved, and be signed by the administrations of the two countries together with the Commission.

The successful conclusion of these projects is quite important for countries that are eager to acquire EU membership. In some sense the fact that a candidate country had successfully concluded a twinning project signalled to the Commission that, in a specific subject, that country had reached the European standard and therefore was ready for accession. This political drive enhanced the risk that demand for technical assistance not be driven by a modernisation objective and that the beneficiary would try to comply only formally with the European standards.

As a result, in order to avoid strategic behaviour, the prime objective of these twinning exercises is to promote an effective application of antitrust law, not just that the appropriate substantive provisions be in place. This has meant that organisational issues also be addressed, like obtaining and maintaining high-quality staff in the authority, organising the authority in a way that would guarantee an efficient decision-making process, making sure that there were enough resources for the most serious cases, etc.

The twinning projects are very good at solving all these problems because the institutions that run them have experience to share, both positive and negative. Furthermore, these projects are not limited to the antitrust authorities, but aim at all stakeholders in the antitrust process, the judiciary, the legal and academic communities, the regulators and the Government, providing very positive effects for competition policy to flourish.

As a result of this technical assistance, effort jointly conducted by the Commission and member States, Estonia, Hungary, Lithuania, Latvia, Poland, Slovakia, Slovenia and the Czech Republic were able to join the European Union in June 2004, while Bulgaria and Romania were able to join 2 years later. All these countries had adopted a domestic antitrust law that was EU-convergent and had proved that they were capable of applying it effectively. Furthermore, the twinning programmes had created a network of antitrust officials on whose expertise the authorities of these new member countries could rely whenever necessary. There is no question that without EU antitrust enforcement these countries would have been much less important and less effective.

CONCLUSION

We have witnessed an impressive increase in the number of regional agreements on competition among developing countries, notably linked with regional efforts to set up free trade zones or common markets. The successes of these regional agreements have been slow and unequal, but useful lessons can be learned from past experiences, in particular because the existing agreements are very diverse in their institutional designs and scope, and it is thus relatively easy to identify the strengths and weaknesses of each one of them. Additionally, there has been one hugely successful regional agreement on competition among developed countries, namely the European Union, and consideration of this experience may be useful when discussing the institutional features of regional agreements on competition in developing countries. The fact that WAEMU is the regional cooperation agreement on competition in the developing world that is closest to the European system and is also the most successful one strongly suggests that the institutional design of such regional agreements is crucial to their success. Needless to say, the institutional design adopted for a regional cooperation agreement on competition is ultimately the result of politically complex choices by the sovereign countries that are parties to the agreement. It is up to each set of negotiating countries to find for themselves, as a function of their political preferences, how they want to organise the relationship between the regional level and the national level in their cooperation agreement. But in considering this very political question, they may want to be informed that, for a system of competition enforcement to function properly: (1) complainants have to be geographically close to the institution in charge, which implies that the relationship between the centre and the periphery needs to be governed in such a way that the incentive of domestic authorities to act is not weakened; (2) antitrust institutions need to be properly funded, so that they attract the right professional people and are able to carry out lengthy investigations; and (3) clarity has to be provided on who is in charge of an investigation – either the regional or the domestic authority – otherwise the whole system would collapse because of litigation on whether the applicable legislation to a specific case should be the Community or the domestic one (the EU principle of '*effet utile*' would be a very good example to follow).

NOTES

1. For example, in a contribution to the Working Group on Trade and Competition at the WTO in 1997, the delegation from Singapore stated:

   > … there are several important economic and policy questions that need to be addressed even before a debate on harmonization as a possible panacea can be embarked upon. These include inter alia:
   > (a) How significant are truly private anti-competitive business practices? There is evidence to suggest that in many instances anti-competitive business practices by firms are either actively or tacitly supported by governments. …
   > (b) If indeed the bulk of private anti-competitive practices are supported by governments, does the WTO not at present provide an adequate means of addressing them?

2. Bulgaria, Gabon, Cameroon, Malawi and South Africa in 1998; Belgium, Indonesia, Thailand, Slovenia, Saint Vincent and Cyprus in 1999; Armenia, Morocco, Lithuania, Moldova, Uruguay, Cape Verde and Fiji in 2000; Slovakia, Ukraine, Bosnia–Herzegovina, Kazakhstan, Saint Lucia, Antigua and Barbuda in 2001; Austria, Azerbaidjan, Latvia, Barbados and Papua New Guinea in 2002; Albania, Algeria, Mauritius, Namibia, Tanzania and Ethiopia in 2003; Jordan, Laos, Saudi Arabia, Vietnam, Jersey, Luxembourg, Singapore, El Salvador and Paraguay in 2004; Serbia, Macedonia, Honduras, Egypt, El Salvador and Austria in 2005; Montenegro, Nicaragua, Colombia, Kazakhstan and Qatar in 2006; China, Mauritius, Nepal and Uruguay in 2007; and Syria and the Faroe Islands in 2008.
3. For an analysis of Latin American free trade agreements and antitrust developments, see Sokol, D. (2008), 'Order without (enforceable) law: Why countries enter into non-enforceable competition policy chapters in free trade agreements', *Chicago-Kent Law Review*, 83, 231–292.

4. See Sokol (2008), under note 3.
5. See Gerber, David (1998), *Law and Competition in Twentieth Century Europe: Protecting Prometheus*, Oxford: Oxford University Press.
6. European Commission (2004), *Commission Notice on Cooperation within the Network of Competition Authorities* (2004/C 101/03).

Index